ACADEMIC READING AND STUDY SKILLS

ACADEMIC READING AND STUDY SKILLS

A THEME-CENTERED APPROACH

SECOND EDITION

Beth M. Pacheco

New York City Technical College

Harcourt Brace Jovanovich College Publishers

Fort Worth Philadelphia San Diego New York Orlando Austin San Antonio

Toronto Montreal London Sydney Tokyo

Publisher	Ted Buchholz
Acquisitions Editor	Michael Rosenberg
Development Editor	Stacy Schoolfield
Project Editor	Publications Development Company
Senior Production Manager	Ken Dunaway
Design Supervisor	Guy Jacobs
Cover Design	Pat Sloan
Composition	Publications Development Company

Cover illustration by Richard C. Karwoski, "Trees and Shadows," © 1979.

Address Editorial Correspondence to: 301 Commerce Street, Suite 3700, Fort Worth, TX 76102

Address Orders to: 6277 Sea Harbor Drive, Orlando, FL 32887
1-800-782-4479 or 1-800-443-0001 (in Florida)

Acknowledgments appear on pp. 317–318

Printed in the United States of America

Library of Congress Cataloging-in-Publication Data

Pacheco, Beth M.
Academic reading and study skills : a theme-centered approach / Beth Pacheco.—2nd ed.
p. cm.
ISBN (invalid) 003555337
1. College readers. 2. Study, Method of. I. Title.
PE1122.P23 1991
428.6—dc20 91-28320
CIP

1 2 3 4 0 1 6 9 8 7 6 5 4 3 2 1

For Mary and Murray M. Margolis
and my brothers, Michael Margolis and Martin Rubin

Preface

Academic Reading and Study Skills: A Theme-Centered Approach, Second Edition is designed for the advanced levels of a college skills sequence. It includes instruction and practice in reading and study techniques; however, it is a departure from the traditional reading text. In its presentation of a thematically unified content base, this text gives students the experience of a content course. Rather than acquaint students with many unrelated, abridged general topics, it directs their skills to the exploration of the unifying theme, *autonomy and the individual,* a concept of both universal and culturally specific importance.

The Theme and the Text

Autonomy has to do with choice. It involves the ability to discern and make choices that lead to fulfillment and happiness. The readings in this text consider autonomy from the perspectives of biology, human ecology, psychology, sociology, archeology, anthropology, human sexuality, mathematics, history, literature, and composition. Ample and broad reading matter allows for selectivity and enrichment by the instructor. Exercises encourage students to work autonomously and cooperatively. Moreover, they guide students to consult themselves, their peers, their instructors and other texts and study aids as resources of valuable information.

Overview

Twelve chapters and two appendixes compose the text. The chapters are self-contained. However, the unifying theme permits for optional questions in the Critical Thinking and Connections sections that draw on the student's accumulating core of information.

The organization of the chapters is generally consistent. Each includes the following activities:

1. *Before Reading:* Questions based on key concepts in the Reading Selection elicit prior information and a focused prereading exchange of ideas and insights.
2. *Reading Selection:* Readings are from college textbooks and related assignments. Earlier readings are adapted for accessibility, while the readings in the later chapters are longer than those in the traditional reading text (though not as long as the typical reading assignment in a postdevelopmental college course).
3. *Vocabulary:* Words are boldfaced in the text. Students may be directed to give brief definitions based on context and word analysis. Short answer exercises reinforce new terms.
4. *Comprehension:* The exercises, which predominantly require short answers, elicit specific information, relationships of ideas, inferences and interpretations. They assist students to understand concepts and writer's technique and prepare them for the open-ended questions in the Critical Thinking and Connections sections.
5. *Study Activity:* The reading selections from across the curriculum provide the content for practicing reading and study skills. Thought pattern, alone and in combination, are stressed as guides for comprehension, note taking and asking questions. Study skills are coordinated to the methodology of a specific discipline. For example, in Chapter 4, the scientific method in research and in Chapter 8, story vocabulary in literature are presented as frames for outlining and summarizing. Chapter 7 models the library research process and Chapter 11 presents math problems from the reading skills perspective.
6. *Critical Thinking:* Questions designed for collaborative and independent assignment require content based responses. Questions unpack conceptual tasks taking students beyond literal comprehension to creative interpretation, application and evaluation of material.
7. *Connections:* Short, related passages are presented for discussion of contrasting styles and points of view.
8. *Topic for Composition:* An optional writing assignment concludes each chapter. The structure as well as the content of a particular reading may be addressed in the assignment.

Appendix I, Vocabulary for the College Student, contains

1. An alphabetized glossary of boldfaced words from the reading selections, thematically related material, and exercises.
2. Common prefixes, suffixes, and word stems

Appendix II contains suggestions for taking short answer tests.

Working with the Text

Before Reading

As you begin each chapter, you will have the opportunity to discuss with your classmates and your instructor a key concept that is developed in the readings and exercises. It is important to participate in this discussion. There are no wrong answers. Each student's contribution sheds new light on the subject and is, therefore, of value to the entire class.

Vocabulary

Unfamiliar and technical terms are highlighted in the text. Circle any other words or phrases that require clarification. Using context and word structure, try to arrive at brief tentative definitions. You may check your work with Appendix I, which contains an inventory of all highlighted vocabulary. If you continue to be uncertain, consult the dictionary and raise questions in class regarding the meaning of words, particularly as they are used in the selections.

Comprehension

Questions in this section throughout the text are directed to the chapter's Reading Selection. They will give you practice in identifying specific information; analyzing the writer's techniques for developing and clarifying main ideas; and making inferences and interpretations. Be sure to give text-based answers—that is, answers that you can support by citing specific passages in the Reading Selection. For this reason, if an answer is stated or suggested in the text, it is worthwhile to note the paragraph number next to your answer. This procedure also makes for a more efficient review. When you review, be sure that you understand the reason for the correct answer and why each of the remaining answers is incorrect.

Study Activity

This section presents techniques for identifying, organizing, and reviewing the information in reading assignments. You will have practice in studying skills, such as note taking, outlining, paraphrasing, and summarizing. Space is provided in the text for brief answers. Use your notebook for developing complete, sufficiently detailed responses.

Critical Thinking

INDEPENDENT AND GROUP WORK

Here you will work independently or with classmates to solve problems by applying principles and concepts from the readings. You will be dealing with abstractions that may have more than one right answer. You must support your theories and opinions with text-based and factual information from your experience. Responses may be briefly summarized in the text; they should be fully developed in your notebook.

Connections

Each chapter has material that is thematically connected to the chapter's Reading Selection. You will encounter contrasting and supporting points of view and will experience different forms of expression, including short stories and poetry.

Topic(s) for Composition

These writing assignments call on you to use what you have learned through reading, questioning, and discussion as you have progressed through the chapter.

New in the Second Edition

- A chapter on reading mathematics
- A chapter that focuses on autonomy and cooperation as dual aspects of the environmental movement
- A revised note taking chapter with a full-length essay and extensive text from various disciplines for note taking practice
- An additional short story for analysis and summarizing, Distance from the critically acclaimed collection, *What We Talk About When We Talk About Love* by Raymond Carver
- More poetry and short fiction, much of it cross-cultural, in the Connections section of several chapters
- Theme-related writing assignments that draw upon reading content

- A refined apparatus and reorganization particularly in earlier chapters that present reading skills such as finding main ideas, categorizing details, and using patterns of organization as structures for analysis
- Presentation of library research earlier in the text so that students have more time to apply the process to their own research projects
- Instruction in summarizing the case study and the argumentative essay using mapping as a preliminary step.

Retained from the First Edition

- Thematically related readings that are excellent examples of academic writing and literature. Some are classics in their respective disciplines.
- Exercises that focus thinking on reading and develop informed communication on academic issues and subjects.

ACKNOWLEDGMENTS

I'm pleased to acknowledge the fine teachers and students who have contributed to this edition of *Academic Reading and Study Skills.* Thanks to Brenda Bass, Belle Cohan, Margerie Tenner, Alice Richardson, Serena Nanda and Darrow Wood for crossing the curriculum. Thanks to my many comrades in College English, especially Jean Dyer, Joan Russell and Mary Winslow. Thanks to Marcos Pacheco for his keen illustrations, to Tara Mehrbach for adding Mother Earth and to Joan Gregg for all of our collaborative endeavors. Special thanks to Benjamin Pacheco for his expertise in many areas.

Reviewers who have given me very good suggestions are Rose Austin, North Harris Community College; Virginia Blasengame, Franklin University; Ida Egle, Santa Rosa Junior College; Robin Erwin, Niagara University; Roger George, Bellevue Community College; Barbara Henry, West Virginia State College.

I am also grateful to my editors at Harcourt Brace Jovanovich, Michael Rosenberg, for his confidence and Stacy Schoolfield, for her fine ideas in developing the manuscript. Thanks to Nancy Land for the final touch.

Beth M. Pacheco
New York City Technical College (CUNY)

Contents

1 **Motivation** *1*

Previewing: Courses, Classes, and Texts

Before Reading *2*

Reading Selection *2*

"Maslow's Hierarchy of Needs" by Janice Gibson

Abraham Maslow's theory explains motivation—the single most necessary element for academic success.

Vocabulary *5*

Comprehension *6*

Critical Thinking *9*

Questions for Independent and Group Work

Connections *10*

How Close to Self-Actualization Are You?

Topic for Composition *11*

Study Activity *12*

Previewing: Courses, Classes, and Texts

Organizing the Semester
Time Management
Previewing College Texts
Previewing a Chapter

2 **A New Style of Aging** *17*

Thinking Academically

Before Reading *18*

Reading Selection *18*

"A New Style of Aging" by Margaret Mead

In this cross-cultural study of aging, anthropologist Margaret Mead suggests that the value Americans place on autonomy has had a destructive effect on people of all ages in our society.

Vocabulary *22*

Comprehension *24*

Study Activity *26*

Thinking Academically

Essay Directions
Anticipating Essay Questions
Preparing to Write: The Note Outline

Critical Thinking *29*

Questions for Independent and Group Work

Connections *29*

"Aunt Sue's Stories" by Langston Hughes
"The Sampler" by I.V. Morris

Topic for Composition *33*

3 Love and Marriage *35*

Central Ideas and Supporting Details in Textbook Passages

Before Reading *36*

Reading Selection *36*

"Love and Marriage: An Historical View" by Susan M. Garfield

This reading for a course in human sexuality traces the history of love's role in (and outside of) marriage from ancient Greece to modern times.

Vocabulary *39*

Word History: Etymology

Comprehension *42*

Study Activity *45*

Central Ideas and Supporting Details

A Technique for Identifying Central Ideas and Supporting Details
How Ideas Relate
Expressing Central Ideas
Reading for Details

Critical Thinking *54*

Questions for Independent and Group Work

Connections *54*

Cross-cultural Voices on the Subject of Love
"Evening Star" by Shu Shan Cheng from "In Praise of Krishna"

"On Marriage" by Kahlil Gibran

Topics for Composition *57*

4 **Learning Culture** *59*

Thought Patterns in College Textbooks

Before Reading *60*

Reading Selection *60*

"Learning Culture" by Serena Nanda

Anthropologist Serena Nanda compares child rearing practices in industrial and traditional societies focusing on adolescence.

Vocabulary *63*

Extending Vocabulary with Word Forms

Comprehension *65*

Study Activity *68*

Thought Patterns in College Textbooks

Writers and Readers Use Thought Patterns
Signal Expressions
Models of Thought Patterns

Exercises *74*

Critical Thinking *81*

Questions for Independent and Group Work

Connections *81*

"If" by Rudyard Kipling

Topic for Composition *83*

5 **Pygmalion in the Classroom** *85*

The Scientific Method: Outlining Experimental Material

Before Reading *86*

Reading Selection *86*

"Pygmalion in the Classroom" by Robert Rosenthal and Lenore Jacobson

Does a teacher's expectations of a student's ability have an effect on how well the student learns? This reading in Educational Psychology describes an experiment designed to answer this question.

Vocabulary *90*

Comprehension *92*

Study Activity *95*

Outlining Experimental Material

Terms in the Scientific Method
Using Scientific Terminology
Applying Scientific Terminology

Critical Thinking *98*

Questions for Independent and Group Work

Connections *98*

From "Growing Up" by Russell Baker

Topic for Composition *101*

6 Lucy in the Sky *103*

Making Notes in the Textbook

Before Reading *104*

Reading Selection *104*

"Lucy" by Donald Johanson and Maitland A. Edey

Working autonomously and as a team, scientists including biologists, geologists, and paleontologists discover an important skeleton. They named her Lucy after the Beatles' song, "Lucy in the Sky with Diamonds"

Vocabulary *111*

Comprehension *113*

Study Activity *114*

Making Notes in the Textbook

Why Mark the Textbook?
Annotating: Developing a System of Symbols

Exercises *117*

Critical Thinking *126*

Questions for Independent and Group Work

Topic for Composition *127*

7 Liberty Looked from Every Star *129*

Doing Library Research

Before Reading *130*

Reading Selection *130*

"To My Old Master . . ." by Jourdan Anderson

Anderson's ironic letter is a response to the invitation of his former master to return with his wife and children to the plantation where they had been slaves.

Study Activity *133*

Doing Library Research

Selecting a Topic
Using Questions to Narrow a Topic
A Final Note on Selecting a Topic
Locating Sources

High Tech/Low Tech: The Computer Database/The Card Catalogue

Finding Books in the Stacks

In the Reference Room

Encyclopedias
Bibliographies
Indexes to Periodicals
Readers' Guide

Exercises

Where Are Periodicals Located?
Newspaper Indexes
Other Valuable Indexes

Recording Sources

Preparing a Working Bibliography
Preparing for Final Documentation

Evaluating Sources

Preliminary Reading
Applying the Criteria for Selection

Formulating a Thesis

Critical Reading for Working
Outlining the Paper
Abstracting Information

Connections *162*

"From My Bondage and My Freedom" by Frederick Douglass

8 Rites of Passage *169*

Analyzing and Summarizing the Short Story

Before Reading *170*

Reading Selection *170*

"A Summer's Reading" by Bernard Malamud

Self-respect is the first step towards autonomy for the high school drop-out who is the hero of this short story.

Vocabulary *177*

Introducing Figurative Language

Comprehension *179*

Critical Thinking *181*

Questions for Independent and Group Work

Study Activity *182*

Summarizing the Short Story

Story Elements (Story Vocabulary)
Patterns of Organization
Story Elements as a Foundation for Summarizing
Guided Summary

Connections *189*

"Distance" by Raymond Carver

Comprehension *197*

Study Activity *200*

Topics for Composition *201*

9 Joey, "A Mechanical Boy" *203*

Summarizing the Case Study

Before Reading *204*

Reading Selection *204*

"Joey: A Mechanical Boy" by Bruno Bettelheim

Joey is an autistic child. Autonomy is control of the self; autism, in contrast, is being locked into the self, unable to establish emotional ties to others. In this fascinating case study, Bettelheim finds the key to Joey's freedom.

Vocabulary *214*

Comprehension *216*

Critical Thinking *218*

Questions for Independent and Group Work

Study Activity *219*

Summarizing the Case Study

The Case Study
Case Study Vocabulary
The Summarizing Process
Guided Case Study Summary

Connections *224*

from "This Stranger My Son" by Louise Wilson

Topic for Composition *225*

10 The Green Decade *227*

Summarizing the Essay

Before Reading *228*

Reading Selection *228*

"Earth Day 1990: Threshold of the Green Decade" by Denise Hayes

Environmentalist Denis Hayes addresses an issue of tremendous importance to college students: saving the earth and the creatures who share it with us.

Vocabulary *239*

Comprehension *241*

Critical Thinking *244*

Inference Questions for Independent and Group Work

Study Activity *245*

Summarizing the Essay

Connections *246*

Letters to the Editor

Topic for Composition *246*

11 Easy as A, B, and C *249*

Reading Mathematics

Before Reading *250*

Reading Selection *250*

"A, B, and C: The Human Element in Mathematics" by Stephen Leacock

Stephen Leacock, a story telling mathematician, insists that math problems have adventure, industry and romance for those who read closely and carefully.

Vocabulary *254*

Comprehension *255*

Study Activity *257*

Reading Mathematics

Basic Math Terms
Language of Mathematics
Algebraic Symbols
Mathematical Statements
Word Problems
Diagramming and Designing a Table
Identifying Essential Information
Estimating
Steps in Problem Solving
More Word Problems

Connections *272*

"Boarding-house Geometry" by Stephen Leacock

Topic for Composition *273*

12 Common Sense: Declaring Independence *275*

The Formal Outline

Before Reading *276*

Reading Selection *277*

"A Struggle for Autonomy Leads to 'The Declaration of Independence'" by John B. Harris and Richard B. Sullivan

Vocabulary *281*

Comprehension *283*

Study Activity *285*

The Formal Outline

Notation
Outlining Detailed Factual Material

Critical Thinking *290*

Questions for Independent and Group Work

Connections *292*

"En La Brecha" by Jose de Diego with English translation

Topics for Composition *294*

APPENDIX I Word Inventory *295*

Prefixes, Suffixes, Stems *300*

Word Stems

Suggestions for Extending General and Technical Vocabulary *304*

General Words
Specialized or Technical Words

Critical Reading and Writing Terms *304*

APPENDIX II Techniques for Taking Short Answer Tests *307*

Preparing for Short Answer Tests *307*

Overview and Integrate Course Content

General Suggestions for Taking Short Answer Tests *310*

Specific Suggestions for Different Types of Short Answer Tests *311*

True-False
Matching
Multiple-Choice

General Suggestions About Language *312*

Anticipating the Answer

Reading Tests *315*

What motivates these college athletes and their instructor? Are their goals physiological, aesthetic, or both?

1

Motivation

Previewing: Courses, Classes, and Texts

Has the road been hard?
The road is everything.

—*Willa Cather*

Before Reading

As you begin each chapter of the text, you will have the opportunity to discuss with your classmates and your instructor a key concept that is developed in the readings and exercises. Motivation is an appropriate concept for the first chapter of a college-level text. Students generally begin their courses and their texts with great expectations. They have goals, energy, and direction—the potential for success. In the language of educational psychology, they are highly motivated.

There are many theories regarding the source and nature of motivation, the power that takes men and women toward achievement. The following selection is from a text in educational psychology. It describes psychologist Abraham Maslow's theory of motivation, which is based on the study of such unique and autonomous individuals as Abraham Lincoln, Eleanor Roosevelt, and Martin Luther King.

Consider for a moment the source of your own motivation. To do this, first try to describe your academic and career goals. Now try to express why you have selected these goals. Your reasons for working and struggling are your motivation.

READING SELECTION

As you read, notice the boldfaced words. Circle any other words or phrases that require clarification. Using the context in which they appear and your knowledge of word parts, try to arrive at tentative definitions. When you have completed the reading, you may record your tentative definitions in the space provided in the Vocabulary section following the selection. You may want to check your work with Appendix IA, Word Inventory, which includes many of the unfamiliar words and technical terms in the text. If you continue to be uncertain, use your dictionary and raise questions in class about the meanings of words.

Maslow's Hierarchy of Needs

By Janice Gibson

1 Abraham Maslow conceived of men and women as born with a **hierarchy** of needs (see Figure 1). He divided these needs into two groups: lower or deficiency needs and higher or growth needs. According to Maslow, needs on the lower levels must be satisfied, before needs further up on the scale make themselves felt.

Deficiency Needs

2 The lower or deficiency needs seek to overcome negative states such as hunger, fear, loneliness, and insecurity.

7. *Self-actualization* needs: need for self-fulfillment and realizing one's individual potential.
6. *Aesthetic* needs: need for beauty and order.
5. *Cognitive* needs: needs to know and understand and explore; curiosity.
4. *Esteem* needs: needs for achievement, approval, competence, recognition.
3. *Love* needs: needs for acceptance and belonging.
2. *Safety* needs: needs to feel secure and safe, out of danger.
1. *Physiological* needs: hunger, thirst, air.

Figure 1 *Hierarchy of needs.*

Physiological Needs

3 Physiological needs, the most basic of all, must be gratified before any higher needs can fully **emerge.** If physical needs are not met, we become preoccupied with these deficiencies. The thoughts and fantasies of a starving person, for instance, will be dominated by images of food. Even his or her dreams will center on food themes. Teachers are aware of the fact that hungry children have difficulty paying attention in school.

Safety Needs

4 Next in the hierarchy are safety needs. On occasion they **dominate** the lives of adults. It is in the lives of infants and children, however, that safety needs are most clearly expressed. During the first years of life, human beings are most helpless and most in need of a stable and orderly environment. When a child's world is disrupted, safety needs come to dominate growth and development. An illustration of this is Maslow's example of a toddler, who, in his mother's company, slowly and cautiously explored a strange room. While his mother was present, he gradually became more adventurous in his explorations. When his mother suddenly left, the toddler immediately stopped exploring and looked **frantically** for her. To quote Maslow: "Growth forward customarily takes place in little steps and each step forward is made possible by the feeling of being safe, or operating into the unknown from a safe home port, of daring because retreat is possible" (1974).

Love and Belonging Needs

5 Third in Maslow's hierarchy of needs is love and belonging. Once an individual feels safe in his home environment he will turn to others beyond the home for fulfillment. Friendships, love relationships, and group acceptance emerge as the dominant concerns at this

point. According to Maslow, when a person is **thwarted** in satisfying this need, maladjustment and even mental illness may **ensue**.

6 Educators and child psychologists are aware of the importance of this need in the lives of school-age children. If a child experiences difficulty in getting along with his classmates and teachers, it is highly unlikely that while in school he will be successful. For a young child, school is the first real testing ground for establishing his proper place among other children. If the child fails, school can become a **hostile** environment associated with much fear and anxiety.

Esteem Needs

7 Next in Maslow's hierarchy are esteem needs. In this category he includes both the need for self-respect and the need for respect from others. From self-respect comes confidence, independence, freedom. From the respect a person receives from others comes a sense of **prestige** and appreciation. If these needs are not satisfied, a sense of inferiority will emerge; the individual will constantly be concerned with his own **inadequacies**. At the same time, he will fear the **condemnation** of others.

Growth Needs

8 The higher needs in Maslow's hierarchy, (Figure 1, levels 5 and 6) include such positive and important human objectives as knowledge, goodness, order, and beauty. Growth needs, unlike the basic needs, are not actually hierarchical in order. One can be substituted for another.

Self-Actualization

9 The last and most far-reaching need is the need for what Maslow terms self-actualization. He defines this need as follows: ". . . the desire for self-fulfillment, namely . . . the desire to become more and more what one is, to become everything that one is capable of becoming" (1974). According to this definition, each person must find for himself his own path towards self-actualization.

10 Maslow believes that each of us can progress naturally from the fulfillment of one need to the next, steadily moving towards self-actualization. He maintains, however, that a warm accepting supportive environment is necessary for self-actualization. Without such an environment, an individual cannot satisfy his safety needs, and because of the consequent anxiety, he will not progress beyond this point.

Vocabulary

The following words are boldfaced in the reading selection. The numbers in parentheses refer to the paragraphs in which they first appear. Write a synonym or brief definition for each. Add other unfamiliar terms and their meanings to the list.

WORD OR PHRASE	SYNONYM OR BRIEF DEFINITION
hierarchy (1)	system of importance - higher + lower order members
emerge (3)	come out
dominate (4)	take control of
frantically (4)	wildly, in a panic
thwarted (5)	prevented from accomplishing sth.
ensue (5)	follow
hostile (6)	unfriendly.
prestige (7)	worth, value, success
inadequacies (7)	lacks,
condemnation (7)	be against sth/so
aesthetic (Fig. 1)	visual / beauty
cognitive (Fig. 1)	mental
esteem (Fig. 1)	being liked / approval
physiological (Fig. 1)	physical.

YOUR ADDITIONS

deficiency preoccupied gratified infant disrupted home port maladjustment anxiety inferiority

A. Match the underscored word in the phrase on the left to its synonym in the column on the right.

Example	b mental illness may ensue	a. deficiencies
1.	e first in the hierarchy	b. follow as a result
2.	a concerned with his own inadequacies	c. usually
3.	c customarily takes place	d. frustrated
4.	d when a person is thwarted	e. graded series
5.	f school, a hostile environment	f. unfriendly

B. Complete each sentence with the appropriate word from the following list: prestige; consequent; disrupts; physiological; frantically; preoccupied.

Example Food, shelter, and sleep are examples of physiological needs.

1. The anxious child searched frantically for her father.
2. Recognition of achievement brings prestige to a person.
3. A hungry child will be preocupied with thoughts of food.
4. Divorce often disrupts. a child's world.
5. When the struggle for safety is all-consuming, the consequent anxiety limits growth and development.

Comprehension

Questions in this section are directed to the chapter's reading selection—"Maslow's Hierarchy of Needs," in Chapter 1. They will give you practice in identifying specific information, analyzing the writer's techniques for developing ideas, and making inferences and interpretations based on what you have read.

In reviewing your work, be sure that you understand the reason for the correct answer and the reasons why each of the remaining answers is incorrect.

SPECIFIC INFORMATION

Questions may require you to return to the selection to retrieve accurate information.

A. According to Maslow, children's growth forward is possible because retreat is

1. impossible.
2. shameful.
3. possible.
4. difficult.

B. When their physiological needs are not met,

1. hungry children are inattentive.
2. failing children are hostile toward school.
3. toddlers become overcautious in exploration.
4. adolescents develop feelings of inferiority.

C. The higher needs in the hierarchy

1. are less important than the basic needs.
2. may be met simultaneously.
3. can substitute for each other.
4. emerge in chronological order.

ANALYSIS

Items may include quoted passages from the reading selection. Questions will focus your attention on the relationships of ideas. In later chapters, questions will direct you to closely examine language choice and language function.

D. The following statements express

1. three separate cause-effect relationships.
2. the same point three times.
3. a series of contradictions.
4. a chain of cause-effect relationships.

"If the child fails, school can become a hostile environment associated with much fear and anxiety."

"When a child's world is disrupted, safety needs come to dominate growth and development."

"If physical needs are not met, we become preoccupied with these deficiencies."

E. In the following paragraph, the author has *not* included

1. clarification of a term.
2. explanation of a term.
3. an illustrative case.
4. a central idea.

Next in Maslow's hierarchy are esteem needs. In this category he includes both the need for self-respect and the need for respect from others. From self-respect comes confidence, independence, freedom. From the respect a person receives from others comes a sense of prestige and appreciation. If these needs are not satisfied, a sense of inferiority will emerge; the individual will constantly be concerned with his own inadequacies. At the same time, he will fear the condemnation of others.

F. The central or unifying idea behind Maslow's hierarchy is that unmet needs

1. must be treated in psychotherapy.
2. eventually become unimportant and are ignored.
3. both stimulate and place limits on an individual's direction in life.
4. encourage self-sufficiency and autonomy.

G. The author's intention is to

1. inform the reader of the specifics of Maslow's theory of motivation.
2. present the reader with successful child-raising techniques.
3. entertain and amuse the reader.
4. persuade the reader that Maslow's is the best theory of motivation.

INFERENCES AND INTERPRETATIONS

Questions may require you to make assumptions based on what you have read; they may direct you to apply abstract concepts introduced in the reading selection to real life situations.

H. In paragraph 4, the author suggests or implies, but does *not* specifically state, that

1. when there is disruption in their lives, children develop strength and confidence.
2. when a child's world is disrupted, safety needs dominate growth and development.
3. when the home is disrupted, children must find refuge from insecurity and anxiety.
4. when there is upset at home, children turn to other children for acceptance and approval.

I. For Maslow, which of the following probably has the *least* influence on growth and development?

1. Competition
2. Affection
3. Approval
4. Organization

J. A reasonable assumption based on Maslow's theory is that a teacher can help a student who lacks confidence by

1. giving problems that are within the student's ability to solve and praising the student's efforts.
2. making frequent inspirational speeches to the student.
3. isolating the student from the rest of the class for intensive private instruction.
4. counseling the student to change majors.

Critical Thinking

QUESTIONS FOR INDEPENDENT AND GROUP WORK

In this section, you will be working independently or with classmates to solve problems. *You will be dealing with abstractions for which there may be more than one right answer.* You must support your theories and opinions with text-based and factual information.

A. Read and discuss the following list of activities. Label each with the need which, for you, it fulfills in Maslow's hierarchy (refer to Figure 1).

	YOUR RESPONSE	***GROUP RESPONSE***
1. Getting a part-time job		
2. Exercising regularly		
3. Creating a technical artistic or fashion design		
4. Tutoring a peer		
5. Joining a campus organization		
6. Hearing a symphony		
7. Using a computer		
8. Earning an A on an exam		
9. Being changed and fed		
10. Breaking a bad habit or addiction		

B. Use Maslow's hierarchy to analyze several magazine or television advertisements. (Select at least one political advertisement.)

1. Name the product.

2. Describe the image.

3. State the message.

4. Which consumer (or voter) needs does the advertisement address?

C. Hierarchy is defined as a body of persons classified by rank or authority. Apply the term to these organizations.

1. Your college

2. A team: baseball, soccer, swimming, or any other

3. The American federal government 

4. The Catholic Church

Connections

In the Connections section, throughout the text, you will have the opportunity to read and discuss material that is thematically related to the chapter's reading selection.

HOW CLOSE TO SELF-ACTUALIZATION ARE YOU?

Maslow has listed characteristics of self-actualized people. Read each characteristic and rate yourself on a scale of 1 to 10. Don't be discouraged if, at this point in your life, your score is low. Remember, Maslow considered Abraham Lincoln, Eleanor Roosevelt, and Albert Einstein "10s."

CHARACTERISTICS OF SELF-ACTUALIZED INDIVIDUALS

1. Efficient perception of reality: You don't demand simple answers. You accept life with all of its complexities.

   Self-rating ______

2. Acceptance of self and others: You aren't apologetic about yourself or your beliefs. You are also open to and accepting of others.

   Self-rating ______

3. Spontaneity: You are not concerned with impressing others. You feel free to think and act spontaneously, but you are careful not to intentionally distress other people.

   Self-rating ______

4. Detachment: You need privacy. You are not antisocial, but you do value the times you spend alone.

Self-rating ______

5. Autonomy: You venture beyond your own cultural background. You have a real sense of joy in experiencing all aspects of life.

Self-rating ______

6. Social interest: You have a strong sense of the unity and brotherhood among all human beings and are relatively free of prejudice and jealousy.

Self-rating ______

7. Interpersonal relationships: You have a small number of very deep and rich friendships with both men and women.

Self-rating ______

8. Welcomes challenge: You enjoy the work involved in achieving a goal as much as the achievement of the goal itself.

Self-rating ______

9. Sense of humor: Your humor is constructive rather than destructive. You do not hurt people or put them down.

Self-rating ______

10. Creativity: In your everyday life you tend to be original and inventive.

Self-rating ______

Total ______

Total ÷ 10 = ______

Which do you think are the most desirable characteristics listed here?

Topic for Composition

Abraham Maslow based his theory of self-actualization on the lives of outstanding men and women. Write a descriptive sketch of either a public figure or a personal acquaintance whom you believe has achieved self-actualization, that is, "become everything he or she is capable of being." You may use Maslow's list to develop your answer.

Study Activity

In this section, you will learn techniques for identifying, organizing, and reviewing the information in reading assignments which provides background for lectures, class discussions, quizzes, and examinations. You will also practice study skills such as note-taking, outlining, paraphrasing, and summarizing.

PREVIEWING: COURSES, CLASSES, AND TEXTS

ORGANIZING THE SEMESTER

Organization, according to this chapter's reading selection, is crucial to human growth and achievement. Many students find that a study schedule is a good technique for establishing order and balance in their busy lives.

A. Make a list of your responsibilities this semester. Arrange them in a hierarchy with your most pressing responsibility at the top and your least pressing responsibility at the bottom.

1.

2.

3.

4.

5.

6.

7.

B. Use the information in Exercise A to plot your schedule of activities for a week. On the form in Figure 2, record your classes, work hours, family commitments, and studying time. An hour of class generally requires an hour of preparation; therefore, if you are taking a course that meets three hours a week, you should allot a minimum of three hours to prepare for that class.

TIME MANAGEMENT

If you find a chart of this kind helpful, try revising it after a few days based on the demands of your courses. Now you can identify specific blocks of time just for reading, other blocks for writing, and others just for review. Reviewing sessions will increase in frequency as midterm and final examinations approach.

Time	Monday	Tuesday	Wednesday	Thursday	Friday	Saturday	Sunday
8.							
9.							
10.							
11.							
12.							
1.							
2.							
3.							
4.							
5.							
6.							
7.							
8.							
9.							
10.							

Figure 2 *There is probably little time left in your schedule for leisure activities. A reality of student life is that successful students work very hard. According to Abraham Maslow, the first characteristic of a self-actualized individual is an "efficient perception of reality and comfortable relations with it."*

PREVIEWING COLLEGE TEXTS

You preview texts by skimming through to see what topics they encompass, to understand how the material is organized and visually presented, and to locate the following important study aids:

Title page Gives important bibliographical information needed for papers and research projects, including the author, title, publisher, place, and date of publication.

Preface (Sometimes called the Foreword or Introduction.) Generally includes a statement of the author's philosophy regarding the subject of the text. Reading the Preface to a text is important because it often contains information to help you get the most from the text.

Contents An overview of the entire text, the topics covered, the order of presentation, and page references.

Glossary An alphabetical listing of technical terms and their definitions.

Bibliography A list of the author's sources including texts, journals, and articles. Items are listed alphabetically according to authors' last names. The bibliography can give you good leads for your subject-related research projects.

Appendix Supplemental useful material.

Index Alphabetical detailed listing of persons, places, and concepts which the text contains, with page references. The Index is the most efficient reference for finding specific information.

Type The different kinds of print throughout the text are visual indications of relationships and levels of subordination between titles, topics, and subtopics. Italics and boldface are used to bring important terms to the reader's attention.

C. Preview this text. Then consult the text's study aids to answer the following questions:

1. In the Preface, what unique feature of the text does the author stress?

2. In the Contents, which reading selection looks the most interesting to you?

   Which of the study techniques do you need to develop?

3. Will the appendices be useful?

PREVIEWING A CHAPTER

Looking ahead is the best strategy for anticipating obstacles and identifying study aids. To preview a text chapter, follow these steps:

1. Leaf through the chapter to ascertain its length. Estimate how long you will take to complete the chapter, and make your time allowance. If you cannot complete the chapter in one sitting, place a marker at the page that you intend to reach.

2. Look for study aids such as prereading questions, chapter summary, illustrations, end-of-chapter questions, and lists of key concepts or terms. Read this material first. Reading the summary questions or designated terms before reading the chapter alerts you to the critical points of information in the text.

3. Note the title, topics, and subtopics and how they relate. In an introductory social science text, the author often progresses from general to specific, focusing on defining, clarifying, and illustrating unfamiliar terminology. The selection "Maslow's Hierarchy of Needs" begins with a major concept, a psychological theory. This general statement is followed by topics and subtopics, which are the component parts of the theory:

Title: **MASLOW'S HIERARCHY OF NEEDS**

Topic: **Deficiency Needs**

Subtopics:
Physiological Needs
Safety Needs
Love and Belonging Needs
Esteem Needs

Topic: **Growth Needs**

Subtopic: **Self-Actualization**

4. As you preview, turn title, topics, and subtopics into mental questions that alert you to the crucial points in the text. Use question words that elicit information, such as *who, what, when, why, where,* and *how.* For example, the title of the reading selection suggests the following questions to the reader:

Who is Abraham Maslow?

What is a hierarchy of needs?

How does it work?

The subtopic "Physiological Needs" suggests the following questions to the reader:

What are physiological needs?

Who experiences them?

How do they affect motivation?

D. Practice formulating mental questions. In "Love and Marriage," the reading selection in Chapter 2, you will encounter the "courtly love." Write a few information questions that the topic suggests to you.

What

Who

Where

When

In summary, to preview a text chapter, examine the chapter for length; give yourself a time allowance; preread all study aids; and turn the title, topics, and subtopics into questions for which you will read to find answers.

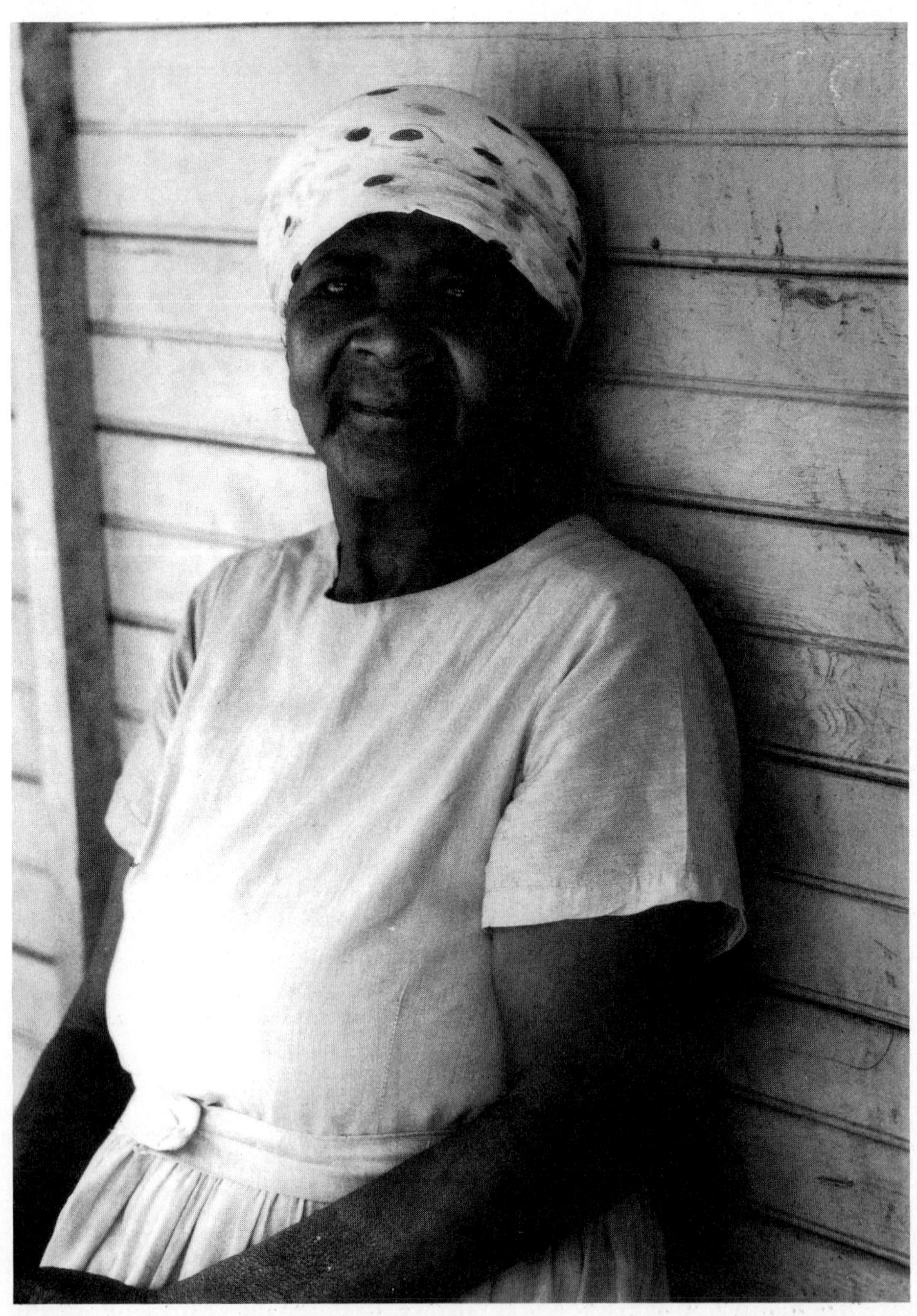

Jamaican society appreciates the beauty, values the wisdom, and welcomes the active participation of its older members. To what extent is this true of our own society?

2

A New Style of Aging

Thinking Academically

The only medicine
for suffering, crime
and all other woes of
humankind, is wisdom.

—*T. H. Huxley: Science and Education IV*

Before Reading

In this chapter's reading selection, "A New Style of Aging," anthropologist Margaret Mead suggests that the American ideal of autonomy has had a destructive effect on our society, particularly on the lives of the elderly.

Before you read the selection, consider the following statement: The elderly in America are treated like machinery that is discarded when it is no longer useful or up-to-date. Is the comparison between older Americans and old machines accurate? Support your answer with your own experiences.

READING SELECTION

A New Style of Aging

By Margaret Mead

1 It is useful in discussing aging to talk about different cultural styles, to look at what is happening in other societies, in older societies. I would like particularly to talk about the need to develop a new style of aging in our own society, and to suggest that we could do more for the older American than we are doing at present. Everyone who is aging has a chance to develop this new style. Everyone who is working with old people can contribute to this new style.

2 Young people in this country have been accused of not caring for their parents the way they would have in the old country, in Puerto Rico, in the Old South or in Italy. This is true, but it is also true that the old people in this country have been influenced by an American ideal of independence and autonomy. The most important thing in the world is to be independent. So old people live alone, perhaps on the **verge** of starvation, in time without friends—but we are independent. This standard American style has been forced on every ethnic group in the country, although there are many groups for whom the ideal is not practical. It is a poor ideal and pursuing it does a great deal of harm.

3 This ideal of independence also contains a tremendous amount of unselfishness. In talking to today's young mothers, I have asked them what kinds of grandmothers they are going to be. I have heard devoted, loving mothers say that when they are through raising their children, they have no intention of becoming traditional grandmothers. They are astonished to hear that in most of

the world, throughout most of its history, extended families of 3 or 4 generations live under the same roof. We have overemphasized the nuclear family unit—father, mother, small children. We think it is wonderful if Grandma or Grandpa, if still alive, will live alone.

4 We have reached the point where we think the only thing we can do for our children is to stay out of their hair, and the only thing we can do for our daughter-in-law is to see as little of her as possible. Old people's homes, even the best, are filled with older people who believe the only thing they can do for their children is look cheerful when they come to visit. So in the end, older people have to devote their energies to "not being a burden."

5 We are beginning to see what a tremendous price we've paid for our emphasis on independence and autonomy. We have isolated old people and we've alienated children and young people from their grandparents.

6 One of the reasons we have as bad a generation gap today as we do is because grandparents have copped out. Young people are being deprived of the thing they need most—perspective, to know why their parents behave so peculiarly and why their grandparents do the things they do.

7 In peasant communities where things didn't change and where people died in the beds they were born in, grandparents taught the young what the end of life was going to be. So you looked at your mother, if you were a girl, and you learned what it was like to be a bride, a young mother. Then you looked at your grandmother and knew what it was like to be old. Children learned what it was to age and die while they were very small. They were prepared for the end of life at the beginning.

8 It is interesting to realize that early in human society we developed a method of keeping old women alive. Human beings are the only primates that have a menopause. So women do stop having babies, and if they haven't died by the time they stop, women can become quite strong and can live quite a long time. For countless centuries old women have been around who knew things that no one else knew—that 16, 20, 30 years ago there was a hurricane or a famine and people survived. The old women remembered what people did in the past. Today, however, such memories are no longer useful. We can be dead certain that when our grandchildren reach our age, they will not be living as we live today.

9 Today, grandparents and old people in general have something quite different to contribute. Their generation has seen the most change in the world, and the young today need to learn what this change has been. They need to know about their past before they can understand the present and plot the future.

10 Young people also need reassurance that change does not mean an end to the world, but merely an end to the world as they first saw it. Older people remember that we have had periods of disorder in this country before. Some of them can remember the Time of Troubles in Ireland. Some of them remember the riots after World War I and those during World War II, and they remember that we lived through them. Because the ties between generations have been broken, young people have lost their **perspective**.

11 Normally we talk about the heartless young people who don't have room for their parents in their lives, much less in their apartments. But old people today have tremendous advantages, and these advantages make them much less dependent.

12 We all look so young to each other. Sometimes we kid ourselves that we look young to the young, which is nonsense. But we have our hair cut and styled in the most modern fashion, dye it in the most modern colors. It is wonderful how young your old friends look. Old people have never been cheered up in this way before.

13 My grandmother may have been treated with a certain respect, but she was formally dressed in a way that her grandmother had been, in a way that made her feel old. Today, we dress old people in a way that makes them feel young.

14 On the subways I've been riding for 50 years, two things have happened: People have stopped giving up their seats to the old, and old people have stopped accepting seats when they are offered: "I'll stand, thank you."

15 What we need to do is find a style of aging that will keep and foster this independence, but will encourage old people to think in terms of what they can do for someone else. If we are going to change the style, the relationship between the young and old, older people will have to take the lead by finding ways in which to relate either to their own grandchildren, or to someone else's.

16 As long as we say that youth has no need for age, that young people in this country aren't interested in old people, in seeing them or listening to them, there will be an enormous number of things in our society that are not being done, but which could be

done by old people. It is true that it is very hard to get employment if you look the least bit old. But there are many things to be done in society that don't have to be done under the **auspices** of employment agencies.

17 What we need in this society more than anything else is warm bodies who can sit by a door, answer a telephone, stay around until the plumber comes. There are masses of people sitting around being independent and keeping healthy who could be sitting in somebody's house freeing that person to get out and go to work.

18 We are beginning to think about day care centers and we ought to bring older people in. PTA's should encourage older people to participate, not throw out the mothers the minute their last children leave the school.

19 The Soviet Union now has "block grandmothers." People who have been social workers or teachers and have had experience caring for people are paid a regular salary in a housing project to be a grandmother. When there's an accident in the playground, the mother can hand her the baby. When a mother doesn't know what to do, she can ask the advice of the "grandmother." The grandmother function has been **institutionalized**.

20 This country is filled with widows who sit in their houses polishing furniture instead of being of any use to the world. They'll tell you that nobody wants them, that nobody listens to old people anymore, but it isn't true. Or it's only as true as they make it true.

21 There isn't any reason why society shouldn't be reorganized along new lines by finding places where old people are really useful. Old people themselves have to begin asking the question, "Where and how can I continue to make a contribution?"

22 What we want is for people when they are about 50—when they begin to think about aging—to consider also the end of their lives. People need to know that you can make living wills. You can decide to let your eyes be used by somebody else, or your heart, or your kidneys. If you start very early thinking that you can make a contribution when you die, you will develop a different attitude towards death.

23 You can also **stipulate** that you do not want to be kept artificially alive, by blood transfusions or in other ways. You can feel that you have some control over the end of your life, making sure that your relatives don't beggar themselves for the funeral or exhaust the family's financial resources prolonging life in a hopeless illness.

24 There are 1,000 ways old people can contribute if we only set up the housing, the neighborhoods, the living arrangements that make it **feasible** for them to do so.

Vocabulary

The following words are boldfaced in the reading selection. Write a synonym or brief definition for each. Add other unfamiliar terms and their meanings to the list.

WORD OR PHRASE	***SYNONYM OR BRIEF DEFINITION***
verge (2)	
perspective (10)	
auspices (16)	
institutionalized (19)	
stipulate (23)	
feasible (24)	

YOUR ADDITIONS

A. Match the italicized word in the sentence to its most appropriate dictionary definition.

1. "So old people live alone, perhaps on the verge of starvation, in time without friends—but we are *independent.*"
   a. politically autonomous
   b. free from the influence, guidance, or control of another
   c. self-reliant
   d. not having to work for a living

2. "Because the ties between generations have been broken, young people have lost their *perspective.*"

a. techniques for representing three-dimensional objects on two-dimensional surfaces
b. any picture in perspective
c. a vista
d. the appearance of objects in depth
e. the relationship of aspects of a subject to each other and to a whole

3. "What we need to do is to find a style of aging that will keep and *foster* this independence. . . ."
a. to bring up; rear; nurture
b. to promote the development or growth of; encourage
c. to nurse, cherish; foster a secret hope
d. receiving, sharing, or affording parental care, though not legally or biologically related

4. ". . . making sure that your relatives don't *beggar* themselves for the funeral . . ."
a. one who solicits alms for a living
b. one who has no money; an impoverished person
c. to make a beggar of
d. to exhaust the resources of

5. "There are 1,000 ways old people can contribute if only we set up the housing, the neighborhoods, the living arrangements that make it *feasible* for them to do so."
a. capable of being done or carried out; possible; as a feasible plan
b. likely; plausible, as a feasible story
c. capable of being used or dealt with successfully; suitable, as land feasible for cultivation

6. But there are many things to be done in society that don't have to be done under the *auspices* of employment agencies."
a. protection or support; patronage
b. a portent, omen, or augury, especially when observed in the action of birds
c. observation of and divination from the action of birds

7. "This *standard* American style has been forced on every ethnic group. . . ."
a. flag, banner, or ensign
b. degree or level of excellence
c. a pedestal or stand
d. substantially uniform, well established, and widely accepted

Comprehension

SPECIFIC INFORMATION

A. Mead's "new style of aging" is for the elderly to

1. become less autonomous, more dependent.
2. use their autonomy to benefit society.
3. dye their hair in the most modern color.
4. develop their creative and artistic potential.

B. Mead indicates that in the past, succeeding generations had ___________ life experiences.

1. similar
2. vastly different
3. uneventful
4. astonishing

C. Which of the following does Mead *not* include among the contributions the elderly could make?

1. their warm bodies
2. their dead bodies
3. their experience
4. their Social Security benefits

D. According to the selection, children in ______________ families can observe the stages of live.

1. South American
2. nuclear
3. extended
4. broken

E. Mead feels that the older generation has much to teach the younger generation because the former has survived

1. hurricanes.
2. tragedy.
3. change.
4. the depression.

ANALYSIS

F. The pronoun *we* in the sentence "It is interesting to realize that early in human society *we* developed a method of keeping old women alive" refers to

1. the human species.
2. American society.
3. the author and other elderly people.

G. The pronoun *we* in the sentence "*We* all look so young to each other." refers to

1. the human species.
2. American society.
3. the author and other elderly people.

H. The pronoun *we* in the sentence "*We* are beginning to think about day-care centers and *we* ought to bring older people in" refers to

1. the human species.
2. American society.
3. the author and other elderly people.

I. A main idea of the selection is that the value placed on independence has resulted in ________________ for the elderly.

1. modern fashions
2. self-actualization
3. isolation and unhappiness
4. extended families

J. Margaret Mead puts the onus, the responsibility, for the generation gap on

1. the elderly themselves.
2. the Soviet Union.
3. American youth.
4. the economy.

INFERENCES AND INTERPRETATIONS

K. Mead suggests or implies, but does not actually state, that

1. when our children are our age, they will not be living as we do.
2. our training and experience will not be of great value to our children when they become adults.
3. our adult children will probably consult us regularly for our insights and expertise.

L. List some specific history-changing events which your grandparent's generation experienced:

M. Why does Mead say, "people no longer die in the beds they were born in?"

Study Activity

THINKING ACADEMICALLY

Subjective or essay questions require responses which give the instructor the opportunity to examine your mastery of the course content in four ways: (1) how well you remember essential information; (2) how well you can synthesize and put together different aspects of the subject; (3) how well you can apply course content to particular cases; and (4) how well you can communicate what you have learned.

Essay Directions

Essay questions include a direction verb such as those defined in the following list. The words are grouped according to the types of tasks which they direct the student to perform.

Enumerate, or **List** To present your points, one by one, making them as concise as possible

Trace To follow the course or trail of something; to give a description of progress from one point in time to another

Define To give the meaning of a term or theory, often with an illustration to clarify

State To answer briefly and to the point, usually omitting details, examples, and illustrations

Summarize To present in condensed form principles, facts, ideas, or explanations, often omitting details, examples, and illustrations

Illustrate To clarify an idea by presenting a diagram, figure, statistic, or example (exemplify)

Explain To make clear; to give reasons for conditions or results; to tell how something works

Relate To show relationships by emphasizing how ideas or conditions or people connect; to show how one thing causes or is caused by another; to show how things are alike or different

Compare To show differences but emphasize similarities between objects, people, events, or ideas

Contrast To emphasize differences between objects, people, events, or ideas

Criticize, Judge, or **Evaluate** To express your own judgment of objects, works, issues, or ideas, giving weight to both positive and negative points

Discuss, Consider, or **Describe** To provide a full and detailed answer, examining the subject from different perspectives and presenting both sides of any argument

Justify To give reasons that support an idea, condition, or point of view

Anticipating Essay Questions

The material covered in lecture, class discussion, and text generally determines the kinds of questions the instructor will ask. A good technique for preparing for an essay exam is to try to anticipate the questions. Use the definitions given above to determine which word the instructor would use in framing the following essay questions.

1. In class discussion, students have referred frequently to the term "generation gap." The instructor wants to know if they understand the term.

   a. enumerate
   b. evaluate
   c. define
   d. compare

2. The instructor and students have discussed Margaret Mead's concept of a new style of aging. The instructor wants the students to express the concept and to give an opinion of its merits.

   a. discuss
   b. state and evaluate
   c. describe and justify
   d. define and enumerate

3. Mead has suggested specific contributions that elderly people can make to our society. The instructor wants to know if the students are aware of them.

   a. describe
   b. define
   c. illustrate
   d. enumerate

4. The instructor wants the students to consider the position of the elderly in our society and in "peasant" societies, concentrating on the differences.

   a. criticize c. contrast
   b. describe d. justify

5. The instructor has assigned the essay "A New Style of Aging." The instructor wants the students to pick out the main points and bring them together into a concise statement.

   a. trace c. compare
   b. evaluate d. summarize

6. The instructor wants the student to comment at length on the following statement: "One of the reasons we have as bad a generation gap today as we do is because grandparents have copped out."

   a. compare and contrast c. discuss and illustrate
   b. describe d. summarize

7. The instructor has assigned a chapter in Mead's much earlier work *Coming of Age in Samoa.* The instructor wants the students to show connections between the chapter and the essay "A New Style of Aging."

   a. trace c. relate
   b. define d. evaluate

Preparing to Write: The Note Outline

A good essay answers the question and develops the answer with details. Inexperienced essay writers, however, tend to make the same point over and over again. Therefore, it is worthwhile to take the time to make a note outline of major and minor points before you begin to write.

Study the following essay question and the outline for the essay answer.

State and evaluate Margaret Mead's suggestion for a new style of aging.

Mead's new style of aging encourages contribution and participation.

Good idea:

1. Uses skills now being wasted
2. Brings generations together
   a. Gives young perspective on change
   b. Old model stages of life
3. Gives elderly fulfillment

Bad idea: 1. Some old people don't want to work anymore
2. Some don't want to be around the young
3. Mead unrealistic about money for projects

Evaluation: For the most part, good idea—benefits all ages

Critical Thinking

QUESTIONS FOR INDEPENDENT AND GROUP WORK

A. Work independently or with your classmates to develop note outlines for at least *two* of the following essay questions.

1. Define and justify, from your experience and what you have read, Margaret Mead's term "generation gap."

2. Enumerate the specific contributions which, according to Mead, the elderly can make to our society.

3. Contrast the position of the elderly in the modern United States and in more traditional societies—"the old country" or "Old South."

4. Discuss and illustrate Mead's point that the elderly have "copped out" by referring to this chapter and other sources of information.

Connections

A. Read or listen to "Aunt Sue's Stories" by Langston Hughes. Relate the viewpoint to that expressed in Margaret Mead's "A New Style of Aging."

Aunt Sue's Stories
By Langston Hughes

Aunt Sue has a head full of stories.
Aunt Sue has a whole heart full of stories.
Summer nights on the front porch
Aunt Sue cuddles a brown-faced child to her bosom
And tells him stories.

Black slaves.
Working in the hot sun.
And black slaves
Walking in the dewy night,
And black slaves
Singing sorrow songs on the banks of a mighty river
Mingle themselves softly
In the flow of old Aunt Sue's voice,
Mingle themselves softly
In the dark shadows that cross and recross
Aunt Sue's stories.

And the dark-faced child, listening,
Knows that Aunt Sue's stories are real stories.
He knows that Aunt Sue never got her stories
Out of any book at all,
But that they came
Right out of her own life.

The dark-faced child is quiet
Of a summer night
Listening to Aunt Sue's stories.

Is "Aunt Sue" a traditional or modern figure?

Briefly describe someone you know who plays a similar role.

B. Read the short story "The Sampler," by I. V. Morris. Consider the character of the elderly gentleman in the light of Margaret Mead's theories on aging and autonomy.

The Sampler
By I. V. Morris

1 In a certain store where they sell plum puddings a number of these delicious articles are laid out in a row during the Christmas season. Here you may select the one which is most to your taste, and you are even allowed to sample the various qualities before coming to a decision.

2 I have often wondered whether this privilege was not imposed on by people who had no intention of making a purchase, and one day when my curiosity drove me to ask this question of the shop girl, I learned it was indeed the case.

3 "Now there's one old gentleman, for instance," she told me, "who comes here almost every week and samples each one of the puddings, though he never buys anything and I suspect he never will. I remember him from last year and the year before that too. Well, let him come if he wants it that bad, say I, and welcome to it. And what's more, I hope there are a lot more stores where he can go and get his share. He looks as if he needed it all right, and I suppose they can afford it."

4 She was still speaking when an elderly gentleman limped up to the counter and began scrutinizing the row of puddings with great interest.

5 "Why that there's the very party I've been telling you about," whispered the shop girl. "Just you watch him now." And then turning to him: "Would you like to sample them, sir? Here's a spoon for you to use."

6 The elderly gentleman, who as the novelists say was poorly but neatly dressed, accepted the spoon and began eagerly to sample one after another of the puddings, only breaking off occasionally to wipe his red eyes with a large torn handkerchief which he drew from the breast pocket of his shoddy overcoat.

7 "This is quite good," he declared of one variety, and when he came to the next, "This is not bad either, but a trifle too heavy." All that time it was quite evident that he sincerely believed that he might eventually buy one of these puddings, and I am positive that he did not for a moment feel that he was in any way cheating the store. Poor old chap. Probably he had come down in the world and this sampling was all that was left him from the time when he could

afford to come and select his favorite pudding, which he would later carry home under his arm.

8 Amidst the throng of happy, prosperous-looking Christmas shoppers, the little black figure of the old man seemed incongruous and pathetic, and in a burst of benevolence, one of these bursts which so often bring pain instead of joy, I went up to him and said:

9 "Pardon me, sir, will you do me a favor? Let me purchase you one of these puddings. It would give me such pleasure."

Make a hypothesis here. What is the elderly gentleman going to do?

Now read the author's conclusions in the following paragraphs:

10 He jumped as if he had been stung and the blood rushed to his face.

11 "Excuse me," he said with more dignity than I would have thought possible considering his appearance, "I do not believe I have the pleasure of knowing you. Undoubtedly you have mistaken me for someone else." And with a quick decision he turned to the shop girl and said in a loud voice, "Kindly pack me up this one here. I will take it with me." He pointed at one of the largest and most expensive of the puddings.

12 In surprise, the girl took down the pudding from its stand and proceeded to make a parcel of it, while he extracted a worn little black pocketbook and began counting out shillings and sixpenny pieces on to the counter. To save his "honor" he had been forced into a purchase which he could not possibly afford and which probably meant many bitter privations in other things. How I longed for the power to unsay my tactless words. It was too late though, and I felt that the kindest thing I could do now would be to walk away.

13 "You pay at the desk," the shop girl was telling him, but he did not seem to understand and kept trying to put the coins into her hand. And that was the last I saw or heard of the old man. Now he can never come there to sample plum puddings anymore.

Topic for Composition

Discuss with an older person Margaret Mead's assertion that the elderly are treated differently in other societies and consequently play a different role in those societies. Prepare a list of questions for the discussion. Then summarize the results in a brief essay.

Twentieth century dancers eloquently portray the Renaissance lovers who become husband and wife in Shakespeare's "Romeo and Juliet." Can people love deeply, yet remain autonomous?

3

Love and Marriage

Central Ideas and Supporting Details in Textbook Passages

> . . . the desire and pursuit of the whole is called love."
>
> —*Aristophanes from Symposium* of Plato c.a. 400 B.C.

Before Reading

This chapter addresses two subjects about which most of us have fairly strong opinions—love and marriage. The reading selection, which was written for a course in human sexuality, traces the history of love's role in marriage beginning with the ancient Greeks and concluding with modern times. How do you define love?

- Is the love one feels for a sweetheart, friend, parent, spouse, child, the same emotion? How are these loves different?
- Can you note a culture in which love is not a requirement for marriage?
- What is the basis for marriage in this culture?
- Do you think that people can love and remain autonomous at the same time?

READING SELECTION

As you read, examine how the author states and clarifies important points within one or more paragraphs. Try to distinguish the central or unifying ideas from their supporting details.

Love and Marriage: An Historical View

By Susan M. Garfield

1 The ancient Greeks perceived a schism between sexual and spiritual love. They **distinguished** between *eros,* **carnal** love associated with the sensual, physical and sexual aspects of love and **agapé**, spiritual love which is associated with protective and altruistic feelings. **Agapé** is the non-demanding side of love, which is demonstrated, for example, in parents' love for their children and in the genuine concern that we have for the life and growth of those whom we love.

2 Although **eros** and **agapé** may have occurred in the ancient Greek marriage, a man married primarily in order to increase his estate and to insure its continuity by producing children. According to the Greek philosopher Demosthenes, the appropriate age for marriage was eighteen for a woman and thirty-seven for a man; the appropriate role for a wife was "to provide . . . legitimate children and to grow old faithfully in the interior of the house." Greeks regarded heterosexual domestic relations as a normal part of a man's

life cycle, but they did not assume that the major love of a man's life would be his wife.

3 Greek culture considered women to be inferior to men; conversely, it celebrated what it perceived to be the greater physical beauty of young boys and the intellect of mature men. Apparently, the male homosexual relationship—and we do not know how **prevalent** such relationships were—was that of an older man and a youth. It was believed that the unity of *eros* and *agapé* might be realized in such relationships. The underlying assumption was that the young boy would himself grow up, in time, marry, continue his family line, and engage in normal masculine activities. Then, at sometime in his life, he might, in turn, have a relationship with a younger man or boy. A man's liaisons with boys and with **heterae**, women who were educated and independent in Athenian society, were not considered threats to marriage.

4 Christianity, following Jewish tradition, condemned homosexuality and drew a distinction between love and sex. Under the influence of the church, sexuality was suppressed, and women were idealized as nonsexual beings. The idealization of women reached its **zenith** in mariolatry, the adoration of the Virgin Mother.

5 In the eleventh century courtly love, a new male-female relationship emerged, which combined the idealization of women with **chivalry**, the knights' code of honor. Love became a novel and fashionable subject of discussion among aristocrats, who, in their formal "courts of love," argued its merits, described its characteristics and even devised rules to regulate lovers' behavior. Love came to mean a romantic relationship with someone other than one's spouse. It was synonymous with desire, yearning for what one could never entirely possess.

6 A **liaison** was formed between a knight and a lady, a woman whose husband, more than likely, was away for many years fighting a crusade. The knight pledged unselfish service to the lady. She was his source of inspiration. He fought tournaments in her honor and praised her goodness and beauty in song and poetry. In keeping with the Christian contempt for sex, chastity was observed in these affairs. Occasionally, the "purity" of the love was put to the test, when a couple slept together nude but refrained from sexual intercourse.

7 The courtly love relationship developed out of the social conditions of medieval life. Marriage in the Middle Ages had several clearly defined functions: financial benefits, personal protection,

procreation, but love was not among them. Romantic love and marriage were two separate entities that fulfilled separate needs. If marriage entailed obligation, love, on the contrary, was freely extended and returned. It enabled men and women to experience feelings of tenderness for one another; it introduced gentleness and restraint into the male-female relationship, and it ensured sexual **fidelity** in marriage. As knighthood declined, however, so did the sexual inhibitions of romantic lovers, and love and sex began to merge, at least, outside of marriage.

8 The Renaissance period continued to deny the existence of love in marriage. A European nobleman may have had as many as three women in his life: a wife for representative purposes, a mistress for aesthetic conversation and a woman to fulfill his sexual needs. Yet, sometime during the Renaissance the idea that sex and romantic love could exist in marriage and that romantic love was a prelude to marriage began taking hold. Romantic love assumes that it is not necessary to have a separation between spiritual love and marital sex relations and that the latter is **sanctified** by the former.

9 Surprisingly, the Puritans of the seventeenth century, whom we regard in a very different light, were, in fact, appreciative of physical closeness coupled with emotional warmth. It is true that they put people in the stocks for committing what we consider minor social **transgressions** such as gossiping, but they also engaged in **bundling**, where sweethearts spent long cold winter nights together in bed fully clothed. A New England custom for two centuries, **bundling** afforded several practical benefits: warmth, privacy, the avoidance of a return journey in treacherous darkness. Moreover, the Puritans apparently considered sex a good and natural part of marriage. Pastor Daniel Rogers preached to his congregation, "Married love is a sweet compound of spiritual affection and carnal affection, and this blend of the two is the vital spirit and heartblood of wedlock."

10 In the eighteenth and nineteenth centuries, politics, economics and technology combined to underscore the need for stable **monogamous** family life. Revolutions tumbled monarchs and leveled aristocratic regimes; common folk, citizens of new democracies, could not afford various companions to meet various needs. Moreover, the industrial revolution fostered the idea that the family was a refuge, a safe harbor, from the **isolation** and **alienation** of a rapidly industrializing society. Kindness, altruism, self-sacrifice,

peace, harmony: all were to be found in the ideal nineteenth-century Victorian family.

11 What happened to sex? The Victorians had large families, but sexual desire was regarded as an exclusively male phenomenon, women were supposed to be passionless, actually devoid of sexual feeling. Men sought sexual fulfillment outside of marriage, and prostitution flourished on a grand scale. A double standard of behavior was recognized: Men had far more sexual freedom than women and women were categorized as "good" and "bad." Men married the former; they had sexual relations with the latter.

12 By the mid-twentieth century, particularly in Western countries, romantic love had become a prerequisite for marriage. However, soaring divorce rates indicated that the romance requirement was having a disruptive effect on the institution of marriage itself. In explanation, psychologists suggested that we often seek in our mates those qualities which we, ourselves, lack. The resulting personality clash can destroy even the strongest romantic attraction. Moreover, a changing self-image was held by women who were less willing to play traditional nurturing roles. Eager to achieve autonomy and outspoken about their own emotional needs, many women felt that marriage with or without romance was not as important a factor in their lives as it had been for their mothers and grandmothers.

13 As the twenty-first century approaches, modern romantics are experimenting with various forms of marriage: marriage by contract; homosexual marriage; childless marriage; celibate marriage; and informal marriage (living together without benefit of ceremony). The search for *eros* and *agape,* together forever, continues.

Vocabulary

The following words are boldfaced in the reading selection. Write a synonym or brief definition for each. Add other unfamiliar terms and their meanings to the list.

WORD OR PHRASE	SYNONYM OR BRIEF DEFINITION
distinguished (1)	
carnal (1)	

WORD OR PHRASE	SYNONYM OR BRIEF DEFINITION
prevalent (3)	
zenith (4)	
chivalry (5)	
liaison (6)	
procreation (7)	
fidelity (7)	
sanctified (8)	
transgressions (9)	

YOUR ADDITIONS

WORD HISTORY: ETYMOLOGY

Language, like other important aspects of the human condition, is constantly evolving. The science of the evolution of language is *etymology*. Etymologists trace words back to their original forms. English in its original form, Old English, was a Teutonic language brought to Britain by Germanic invaders in the fifth century and modified by contact with the Celtic peoples who inhabited the islands.

The history of English reveals the influence of politics and geography on language development. Through several centuries, invading armies, particularly the Danes, brought new words into the language. Middle English, which emerged after the Norman Conquest in 1066, was a blending of Old English and Norman French. The Renaissance period is particularly noted for the great influx of vocabulary from the classical languages, Latin and Greek, and from French, Italian, and Spanish. According to the *American Heritage Dictionary of the English Language,* the English adopted words right and left, and enough words survived to make the vocabulary perhaps the largest of any language with a rich store of synonyms from different language sources. For example, English has the synonyms *royal* (French), *kingly* (Old English), and *regal* (Latin).

When consulting your dictionary, you should be sure to check the etymology of an unfamiliar word because it may provide an association that will help you to remember a new definition. The following table lists the original

Form	Source	Meaning
aesthetikos	Greek	sense perception
alius	Latin	from
aristos	Greek	best
alter	Latin	to others
carnalis	Latin	flesh
caelebs	Latin	unmarried
cheval	French	horse
creare	Latin	create
demos	Greek	common people
domus	Latin	house
fides	Latin	faith
genos	Greek	race
gamos	Greek	marriage
heteros	Greek	other
homos	Greek	same
idea	Greek	model, form
insula	Latin	island
kratos	Greek	power
monos	Greek	one
void	French	empty
sanctus	Latin	holy
skhisma	Greek	split, division
transgredic	Latin	to step across
psyche	Greek	soul

forms of words that appear in the reading selection. Study the list and then complete exercise A. (A comprehensive list of word elements—prefixes, suffixes, and stems—appears in Appendix B.)

A. Match the underscored word in the phrase on the left to its synonym in the column on the right by writing the letter in the appropriate space.

Example ___j___ protective and altruistic feelings

1. ___a___ heterosexual domestic relations
2. ___i___ combined idealization of women with chivalry
3. ___b___ leveled aristocracies

a. Traditional marriage
b. Rule of the "best"
c. One mate
d. Separation from the mainstream

4. __c__ stable monogamous family life — e. Reproduction

5. __d__ isolation and alienation of industrialized society — f. Made sacred

6. __e__ financial benefits, protection and procreation — g. Physical, sensual

7. __f__ the latter is sanctified by the former — h. Empty

8. __g__ eros, carnal love — i. Adoration

9. __h__ devoid of sexual feeling — j. Generous

10. __k__ schism between physical and spiritual love — k. Split or separation

Comprehension

SPECIFIC INFORMATION

A. Arrange the following historical periods in chronological order by numbering them in the spaces provided. Begin with Ancient Greece.

__2__ Middle Ages

__1__ Ancient Greece

__5__ Victorian Era

__4__ Puritan North America

__3__ Renaissance

B. According to the reading selection, what was not a major force strengthening the monogamous family union in the eighteenth and nineteenth centuries?

1. Economics
2. Revolution
3. Industrialization
4. Romance

C. The historical period in which women's needs and ambitions became an issue in marriage is

1. the Middle Ages.
2. modern times.
3. the Renaissance.
4. the Victorian era.

ANALYSIS

D. Which of the following is an illustrative detail?

1. The Greeks perceived a schism in love.
2. Victorians denied women's sexuality.
3. Marriage in the Middle Ages had specific functions.
4. *Agapê* is demonstrated in the love of parents for their children.

E. In the sentence "Romantic love assumes it is not necessary to have a separation between spiritual love and marital sex relations and that <u>the latter</u> is sanctified by the former," the underscored term refers to

1. romantic love.
2. marital sex relations.
3. spiritual love.
4. separation.

F. Reread paragraph 10 of the reading selection. The second and third sentences ________________ the first sentence.

1. illustrate
2. explain
3. restate
4. contradict

G. The central or unifying idea of the reading selection is that throughout history

1. people have married for love.
2. the primary function of marriage has been procreation.
3. the Greek marriage has been viewed as the ideal marriage.
4. the relationship between love and marriage has not been consistent.

INFERENCES AND INTERPRETATIONS

H. The author implies, but doesn't specifically state, that the Puritan character is generally considered to be

1. fun loving and lighthearted.
2. dramatic and imaginative.
3. unfeeling and inhibited.
4. natural and sensual.

Explain your answers to questions I and J in the space provided. With which historical period do you associate the feelings expressed in the following verses?

I. Unfortunate Coincidence

By Dorothy Parker

By the time you swear you're his,
  Shivering and sighing,
And he vows his passion is
  Infinite, undying.
Lady, make a note of this,
  One of you is lying.

1. Ancient Greece
2. Middle Ages
3. Renaissance
4. Victorian Era

because

J. Indian Summer

By Dorothy Parker

In youth, it was a way I had
  To do my best to please,
And change, with every passing lad,
  To suit his theories.
But now I know the things I know,
  And do the things I do;
And if you do not like me so,
  To hell, my love, with you!

1. Renaissance
2. Industrial Revolution
3. Puritan
4. modern times

because

Study Activity

CENTRAL IDEAS AND SUPPORTING DETAILS

Often in textbooks, one sentence will clearly express the unifying or central idea of a paragraph or of a series of closely related paragraphs. At other times, however, particularly when material is abstract and complex, ideas expressed in two or more sentences combine to form a central idea, a broad inclusive statement. The remaining sentences contain details that relate to the central idea by explaining, illustrating, or restating it.

A TECHNIQUE FOR IDENTIFYING CENTRAL IDEAS AND SUPPORTING DETAILS

A general indication of comprehension is the ability to express in your own words what you have read. You can master a technique for expressing central ideas and details in textbook passages by asking and answering information questions as you read:

1. To determine the subject, ask "*What* is this about?" To bring the subject into focus, ask "*When, Why,* and *Who* is it about?" These questions will yield various related aspects of the subject which you can combine into a logical phrase. The subject may actually serve as a title for the passage.
2. To determine the central idea, ask "What general and inclusive point is the author making about the subject?" The answer, the central idea of the passage, should be stated in a complete sentence.
3. To determine the details and their specific functions in the passage, ask "What statements explain, illustrate, or restate the central idea?" (The list of signal words on page 00 will help you.) Details may be expressed in a few related words and phrases.

Model A

Reread paragraph 1 of the reading selection, "Love and Marriage." Then study the following questions and answers:

What is the passage about?	Ideas of love
When?	Ancient times
Where?	Greece
	(the subject) Ancient Greek ideas of love

What is the author saying about ancient Greek ideas of love?

(the central or unifying idea)
The ancient Greeks saw a division of love into *eros,* physical love, and *agapé,* spiritual love.

What points explain, illustrate, or restate the main idea?

(explanatory details)
1. *Eros*—unthinking, sexual physical love
2. *Agapé*—nondemanding, altruistic love
(illustrative details)
3. *Agapé*—parents' love for child, genuine concern for the other

Model B

Read the following paragraph and study the questions it raises and their answers.

> The joining of love and marriage is a relatively new phenomenon in human history. In the past, marriages were arranged for economic and traditional reasons, not for love. In ancient Greece, for example, love between two men was the ideal and marriage was another state altogether. In medieval Europe and even later, love, for a man and a woman, was something experienced outside of marriage. In many cultures this pattern has continued into this century, but the influence of Western industrialized society is initiating changes.

What is the passage about? — Love and marriage

When? — In human history

Where? — The west and other cultures (the subject) Love and marriage in human history

What is the author saying about love and marriage in history?

(the central or unifying idea)
Love in marriage is a new experience. (explanatory details)

What details explain, illustrate, or restate the central idea?

1. Marriages have been arranged for economic and traditional reasons.
(illustrative details)
2. Greeks—love between two men, not husband and wife
3. Medieval Europe—love outside marriage
(restatement)
4. Western industrialized society is changing the pattern.

Model C

The central or unifying idea is often, but not always, found at the beginning of a paragraph. In the following passage, the details, examples of the central idea, lead the reader to this important point. The pattern can be compared to an addition problem. The details add up to the central or unifying idea.

> What is love? can you define it, conceptualize it, sort out its essential components? Is the love you feel for your sweetheart, friend, parent, child the same emotion?

Let us focus our discussion for the present on romantic love, the kind that is claimed to justify a commitment to marriage.

> Reiss (1971) calls this "courtship love" and defines it as a "type of intense emotional feeling developing from a primary relationship involving a single male and female and consisting of rights and duties similar to those of a husband and wife." Kephart (1972) puts together three characteristics shared by most definitions of love. They are a strong emotional attachment toward a person of the opposite sex; the tendency to think of this person in an idealized manner; and a marked physical attraction. The psychologist Harry Stack Sullivan (1947) says that a state of love exists "when the satisfaction or the security of another person becomes as significant to one as is one's own security." If these three definitions of love can be taken as representative of the social science approach, romantic love is an intense emotional experience that probably varies from person to person and within one person over time.

What is the passage about?	Meaning of love
Who is it about?	Social scientists
When?	Contemporary
Subject:	Love to social science
What is the social science definition of love?	Romantic love is an intense emotional experience that varies and changes within and between individuals.
Details:	Theory 1 Reis Theory 2 Kephart Theory 3 Sullivan = Social science definition of romantic love

HOW IDEAS RELATE

A. Identifying the subject: Circle the subject in each of the following groups of related ideas.

Example husband as authority figure; large families; stable and monogamous; Victorian marriage; home as a safe harbor; sexually unfulfilling

1. sexually chaste; result of social conditions; courtly love; chivalry: the knights' code of honor; idealization of women
2. "a bond of carnal and spiritual affection"; sweethearts bundled; harsh punishments; Puritan contradictions
3. eighteen years old; grew old faithfully; Ancient Greek wife; ignored *beterae;* not husband's major love interest; increased husband's estate
4. condemned homosexuality; idealized women; in Jewish tradition; suppressed sexuality; influence of Christianity
5. shared responsibility; modern marriage; experimental; soaring divorce rates

B. Match the central idea in the column on the left to the details in the column on the right which explain, illustrate, or restate it.

1. ______ The Victorian attitude towards sex created social problems for Victorians and future generations.

2. ______ A variety of forces shaped the structure and philosophy of the Victorian family.

3. ______ The ideal Victorian family was a stable and supportive environment.

4. ______ Women are less focused on marriage than they were in the past.

a. Political revolutions, economic needs, isolation alienation, the common person

b. Kindness, virtue, altruism, self-sacrifice, peace

c. Career goals, self-expression, rejection of nurturing role, physical demands

d. Privacy, warmth, safety, affection

5. ______ Puritan custom of bundling had practical benefits.

e. Double standard, prostitution flourished, emptiness in marriage, devaluation of women

EXPRESSING CENTRAL IDEAS

Read the following passages from the reading selection and thematically related textbook material and specify the subject and the central or unifying idea in the space provided.

A.

The industrial revolution influenced our modern conception of romantic love. Women went to work and encountered a wider choice of possible mates. Technology afforded more leisure time for people to take part in sexually mixed recreational activities. Furthermore, the rapidly growing trade unions brought people together for educational and social as well as political purposes. Yet, family and religion maintained an emotional hold on the youth of the industrial revolution, therefore, sexual attraction that did not have marriage and family in mind was unacceptable. Young people cloaked their physical attraction in the mysterious emotional experience they called love.

Subject:

Central idea:

Do the details explain or illustrate the central idea?

B.

As 19th century Victorian Americans became sexually repressed, they acquired a ridiculous modesty. For example, men and women could visit the art gallery in Philadelphia only in separate groups, lest exposure to nude classical statues cause embarrassment in mixed company. Often statues were draped to spare the female sensibility. When a British tourist asked a young American lady who had fallen off a rock whether she had hurt her leg, she became deeply offended and instructed him that the word "leg" was never used before ladies; in mixed company, she said, the word was "limb." Later the same tourist visiting a ladies' school was stunned to see a square piano with four limbs, each of which, to protect the pupils, had been dressed in little trousers with frills at the bottom.

Subject:

Central idea:

Do the details explain or illustrate the central idea?

C.

In American society love and marriage go together as the song says, "like a horse and carriage." But the belief that "you can't have one without the other" is not common to all cultures. An example of the irrelevancy of love to marriage in cultures other than our own is found in the musical production, "Fiddler on the Roof," which takes place in Czarist Russia. Tevye, an old-world Jewish patriarch, asks his wife of twenty-five years whether or not she loves him. She responds to what she considers an absurd question by replying that he must be ill or upset. She suggests that he lie down. After a while she is sure that he'll feel better. However, Tevye is not satisfied with this response and he repeats his question. His wife then elaborates on the inappropriateness of the question. She's cleaned, cooked and worked for him for twenty-five years and he wants to talk about love? She's lived, fought and starved with him; she's shared her bed with him. Isn't that love? Tevye concludes that it must be and hence they love each other. But this love doesn't mean anything since it has played such an insignificant part in their marriage from the beginning.

Subject:

Central idea:

Does the last sentence really mean what it says? Explain your answer.

D.

The Western conception of romantic love tends to lead towards an idealization of the loved one rather than a realistic view of that person. Consequently romantic love may lead to problems when the daily routines and ordinary tasks and activities of marriage enter the picture. As time passes, a couple finds that their love diminishes as reality settles in. Perhaps the best example to illustrate this point is this story: A student was kissing his fiancée goodnight on the steps of her dormitory when they were interrupted by the student's Japanese roommate who proceeded to lecture them on the fragility of love as a basis for marriage. He said in essence: A western marriage is like a hot tea kettle on a cold stove. After a while the tea (love) cools. What starts out as fireworks soon gets cold. An Asian marriage is like a cold tea kettle on a hot stove. The basis for the relationship is not blind love but rather a true friendship—the love grows out of warm understanding, not passionate physical attraction, and it gets better and better.

Subject:

Central idea:

The student's lecture illustrates the main idea. How well does he make his point?

E.

Romantic love, according to Hunt (1959), may have more to it than has been noted by its critics. First, romantic love accepted women as human beings of value rather than merely as sexual objects; it stressed the concept that lovers should serve and please each other rather than seek to conquer each other. Loyalty and friendship made love a source of support and genuine affection especially in marriage. The more notions about romantic love that were absorbed within marriage, the more marriage came to seem an ideal state and the primary source of individual happiness. It certainly makes people strive for and maintain romantic elements. Some married couples, even after 20 or more years, still have affection and romantic feeling for each other, which they express in many ways, not necessarily by clinging and caressing in public, but by friendliness, pride and admiration for the other person.

Subject:

Central idea:

Can you describe a couple whose marriage is a good example of the central idea?

READING FOR DETAILS

Read the following paragraphs and complete their analysis by noting the details.

A.

The ideas of courtly love were first expressed in the poetry composed by troubadours in Southern France in the second half of the eleventh century. Some scholars believe it is the remnants of classical poetry preserved as folk songs; others cite the source as the love poetry of Moslem Spain. The ideas were taken by professional entertainers who began to write poems glorifying ladies and the act of adoring them from afar. The greatest feudal prince of the region, William IX of Aquitaine, was attracted to the ideal, and soon the composing of lyric love poems became fashionable throughout Southern France.

Subject: troubadour love poetry

Central idea: Troubadour love poetry became popular in southern France late in the eleventh century.

Details:

B.

The same period that saw the development of troubadour poetry witnessed a general improvement in the status of women. The Virgin Mary, who had previously occupied a comparatively minor place in Christianity, became the chief advocate with her son for sinful men and women. In his youth the great Pope Innocent III wrote troubadour poetry to the Virgin. There had always been nunneries, but they had lacked the prestige, wealth and reputation of the great monasteries. Now in France a monastic order for noble women was founded. Thus, throughout Western Europe, the late eleventh century marked a clear appreciation of the status of women in civilization as a whole.

Subject: Troubadour poetry and status of women in eleventh century

Central idea: The period of troubadour poetry marked a rise in the status of women in Western Europe.

Details:

C.

Though passion and marriage continued together in the romantic dream, they were separated in American reality. For one thing the very Declaration of Independence and the formation of the new democratic republic contained a deep and subtle challenge to the ideas of romantic love. Romance, after all, had sprung up in the feudalism of medieval Europe as the pastime of the nobility. The American colonies had no nobility, no feudal institutions, and the new republic pledged itself to liberty, equality and rationality. The bright clear light of the young nation was hard on passion.

Subject: Romance in the young republic

Central idea: Many forces in the new democracy challenged romantic love.

Details:

D.

The socialization of love in our country emphasizes romantic love as the only true basis for a happy marriage. Films, television soap operas, music and magazines reinforce the belief that love alone makes life worth-while. The message is that the strange, apparently irresistible attraction between lovers is perpetual, that it conquers the world's evils and that it is fulfilled by marriage. Commercials bombard individuals with symbols of romantic love. Beginning in childhood and continuing throughout our lives we are exposed to fairy tales and stories with happy-ever-after romantic endings.

Subject: Socialization of romantic love

Central idea: Americans are socialized to believe that romantic love is the only basis for a happy marriage.

Details:

Critical Thinking

QUESTIONS FOR INDEPENDENT AND GROUP WORK

A. Troubadours described the attributes of their loves or the experience of being in love in their music. Do any modern musical artists compose and perform in the troubadour tradition? What are the subjects of today's popular music?

B. The notion of "a lady" comes to us from the Middle Ages. In recent years, feminists have chosen to be called women rather than ladies. What might be their reasons for rejecting the term "lady"? Is one term more desirable to you than the other? Why? Why not?

Connections

CROSS-CULTURAL VOICES ON THE SUBJECT OF LOVE

As you read or listen to each of these poems, once again consider the question, "Can people love deeply yet remain autonomous?" You may want to underscore images (details) that are particularly meaningful for you.

A. This Chinese poem is written for the holiday Double Seven (July 7) when two constellations, Lyra and Aquila, meet in the summer sky. A myth says that the brightest star in the constellation Lyra came to earth in the form of a weaver. She fell in love with a shepherd, Aquila, who, because he was a mortal, could not follow her back to heaven. Once a year, a bridge of birds allows the shepherd to cross to his star.

Evening Star

By Shu Shan Cheng

Clouds dissolve in lovely images
And passion bursts from a shooting star.
On that same day the wind disperses
Morning dew. Two stars unite;
Just once they join, transcending human concourse,
Submerged in yearning.
For one dreamlike moment
They turn their faces from the magpies' bridge.
Love unfading, yearly renewed,
Needs not man's daily meetings to endure.

B. The following verses are taken from "In Praise of Krishna," an Indian poem that has great religious meaning. According to Indian myth, the God Krishna has come to live among mortals and a young village girl, Radha, has fallen in love with him, leaving her home, husband and child to serve him. The emotions that Radha expresses here are those that all men and women feel in their quest for Krishna.

As the mirror to my hand,
the flowers to my hair,
Kohl to my eyes
tambul (sweetness) to my mouth,
musk (perfume) to my breast,
necklace to my throat, ecstasy to my flesh,
heart to my home—

As wing to bird,
water to fish, life to the living—
so you to me.

Love I take on splender
in your splender,
grace and gentleness are
mine because of your beauty

Here Radha laments.

As if a day when no sun came up
and no color came to the earth—
that's how it is in my heart
when he goes away.

O my friend, my sorrow
is unending.

It is the rainy season, my
house is empty,
the sky is filled with seething clouds,
the earth sodden with rain,
and my love far away.

Cruel kama (desire) pierces
me with his arrows:
the lightning flashes; the
peacocks dance
frogs and waterbirds drunk with
delight, call incessantly and
my heart is heavy.
Darkness on earth,
the sky lit with a sullen glare . . .

C. Contemporary Lebanese poet Kahlil Gibran instructs "love one another, but make not a bond of love."

On Marriage

By Kahlil Gibran

Love one another, but make not a bond of love:
Let it rather be a moving sea between the shores of your souls.
Fill each other's cup, but drink not from one cup.
Give one another of your bread, but eat not from the same loaf.
Sing together and be joyous, but let each one of you be alone,
Even as the strings of the lute are alone,
Though they quiver with the same music.
Give your hearts, but not into each other's keeping,
For only the land of life can contain your hearts.
Stand together, yet not too near together.

For the pillars of the temple stand apart,
And the oak tree and the cyprus grow not in each other's shade.

How does each poem view the relationship between love and autonomy?

Topics for Composition

A. Reread the quotation that introduces this chapter. Given the idea that lovers are matched parts of a perfect whole, describe the person who is or could be your perfect "other half."

B. The reading selection traces the history of love through several historical periods. Trace the kinds of love you have experienced, first as a child, then as an adolescent, and now as an adult.

For these two young men, a formal ceremony marks the beginning of adulthood. Do you know of similar rites of passage in your own or other cultures?

4

Learning Culture

Thought Patterns in College Textbooks

All growth is
accompanied by pain.

—Zen proverb

Before Reading

The following reading selection is from a textbook in cultural anthropology. The author compares the child-rearing practices of modern industrial society to those of traditional hunting and farming societies. Think about the quotation that introduces this chapter, "All growth is accompanied by pain." Before reading, consider these questions: What are the different stages of life? List them here: *infancy,* ________________, ________________, __________, ____________________. Which, in your opinion, is the best time of life? ______________ Which may be the most painful? ______________ Why?

READING SELECTION

Technical terms from the reading selection, as defined by the text glossary include:

Anthropology The comparative study of humankind.

Continuity Similar expectations for children and adults.

Culture (general) The learned and shared kinds of behavior that make human adaptation possible.

Culture (specific) The way of life characteristic of a particular society.

Socialization The learning process by which cultural traditions are passed on from one generation to the next. Specifically, the way individuals are taught social roles, moral values, and obedience to authority.

Learning Culture

By Serena Nanda

Cultural Continuity and Discontinuity

1 Anthropologist Ruth Benedict characterized American culture as containing major discontinuities, that is, contradictions between what is expected of children and what is expected of adults. The basic discontinuity between childhood and adulthood for Americans is that children do not take on responsibility until they become adults. Children in our culture are not expected to be responsible. They are expected to play, not work, and few have the opportunity to contribute in any meaningful way to the basic tasks of society. A second major discontinuity is that children are required to be **submissive** to adult authority, but as adults they are expected to be **dominant**. This is especially true for males. Sons must obey their

fathers, but as fathers they must dominate their sons. A third major discontinuity has to do with sex. As children, Americans are not allowed to engage in sexual behavior. For many, just the mere idea of childhood sexuality is **repellent**. As adults, however, especially as men and women marry, sex is considered to be a normal, even valued activity.

2 In great contrast to the discontinuities experienced by the individual learning to participate in American culture is the continuity of socialization among many native American societies. The Cheyenne, a Plains tribe, exhibit a great deal of continuity in their culture. According to E.A. Hoebel, the **ethnographer** of the Cheyenne, Cheyenne children are not treated as a different order of people than are adults. They are regarded as smaller and not yet fully **competent** adults, though, by American standards, their competency is quite astounding. Both boys and girls learn to ride horses as soon as they can walk. By the time they are six little boys ride bareback and use the lasso. By eight boys help to herd the camp's horses. As soon as they can use them, boys get small but accurate bows and arrows. Little girls help their mothers gather wood and carry water.

3 In their play, Cheyenne children both imitate and participate in adult tasks. Until they reach twelve and are ready for real hunting the boys join the girls at "play camp," where the entire routine of camp life is dramatized: Girls "mother" the smallest children and boys carry out the roles of warrior and hunter, catching fish and bringing in birds and rabbits for food. They even **mimic** the rituals of self-torture practiced in the sacred religious ceremony, the Sun Dance.

4 Control of **aggression** is an important value among the Cheyenne, and aggression rarely occurs among adults. The reason is that for the Cheyenne, the needs of the group are paramount to the needs of the individual. Therefore, they learn control at an early age. Infants who cry are not physically punished, but if their apparent needs have been met, the babies will be removed from the camp and their baskets hung in the bushes till they stop crying. This early lesson teaches that one cannot force his or her will on others. Aggression, the loss of control, does not bring reward to children or adults; rather, it results in social isolation.

5 Cheyenne childhood requires a great deal of discipline, responsibility and competence, and these demands are consistent

with the demands on adults. There is no discontinuity between Cheyenne childhood, adolescence and adulthood. The transition to adult status is very easy, being a continuum of what is learned in childhood. For a boy the recognition of this status comes with his first participation as hunter and warrior, which occurs about the age of twelve. This is a real and important event and his achievement is publicly rewarded by his parents' praise and a feast that is given in his honor. Hoebel states, "Cheyenne youths have little reason to be rebels without cause. They slip easily into manhood, knowing their contributions are immediately wanted, valued, and **ostentatiously** rewarded."

Initiation Rites

6 It has been suggested that there is more discontinuity in socialization for males than for females. For girls, the transition to adult status is a continuation of their early life which is organized around the family and caring for others. Boys, on the other hand, are often raised in the company and under the supervision of women. The need for boys to assert their independence from female identification is one explanation for the frequency of male initiation rites which occur in many societies around the world.

7 In many societies a boy between the ages of five to twelve must undergo an initiation, after which he is publicly recognized as a man. This **rite** of passage is frequently lengthy, dramatic and painful, often involving circumcision. During this initiation, a boy must also be taught tribal lore, as well as more practical elements of culture; therefore, some anthropologists see initiation rites primarily as equivalent to the formal schooling received by children in our own society. Still another explanation offered for male initiation rites is that they dramatize the values of society in a context outside of the home. By taking the child out of the home, the initiation rite emphasizes the importance of citizenship—the fact that an individual must be responsible to the whole society, and that society as well as the family has an interest in him. A fourth function is the reaffirmation of the solidarity and importance of the male bond in the society.

The Marginal Status of Adolescents

8 In many societies, adolescents have *marginal status;* that is, they are *not fully incorporated into their culture.* Where cultural

continuity is present, however, as among the Cheyenne, youth are not **marginal**. There is a gradually increasing social participation from childhood through adulthood. In other societies, where there is discontinuity, where a youth must change in order to become an adult, dramatic rituals of initiation ensure that this change is made. In still other societies, like our own, there is a discontinuity, but no ritual. Young men, particularly, are left on their own to "initiate themselves." This may lead to the formation of youth gangs or participation in various group activities in which **peers** socialize each other into the male role. This behavior is frequently, although not always, rebellious and contrary to society's values.

9 As we have seen, there is great variability in the ways that socialization occurs. Many cultures seem far more successful than our own both in providing cultural continuity and meeting the needs of individuals in the different stages of their development.

Vocabulary

The following words are boldfaced in the reading selection. Write a synonym or brief definition for each. Add other unfamiliar terms and their meanings to the list.

WORD OR PHRASE	**SYNONYM OR BRIEF DEFINITION**
submissive (1)	
dominant (1)	
repellent (1)	
ethnographer (2)	
competent (2)	
mimic (3)	
aggression (4)	
ostentatiously (5)	

WORD OR PHRASE	SYNONYM OR BRIEF DEFINITION
rite (7)	
marginal (8)	
peers (8)	

YOUR ADDITIONS

EXTENDING VOCABULARY WITH WORD FORMS

Words are classified grammatically according to how they function in written and spoken communication. Briefly, words that describe are *adjectives;* words that name are *nouns;* words that state action in time are *verbs* and words that modify *adjectives* and tell how and when actions are performed are *adverbs.* (See Appendix II for a list of the common suffixes, word endings that indicate specific grammatical forms.) The following table reviews grammatical forms and functions.

Basic Review of Grammatical Forms and Functions

Form	Function	Example
Noun	Names a person, place, thing, or idea	*Ruth Benedict* *America* *Buffalo* *Maturity*
Verb	States action in time	The Cheyenne *learn* control. Benedict *characterized* them.
Adjective	Describes	*Dramatic* ritual
Adverb	Modifies an adjective; tells how and when actions occur	*Frequently* lengthy *Physically* punished Peers *often* socialize each other.

A. Complete the following word forms chart by filling in the missing words. For verbs, use the infinitive ("to" + the verb). An asterisk indicates that the word rarely takes that form.

	Noun	Verb	Adjective	Adverb
Ex.	dominance	to dominate	dominant	dominantly
1.	competence/y	•	competent	competently
2.	aggression	•	aggressive	
3.	rebellion	to rebel	rebellious	rebelliously
4.	drama	to dramatize	dramatic	dramatically
5.	frequency	to frequent	frequent	frequently

B. Complete each of the following sentences with the appropriate word from the word forms chart:

1. A child's development can be thwarted if he is given tasks he is not ___competent___ to perform.
2. In societies where adolescents are marginal, boys, ___frequently___, if not always, socialize each other into the male role.
3. In a tribal culture, the rite of passage is a very ___dramatic___ event.
4. The Cheyenne discourage self-display and all other forms of ___agression___.
5. An unhappy adolescent may be seen as a ___rebel___ without a cause.

C. Complete each of the following sentences with a word from this list: marginal, ostentatiously, lore, ethnographer, status.

1. One who has the habits and values of two groups but belongs to neither is called ___marginal___.
2. The knowledge and history of a group is its ___lore___.
3. By ___ostentatiously___ rewarding children, parents give them a sense of esteem.
4. An ___ethnographer___ observes, records, and analyzes the social interaction of a particular group.
5. An individual's position in a hierarchy of prestige is his or her ___status___.

Comprehension

SPECIFIC INFORMATION

A. According to anthropologist Ruth Benedict, the following is *not* a major discontinuity in American culture:

1. Children are expected to play, not to contribute.
2. Adults are expected to be dominant, not submissive.
3. Children are expected to share, not to accumulate.
4. In contrast to children, adults are expected to be sexually active.

B. Cheyenne children imitate and contribute to tribal life in

1. the Sun Dance ceremony.
2. the first hunt.
3. the dramatic rituals of initiation.
4. play camp.

C. According to the author, adolescent rebellion occurs in cultures where there is

1. discontinuity and no ritual to mark the transition from childhood to adulthood.
2. continuity and ease of transition from childhood to adult roles.
3. discontinuity and ceremonial recognition of the transition from childhood to adulthood.
4. continuity and joyful celebration of achieving adulthood.

ANALYSIS

D. The central or unifying idea of the reading selection, "Learning Culture," is that

1. adolescence is a universally difficult stage of life.
2. adolescents have marginal status in North American society.
3. the transition from childhood to adulthood is different in different societies.
4. initiation is an important aspect of tribal culture.

E. The author's purpose in paragraph 7 of the reading selection is to present

1. the steps in an initiation rite.
2. reasons for initiation rites.
3. different kinds of initiation rites.
4. society's need for initiation rites.

How many items (steps, reasons, kinds or needs) are presented? 4

F. In paragraph 4 of the reading selection, the practice of removing a crying baby from camp is

1. an example of early socialization among the Cheyenne.
2. a cause of the adult Cheyenne's aggressive personality.
3. the central idea of the paragraph.
4. an illustration of child abuse among tribal people.

INFERENCES AND INTERPRETATIONS

G. Which is an unstated objective of socialization for the Cheyenne?

1. Emotional control
2. Separation of boys from mothers' influence
3. Subordination of the individual's needs to the group's needs
4. Physical endurance and courage

Explain your answers to H, I, and J in writing.

H. For college students, admission, registration, examination, and graduation can be interpreted as

1. tribal lore.
2. rites of passage.
3. examples of cultural continuity.
4. needs in a hierarchy.

I. According to anthropologist Serena Nanda, in comparison to girls, boys, in most societies, have

1. a longer, less demanding childhood.
2. less independence.
3. similar responsibilities.
4. more independence.

J. A story that clearly intends to socialize (teach values) is a

1. comic strip.
2. situation comedy.
3. children's story such as "The Three Pigs."
4. soap opera.

Relate an example of your choice. What value(s) does it teach?

Study Activity

THOUGHT PATTERNS IN COLLEGE TEXTBOOKS

This Study Activity will help you to identify and work with the thought patterns that organize general and detailed information in the textbook narrative. The basic thought patterns—*simple list, time order, cause-effect,* and *comparison (contrast)*—work within and between sentences and within and between paragraphs.

WRITERS AND READERS USE THOUGHT PATTERNS

Writers use patterns to achieve specific purposes. When the purpose is to present a series of related facts or ideas, the pattern is simple listing. When the purpose is to present the steps in a procedure or stages in a process, the pattern is time order. When the purpose is to present reasons for, or the results of events or conditions, the pattern is cause-effect. When the purpose is to examine related elements focusing on their similarities or differences, the pattern is comparison (contrast).

Patterns are used alone or in combination. They tend to appear in combination when material is abstract and theoretical, requiring many illustrations and examples to achieve clarity.

Thought patterns also have several functions for the reader: They alert the reader to the writer's purpose; they focus the reader's attention on unifying or central ideas; they suggest questions that the information in the passage answers; they provide a structure for note-taking.

SIGNAL EXPRESSIONS

Certain words, phrases, and symbols that join ideas indicate particular thought patterns. Once identified, these signal expressions alert the reader to the author's thought processes. Just as traffic signals alert a driver to obstacles, detours, and shortcuts en route to a destination, signal expressions assist the reader in following the development of an idea or an explanation to its conclusion.

How well do you know the common signal expressions? Work through the following sentence level exercises to assess your understanding.

A. Match the concept on the left to that on the right based on the meaning of the underscored signal expression.

____ 1. American adolescents may be marginal unlike
____ 2. American children play games such as
____ 3. Native Americans value cooperation; moreover
____ 4. Children must play; therefore,
____ 5. Children must play; however,

a. bingo, monopoly and jumprope.
b. adolescents in tribal groups.
c. adults must work.
d. they discourage individualism.
e. toys are big business.

B. Rewrite each of the following sentences using alternatives for the underscored signal expressions.

Example: Children must be submissive to adult authority, but as adults they are expected to be dominant.

1. Cheyenne children are regarded as not fully competent adults; although by American standards their competency is astounding.

2. There are several reasons for initiation rites such as public recognition of adulthood, citizenship, education, and solidarity.

3. Cheyenne children learn skills: first, riding, next, using a lasso, then herding horses, and finally caring for younger children.

4. Cheyenne children learn self-control at an early age; as a result, great harmony exists among adults.

5. Anthropologists equate initiation rites with schooling because during these ceremonies children learn the lore of their tribe.

MODELS OF THOUGHT PATTERNS

The following models of thought patterns in passages of varying length and complexity are from material that is thematically related to the reading selection. The passages are grouped according to the thought patterns they exemplify. Each model is followed by an analysis, a written account of the reader's mental observations, particularly the information questions raised as he or she progresses through the text. You may complete each analysis by answering the reader's questions in your notebook.

List

Writing a shopping list before entering a supermarket makes shopping more efficient. Similarly lists permit writers to present closely related ideas or facts in an efficient and clear manner. The reading selection incorporates lists. Paragraph 1 includes a list of closely related ideas—three kinds of discontinuity in American culture. Paragraph 7 lists several reasons for male initiation rites. Reread these paragraphs after examining the following signal expressions that are commonly used in lists.

also	and	Listing by numbers
furthermore	moreover	Listing by letters
another	in addition	Dates
finally	many	Punctuation
such as	various	
examples are	following points	
characteristics are	besides	
include	to illustrate	

A passage may include detailed lists within an overall list. In this case, broad categories often are stated in an introductory sentence and then elaborated in the remaining sentences of the passage as shown in paragraph A.

> A. Communal rites fall into two major categories: (1) rites of solidarity and (2) rites of passage. In the rites of solidarity, participation in dramatic public rituals enhances the sense of group identity, coordinates the actions of the individual members of the group, and prepares the group for immediate or future cooperative action. Rites of passage celebrate the social movement of individuals into and out of groups or out of statuses of critical importance both to the individual and to the community. Reproduction, the achievement of manhood and womanhood, marriage, and death are the principal worldwide occasions for rites of passage.

Pattern:	List
Author's purpose:	To discuss the two major types of communal rites.
Reader's questions:	What are the categories of communal rites? What are the functions of rites of solidarity? What are the functions of rites of passage? What are occasions for rites of passage? No specific rites of solidarity are described. Can you think of some examples?

Time Order

When the author's purpose is to present the steps in a procedure or the stages or phases of a process the pattern is time order. The chronology (that is, the specific order in which items are listed, steps are performed, events occur, or stages emerge) is crucial to meaning. You may wish to review paragraphs 2 and 3 of the reading selection that depict the chronology of the Cheyenne child's enculturation. Before attempting to analyze chronologically presented information, study the following signal expressions used in time order.

before	the process of	subsequently
after	the following procedure	immediately
next	begin	the steps in
soon	while	the phases in
following	later	conclude
when	earlier	

Study paragraph B and complete its analysis.

B. Ethnographers frequently encounter a psychological barrier to effective research which is called *culture shock.* According to anthropologist Kalvero Oberg, culture shock consists of four stages: The first stage, the *honeymoon,* is characterized by feelings of elation and optimism. It is followed by stage 2, the critical period in which the ethnographer has feelings of hostility and superiority towards the people with whom he or she has come to live and work. Often at this time the ethnographer seeks isolation. The third or recovery phase is characterized by the ability to laugh particularly at oneself; it is soon followed by the fourth and final stage, adjustment. In the adjustment phase, ethnographers accept their own marginal status, their appropriate place in the scheme of things.

Pattern: Time order

Author's purpose: To explain the term culture shock by describing its stages.

Reader's questions: How many phases are there in culture shock?
What are the different phases?
What is culture shock?

Cause-Effect

When the author's purpose is to stress the causes (reasons) for events or conditions, or the effects (results or consequences) of events or conditions, the cause-effect pattern is used. For example, paragraph 4 in the reading selection is organized by the cause-effect thought pattern. The cause expressed in the paragraph is that among the Cheyenne, the needs of the group are more important than the needs of the individual; the effect, or result, is that the Cheyenne value and learning self-control at an early age. The remaining sentences indicate how Cheyenne infants are socialized, how they are taught acceptable Cheyenne behavior. Examine the following cause-effect signals.

CAUSE		*EFFECT*	
because of	the reason is	hence	therefore
the causes of	the effects of	thus	consequently
due to	if	result	so
since	why?	outcome	accordingly
			why?

A cause-effect passage will often contain a question and its answer. Study paragraph C which illustrates the analysis of a passage that contains an organizing question.

> C. Rites of passage accompany changes in position or stature that are of general public concern. Why are birth, puberty, marriage, and death so frequently the occasions for rites of passage? Probably because of their public implications: the individual who is born, who reaches adulthood, who takes a spouse, or who dies is not the only person implicated in these events. Many other people must adjust to these momentous changes. Being born defines a new life, and it also brings into existence or modifies the position of parents, grandparent, sibling, heir, age-mate, and many other domestic and political relationships. The function of rites of passage is to give communal recognition to the entire complex of new or altered relationships as well as to changes experienced by the individuals who are the center of attention.

Pattern: Cause-effect

Author's purpose: To give a reason for the celebration of rites of passage at specific times in an individual's life

Reader's question:	Why are birth, puberty, marriage, and death so frequently the occasions for rites of passage?

Comparison and Contrast

When the purpose is to compare two or more objects, ideas, people, or events, the overall thought pattern is comparison. In a statement of comparison, the author generally stresses either similarities or differences. When differences are apparent, the thought pattern is comparison with emphasis on *contrast.* An analysis of comparison (contrast) requires identification of the entities being compared and identification of the subject of comparison. Examine the following expressions used in comparison and contrast paragraphs.

Comparison

both	similarly
likewise	as well as
also	too
share	in common
like	same
more	less

Contrast

but	yet
however	still
unlike	in contrast to
on the contrary	although
even	nevertheless
while	more
less	

In paragraph 5 of the reading selection, Cheyenne boys and girls are compared. The subject of comparison is the degree of discontinuity that each sex experiences. Differences are stressed. Boys experience far more discontinuity in most societies than girls, for whom "the transition to adult status is a continuation of early life . . . ." Read example D and study its analysis.

D. It has been suggested that there is more discontinuity in socialization for males than for females. For girls, the transition to adult status is a continuation of their early life which is organized around the family and caring for others. Boys, on the other hand, are often raised in the company and under the supervision of women. The need for boys to assert their independence from female identification is one explanation for the frequency of male initiation rites which occur in many societies around the world.

Pattern: comparison (contrast), emphasis on differences

Author's purpose: compare boys' and girls' socialization

Reader's question: How does the socialization of boys and girls compare?

Combined Patterns

Patterns overlap as ideas become more abstract and, therefore, require examples and illustrations to achieve clarity. For example, in passages that stress contrasts or similarities, the author frequently presents the causes or results of contrasting or similar conditions. Study paragraph E.

E. The passage of an individual to old age is hardly ever marked by one of the rites of passage. This is partly because it is difficult to tell just when people enter old age, and even more because people rarely like to think of themselves as old. It is true that in many regions, the aged are given a great deal of respect and are highly honored. This is true in China; among some Australian tribes, the elders were so important that these societies are characterized by the term *gerontocracy,* the rule of the aged. This is in marked contrast with the situation in our culture, especially for women. In certain parts of our society, it is still very difficult for a woman to give her age.

Patterns: Comparison (contrast) cause-effect

Author's purpose: To explain why the transition to old age is rarely marked by rites of passage; to compare attitudes to the elderly in different societies

Reader's questions: Why is the transition to old age rarely marked by a rite of passage? How do attitudes towards old age differ in different societies?

Exercises

Analyze the following paragraphs by noting the author's purpose and questions that the information answers. Box the signal expressions as you read.

1 According to a recent census there are over 27 million American teenagers (13–19), about 13 percent of the total population. This is a very significant category in American society for several reasons. First, they are a strong economic force. For example, they account for more than one-fourth of the record sales and more than one-third of the movie audiences. They spend collectively an enormous amount of money on clothes and toiletries. As they shift from fad to fad, fortunes are made and lost in the clothing and entertainment industries. Second, adolescents are a financial burden to society. Most adolescents are in school and not in the labor market. They are furnished with an education that they did not earn. Within each family adolescents and the younger children are economic liabilities. They do not earn their way. The United States is probably the first nation to transform children from family asset as labor to a family liability as student-consumers. A third basis for the importance of this category is that many adolescents are alienated. This results in withdrawal, apathy, or rebellious antisocial behavior.

Pattern:

Author's purpose:

Reader's questions:

2 The end of adolescence is not easily defined, being a combination of physical, intellectual, sociological, legal, and psychological factors. In some societies, adolescence ends at puberty, when an individual has completed sexual development and is capable of producing children. Intellectual maturity is reached when a person is capable of abstract thought. Sociological adulthood may be said to have been attained when an individual is self-supporting or has

chosen a career, or has married, or founded a family. Legal adulthood comes when one can vote, marry without parental permission, enlist in the army, or be responsible for legal contracts. Insurance companies do not consider young men as adults until the age of twenty-five, at which time they no longer have to pay "young driver" premiums for automobile insurance. In the movies, one is either an adult at twelve, when one pays adult admission fee, or at seventeen, when one can see X-rated movies. And in the psychological sense, adulthood is considered to be reached when one has dealt with these tasks of adolescence: discovering one's own identity, becoming independent from one's parents, developing one's own system of values, and becoming able to form mature, independent relationships of friendship and love.

Pattern: List

Author's purpose:

Reader's questions:

3 The pattern of the rites of passage—separation, seclusion, and return—is found in many modern rituals. At college graduation ceremonies, for example, the graduates are assembled somewhere offstage where they put on special costumes. When they march in, they remain segregated from their relatives and friends. They are then given advice by the "guardians" and are handed a ceremonial document. At last they return to their joyous relatives and friends to mingle freely with them once again.

Pattern: Time order

Author's purpose: To show how [illegible] rites of passage patterns exist in modern times by analyzing a college graduation

Reader's questions:

4 Among the Ndembu of Africa this transformation ritual from boyhood to manhood, known as *mukanda,* lasts four months. After a night of feasting and singing the initiates receive a last meal from their mothers (rites of separation). Then they are marched to another camp, known as the "place of dying," where they remain in seclusion under the supervision of a group of male guardians. Here they are circumcised, hazed, harangued and lectured on the rules of manhood (rites of segregation). Finally, daubed in the white clay that signifies rebirth, the initiates are taken back to their families. At first their mothers greet them with songs of mourning, but as each realizes that her son is safe, these turn to songs of jubilation. Again the novices are washed and given new clothes, each performs the dance of war to signify his new status as a man (rites of integration). The function of these rites is not merely to celebrate the changes in the life of an individual but to give public recognition to a new set of roles and relationships in the community.

Pattern: Time order

Author's purpose: To explain/describe the diff. stages in "Mukanda"

Reader's questions:

5 Why is the stage of adolescence in American society a period of stress and strain for so many? The most important reason is that it is an age of transition from one social status to another. There is no clear line of demarcation between adolescence and adulthood. Are people considered adult when they can get a full-time job, when they are physically capable of producing children, or when they can be drafted for military service? Adulthood's beginning in American society is unclear. Thus, adolescence has been defined as the state of being physically mature but not working, sexually mature but not married, "grown-up" but still dependent on parents. Surely much of the acting out by adolescents in the United States can be explained partially at least by these status uncertainties.

Pattern: Cause-effect

Author's purpose: To explain why adolescence is a difficult time in the U.S.

Reader's questions:

6 In a society that permits young children to see adult sexual activity, to watch a baby being born, to become close to death, to have important work to do, to exercise assertive and even dominant behavior, to engage in sex play, and to know precisely what their adult roles will involve, adolescence is relatively free from stress. In societies like our own, however, which consider children as very different from adults, which have completely different expectations for them and which shelter them from much of adult life and responsibilities, the shift from childhood to adulthood is much more discontinuous, and, as a result, much more stressful. Physical factors underlie one's being called an adolescent, but how one's culture handles these physical changes determines the nature of the transition.

Pattern: Comparison (contrast)

Author's purpose:

Reader's questions:

7 The adolescent feels perfectly self-confident up to the moment that he confronts the task of demonstrating his competence. He demands privileges but views their corresponding responsibility as onerous. From the parents' point of view, of course, the ability to bear responsibility is as much a mark of maturity as is having privileges. To the child, by contrast, responsibilities are imposed by adults and, thus, so are degrading tokens of his inferior status.

Pattern: Comparison (contrast)

Author's purpose:

Reader's questions:

8 Child training practices may be adapted to the economic requirements of a society. Such requirements may explain why some societies develop compliant children, while others aim for self-reliant, autonomous individuals. In a cross-cultural study, anthropologists found that agricultural and herding societies are more likely to stress compliance, while hunting societies tend to stress individual

assertion. Their theory is that agricultural and herding societies cannot afford departures from established routines, since such departures might jeopardize the food supply for long periods of time. In contrast, hunters must be free to move about at will.

Pattern: Cause effect-comparison (contrast)

Author's purpose: To show how a societies economic needs can effect child-socialization practies by comparing agricultural and herding societies

Reader's questions:

9 Although most societies socialize boys and girls differently, some societies differentiate between boys and girls much more than others. What accounts for extreme differentiation? Anthropologists suggest that certain conditions make this differentiation more likely. If a society has tasks which require a great deal of physical strength, interchangeability of tasks is less likely. Thus, societies which hunt large animals or which keep large domesticated animals are more likely to have greater sex differentiation. Less differentiation between the sexes seems to be found in societies with nuclear families rather than extended families. With small families, husbands and wives have to interchange roles more, and thus boys and girls have to be socialized more similarly.

Pattern: Cause-effect (comparison/contrast)

Author's purpose: To explain the reasons why some societies differentiate between boys + girls more than others.

Reader's questions:

Critical Thinking

QUESTIONS FOR INDEPENDENT AND GROUP WORK

A. Complete each of the following statements in the space provided. Work within the thought pattern suggested by the signal words.

Example Many cultures are more successful than our own in providing cultural continuity and in meeting individuals' needs in different stages of emotional development; therefore, we should study other cultures carefully.

1. Many cultures are more successful than our own both in providing cultural continuity and in meeting individuals' needs in different stages of emotional development. For example, in traditional societies

2. In our own society, the various ceremonies that mark the transition from one stage of life to another include

3. According to Abraham Maslow, the individual's needs must be met in the following order:

4. In many societies there is pressure on girls to be responsible and obedient and on boys to be self-reliant and independent; consequently, as adults

B. In paragraph 2 on page 75, the author presents a list of criteria for maturity in different aspects of life. Reread the paragraph and, using the following categories, note your own criteria for achieving adulthood.

1. biological:

2. sociological:

3. legal:

4. psychological:

Connections

In the poem, "If," by Rudyard Kipling, a father encourages his son to behave in a manner that reflects the values of their particular culture, upper-class English Victorian society. (You read about Victorian beliefs and behavior in the last chapter's reading selection, "Love and Marriage: An Historical View.")

As you read or listen to "If" you will note that the poem is one long sentence organized by one dominant thought pattern. Answer the questions that follow:

If

By Rudyard Kipling

If you can keep your head when all about you
Are losing theirs and blaming it on you,
If you can trust yourself when all men doubt you,
But make allowance for their doubting too;
If you can wait and not be tired by waiting,
Or being lied about, don't deal in lies,
Or being hated don't give way to hating,
And yet don't look too good, nor talk too wise:
If you can dream—and not make dreams your master;
If you can think—and not make thoughts your aim,
If you can meet with Triumph and Disaster
And treat those two imposters just the same;
If you can bear to hear the truth you've spoken
Twisted by knaves to make a trap for fools,
Or watch the things you gave your life to, broken,
And stoop and build 'em up with worn-out tools:
If you can make one heap of all your winnings
And risk it on one turn of pitch and toss,
And lose, and start again at your beginnings
And never breathe a word about your loss;
If you can force your heart and nerve and sinew
To serve your turn long after they are gone,
And so hold on when there is nothing in you
Except the Will which says to them: "Hold on!"
If you can talk with crowds and keep your virtue,
Or walk with Kings—nor lose the common touch,
If neither foes nor loving friends can hurt you,
If all men count with you, but none too much;
If you can fill the unforgiving minute
With sixty seconds' worth of distance run,
Yours is the Earth and every thing that's in it,
And—which is more—you'll be a Man, my son!

1. The cause-effect thought pattern organizes the entire poem. Quote the lines that express effect:

   (last 2)

2. The poem contains at least 17 conditions for achieving "manhood." Quote one or two lines that you feel need explanation.

   Which conditions reflect your own values?

3. If the last line were changed to "—you'll be a Woman, my daughter!" would you change any of the preceding lines? Explain.

Topic for Composition

Think of a child you know, and write a list of "ifs" for the child's becoming an autonomous adult in our society. You may use the poetic form.

Successful student.

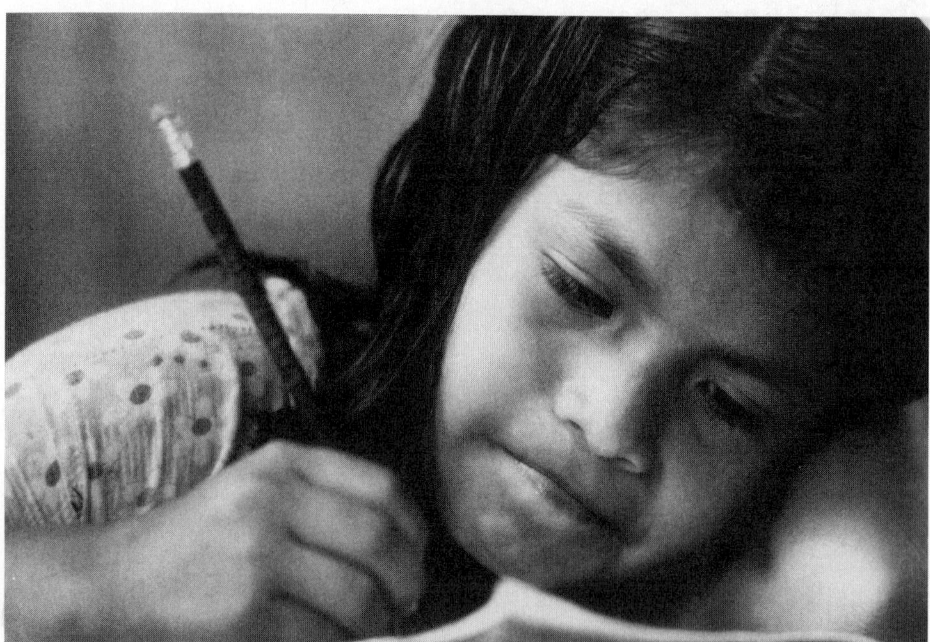

On the first day of school, might a teacher have the same or different expectations for these three children?

5

Pygmalion in the Classroom

The Scientific Method: Outlining Experimental Material

> The curious human mind must and will have things explained whether by mythology, theology or science.
>
> *—Robert E. Lynch and Thomas B. Swanzey, The Example of Science*

Before Reading

Why does success come more readily to some individuals than to others when there is little difference in their basic abilities? Two social scientists, Robert Rosenthal and Lenore Jacobson, have conducted studies of this phenomenon in laboratories and in classrooms. They have found that teacher expectation is a significant factor in student achievement.

Their school study, which is the subject of this chapter's reading selection, is called "Pygmalion in the Classroom." The title is from a Greek myth in which a sculptor, Pygmalion, has such admiration for a female statue which he has created that the statue is transformed into a living woman.

Rosenthal and Jacobson's work suggests that teachers too can be artists. Using the scientific method, these scientists have attempted to demonstrate that, under certain conditions, teachers will find and free special talents in their students. Before reading the selection, identify a teacher who made a difference in your life. When was she or he your teacher? What did this teacher find in *you* that made a difference?

READING SELECTION

The basic technical research terms that appear in the reading selection are defined in the "Study Activity."

Pygmalion in the Classroom

Based on Pygmalion in the Classroom
By Robert Rosenthal and Lenore Jacobson

1 In an experiment in the San Francisco public schools two decades ago, Robert Rosenthal and Lenore Jacobson explored the effect of teacher expectation on pupils' intellectual performance. At the beginning of the school year, teachers were led to believe that specific students in their classes would show considerable academic growth during the school year. The teachers assumed that the students had been designated potential academic "**spurters**" on the basis of their performance on an intelligence test. The children had been selected, however, by means of a table of random numbers, which is to say, their names were picked out of a hat. Eight months later all of the children in the school were tested; those who had been singled out and brought to the attention of their teachers achieved higher scores than their classmates.

2 The purpose of the school experiment was to test the hypothesis of the self-fulfilling prophecy. The essence of this concept is that one person's expectations of another person's behavior can become an accurate prediction of that behavior. It is possible that the prediction may be realized only in the perception of the predictor, but it is also possible that the expectation may be communicated to the other person in **subtle** and unintended ways and consequently influence the person's actual behavior.

3 In order to test for self-fulfilling prophecy in the classroom, the experimenters had to be sure that the teachers' expectations of the students were not based on their knowledge of the students' behavior and achievement in previous terms. Some years earlier, Robert Rosenthal had had no problem in establishing such conditions in a laboratory situation in which laboratory rats rather than students were the subjects. In one experiment, twelve psychology students were each given five perfectly ordinary laboratory rats and told to teach the rats to run a **maze**. Six of the students were told that their rats had been bred for maze "brightness." Six of the students were told that their rats were maze "dull."

4 The results of the experiment indicated that the rats believed to have the higher potential proved to be the better performers. The animals believed to be dull improved for a short period of time and then their performance **slackened**. In fact, twenty-nine per cent of the time they refused to budge from the starting position, compared to eleven per cent for the allegedly bright rats.

5 The student experimenters made ratings of their rats and of their attitudes and behavior toward them. Students who had been led to expect good performance viewed their animals as brighter, more pleasant, and more liable. They also indicated that they had been more relaxed in their handling of the animals, more gentle, friendlier, and less talkative than the experimenters who had been led to expect poor performance. The latter apparently had quite a bit to say to their animals.

6 Although the laboratory experiment tested the effect of both positive and negative expectations, in the school experiment, it was decided, on ethical grounds, to test only the proposition that favorable expectations by teachers could lead to an increase in intellectual competence. With this objective, the experiment was set up in an elementary school in the South San Francisco Unified School District.

7 At the beginning of the experiment in 1964, the teachers were told that further validation was needed for a new kind of test designed to predict academic blooming or intellectual gain in children. In actuality they used the "Flanagan Test of General Ability," a standardized test that was fairly new and, therefore, unfamiliar to the teachers. They had special covers designed for the test which bore the **pompous** title "Test of Inflected Acquisition." The teachers were told that the test would be given several times in the future and that the results would be sent to Harvard University. In May the test was administered to the children in grades one through five.

8 Before Oak School opened the following September, five children in each classroom, about twenty percent of the school population, were designated as potential academic spurters. The teachers were given the students' names in a deliberately casual manner: the subject was brought up at the end of the first staff meeting with the remark, "By the way, in case you're interested in who did what in those tests we're doing for Harvard . . .".

9 The experimental treatment of the children who had been chosen **at random** involved nothing more than giving their names to their new teachers as children who could be expected to show unusual intellectual gains in the year ahead. The difference, then, between these children and the remaining children who constituted the control group was entirely in the minds of their teachers.

10 All children were given the same test after one semester, at the end of that school year, and finally in May of the following year. The results indicated strongly that children from whom teachers expected greater intellectual gains showed such gains (see Figure 1). The gains, however, were not uniform across the grades. The tests given at the end of the first year showed the largest gains among children in the first and second grades. In the second year the greatest gains were among the children who had been in the fifth grade when the "spurters" were designated and who by the time of the final test were completing sixth grade.

11 At the end of the academic year 1964–1965 the teachers were asked to describe the classroom behavior of their pupils. The children from whom intellectual growth was expected were described as less in need of social approval, happier, more intellectually curious, and more interesting than the other children. In short, the children for whom intellectual growth was expected became more alive and autonomous intellectually, or at least were so perceived by their

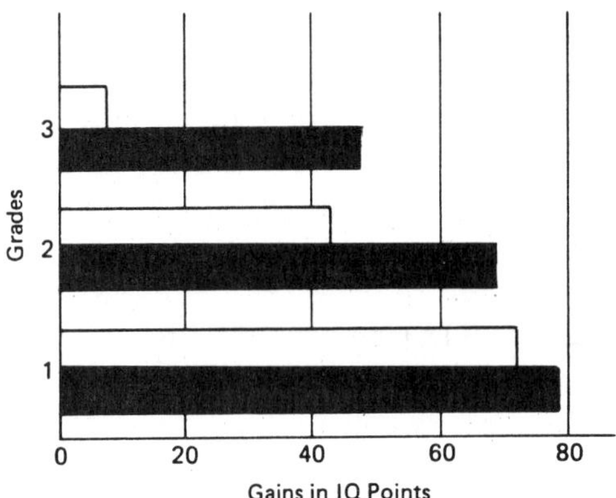

Figure 1 *Children in lower grades showed the most dramatic gains. The chart shows the percentage of children in the first and second grades by amount of their gains in IQ points. Shaded bars represent experimental group children.*

teachers. These findings were particularly striking among the children in the lower grades.

12 An interesting contrast became apparent when teachers were asked to rate the undesignated children. Many of these children had also gained academically during the year. The more intellectually competent these children became, the less favorably they were rated.

13 From these results it seemed evident to the researchers that when children who are expected to gain intellectually do gain, they may benefit in other ways. As "personalities" they go up in the estimation of their teachers. The opposite appeared to be true of children who gain intellectually when improvement is not expected of them. They are viewed as showing undesirable behavior.

14 How is one to account for the fact that the children who were expected to gain did gain? The first answer that comes to mind is that the teachers must have spent more time with them than with the children of whom nothing was said. This hypothesis seems to be wrong, judging from some questions the researchers asked the teachers about the time they spent with their pupils. Also, if teachers had talked more to the designated children, the most likely way of investing more time in work with them, one might expect to see the largest gains in **verbal** intelligence. In actuality, the largest gains were in reasoning intelligence.

15 Rosenthal and Jacobson **have speculated** that the explanation lies in a subtler feature of the interaction of teacher and pupils.

Tone of voice, facial expression, touch, and posture may be the means by which—quite unwittingly—teachers communicate their expectations to their pupils. Such communication might help the children by changing their self-concepts and, hence, their expectations of their own behavior. This is an area in which further research is clearly needed.

16 Why was the effect of teacher expectation most pronounced in the lower grades? The researchers advanced several hypotheses: Younger children may be easier to change than older ones. They are likely to have less well-established reputations in the school. It may be that they are more sensitive to the processes by which teachers communicate their expectations to pupils.

17 It is also difficult to be certain why the older children showed the better performance in the follow-up year. Perhaps the younger children, who by then had different teachers, needed continued contact with the teachers who had influenced them originally in order to maintain their improved performance. The older children, who had been harder to influence at first, may have been better able to maintain an improved performance autonomously once they had achieved it.

18 The Pygmalion experiment raised many new hypotheses. It became evident to the researchers that more attention in educational research needed to be focused on teachers to ascertain how they can effect dramatic changes in their pupils' performance.

Vocabulary

The following words are boldfaced in the reading selection. Write a synonym or brief definition for each in the space provided. Add other unfamiliar terms or meanings to the list.

WORD OR PHRASE	***SYNONYM OR BRIEF DEFINITION***
spurters (1)	
subtle (2)	
maze (3)	
slackened (4)	

WORD OR PHRASE	***SYNONYM OR BRIEF DEFINITION***
pompous (7)	
at random (9)	
verbal (14)	
have speculated (15)	

YOUR ADDITIONS

A. Match the italicized word in the sentence to its appropriate dictionary definition.

1. The students were given laboratory rats of the same *strain.*
   a. tune, air
   b. physical or mental tension
   c. genetic mix, litter

2. The rats believed to have higher *potential* proved to be better performers.
   a. inherent ability, capacity for growth and development
   b. designating a verb form with auxiliaries such as "may" or "can"
   c. work required to bring a unit electric charge to a designated point in a static field

3. The *essence* of this concept is that one person's prediction of another's behavior comes true.
   a. leading principle
   b. concentrated extract of a substance
   c. a perfume

4. Twenty (20) percent of the students were *designated* potential academic spurters.
   a. to point out the location of
   b. to call by a distinctive title, term, or expression
   c. chosen for an office but not yet installed

5. The explanation lies in a *subtle* feature of the interaction between the teacher and pupils: tone of voice, facial expressions, touch, and posture.
   a. highly skillful, expert
   b. difficult to understand or distinguish
   c. artful, crafty

B. Match the underscored word in the column on the left with its synonym in the column on the right:

d	1. self-fulfilling prophecy	a. prevent
a	2. conditions which preclude	b. consistent
c	3. data which were being compiled	c. information organized for analysis
b	4. gains were not uniform	d. prediction
f	5. allegedly brighter rats	e. strongly marked
e	6. the effect of expectations was pronounced	f. supposedly
g	7. chosen at random	g. without a specific plan

Comprehension

SPECIFIC INFORMATION

A. In the Rosenthal-Jacobson studies of the self-fulfilling prophecy, the psychology students and the classroom teachers were

1. intentionally misinformed by the experimenters.
2. designated potential academic spurters.
3. working at cross-purposes with the experimenters.
4. performing dissimilar roles.

B. Conditions for exploring the self-fulfilling prophecy are better in the laboratory than in the classroom, because in a lab

1. genetic inheritance is uncontrolled.
2. the subjects don't have reputations.
3. scientists are unemotional.
4. a rat's performance is clearly predictable.

C. The classroom teachers were led to believe that specific students in their classes

1. were in the control group.
2. were brighter than the other students.
3. were in the experimental group.
4. were potential behavior problems.

D. At the beginning of the term, the actual difference between the students in the two groups was

1. their self-esteem.
2. their motivation.
3. their need to disrupt.
4. their teacher's expectation.

ANALYSIS

E. The reading selection does not contain subtopics. Where in the text is the appropriate position for the following subtopics?

Example The Self-Fulfilling Prophecy above paragraph 2

1. The Laboratory Experiment above paragraph ____
2. The School Experiment above paragraph ____
3. Teachers' Perceptions above paragraph ____
4. Experimental and Control Groups above paragraph ____
5. Explanations and Areas for Future Inquiry above paragraph ____

F. The style of the reading selection is best described as ____.

1. poetic and symbolic.
2. argumentative and provocative.
3. factual and carefully organized.
4. comical and entertaining.

G. The first paragraph of this article is ____ of paragraphs 7 through 10.

1. an illustration
2. an explanation
3. a brief summary
4. a restatement

H. The thesis, or central idea, of the reading selection is that

1. home environment is the key to academic success.
2. the more attention given the student, the more autonomous the student will become.
3. teachers' expectations strongly influence students' performance.

4. age is a decisive factor in determining the extent of a teacher's influence on a child.

INFERENCES AND INTERPRETATIONS

Select the correct text-based answer and explain your choice by completing the statement in the space provided.

Example The behavior of the rats in the laboratory experiment

1. contradicts the self-fulfilling prophecy
2. has no relation to the self-fulfilling prophecy
3. illustrates the self-fulfilling prophecy

because the rats performed according to expectations.

I. At the end of the school term, teachers evaluated their students whose academic achievement came as a surprise as

1. potential academic spurters
2. behavior problems
3. attractive and autonomous

probably because they weren't expecting it.

J. By the end of the term, successful students had developed

1. self-confidence
2. the desire to cooperate
3. a competitive spirit

because their teachers believed in them.

Study Activity

OUTLINING EXPERIMENTAL MATERIAL

The scientific method—the technique for problem solving in the natural and social sciences—imposes order and meaning on isolated, disorganized, random facts and impressions. Your awareness of the scientific method and your understanding of its terminology will assist you to comprehend and take clear notes on the experimental material in textbooks and professional journals.

TERMS IN THE SCIENTIFIC METHOD

Hypothesis A prediction based on observations, facts, and feelings which seems to work but has yet to be tested. A hypothesis will state that the changing or varying of some aspect of a situation will result in a corresponding change in some aspect of behavior. The aspect of a situation that the experimenter changes is called the *independent variable;* it can be regarded as a cause. The resulting change in behavior is called the *dependent variable;* it is an effect.

Procedure A series of clearly defined steps which the experimenter follows in order to find support for the hypothesis. Included in the procedure is a description of the *subject* (people or animals) being studied and the designation of *experimental* and *control* groups.

Experimental group The group that is exposed to the independent variable.

Control group Identical to the experimental group except that it is not exposed to the independent variable.

Result(s) Summary of the collected data resulting from the steps in the procedure, including test scores, responses to interviews and questionnaires, and observed behavior. Results include inferences that the experimenters draw from their observations.

Conclusion(s) Generalization of the results, including inferences to other subjects. The conclusion expresses whether the data support and, therefore, validate the hypothesis. A *theory* is formulated when several experiments validate the same hypothesis. Conclusions will often include suggestions for other hypotheses.

USING SCIENTIFIC TERMINOLOGY

Study the following note outline of Rosenthal's laboratory experiment:

Hypothesis The expectations of experimenters (psychology students) alone will influence the behavior of their subjects (laboratory rats).

Procedure (steps) Twelve psychology students given five subjects (ordinary lab rats of the same strain); 6 students told they had maze-"bright" rats; 6 told they had maze-"dull" rats. Students were directed to teach rats to run a maze. Students completed questionnaire.

Results (including inferences) "Bright" rats did well, "dull" rats did poorly. Students with "bright" rats were gentle, relaxed, quiet; students with "dull" rats were rough, handled rats less, were more talkative. We can infer that students communicated their expectations to the rats, and rats fulfilled students' expectations.

Conclusion Expectations of experimenters alone influenced the behavior of subjects. Hypothesis validated; another hypothesis not suggested.

APPLYING SCIENTIFIC TERMINOLOGY

Read the following statements based on the reading selection, and classify them according to the appropriate scientific term.

Example The students were told that their rats were bright.

1. independent variable
2. control group
3. result

A. One person's prediction of another person's behavior somehow comes to be realized.

1. hypothesis
2. procedure
3. result

B. The more the undesignated children gained, the less favorably they were rated.

1. result
2. conclusion
3. procedure

C. Special covers were printed for the test.

1. control group
2. independent variable
3. procedure

D. The designated children were seen as more appealing, better adjusted, and more affectionate.

1. dependent variable
2. result
3. conclusion

E. Some children gained when improvement was not expected.

1. hypothesis
2. experimental group
3. control group

F. As the children progressed through the grades, they were given tests at the appropriate level.

1. hypothesis
2. procedure
3. conclusion

G. Younger children may be easier to change than older children.

1. control group
2. new hypothesis
3. procedure

H. Twenty percent of the children were designated as potential academic spurters.

1. control group
2. experimental group
3. result

I. The children who were expected to gain did gain.

1. independent variable
2. conclusion
3. dependent variable

J. Older children may be better able than younger ones to maintain improved performance autonomously once they achieve it.

1. result
2. new hypothesis
3. independent variable

Critical Thinking

QUESTIONS FOR INDEPENDENT AND GROUP WORK

A. Because the Pygmalion experimenters were concerned with ethics, they decided to test only for the effect of positive expectations on pupils' performance. Define ethics.

1. What change in the procedure would be made to test for the effect of negative expectations?

2. Suppose you had been a student in the control group in the actual experiment 20 years ago. What would your feelings be about the ethics of that experiment today?

B. Do students' expectations of their teachers' abilities influence their [the students'] academic performance? Explain.

What procedure would you use to test this hypothesis?*

Hypothesis:

Procedure:

Experimental Group (including independent variable):

Control Group:

Ways of evaluating teachers' affectiveness:

Connections

In this brief essay from his autobiography, *Growing Up,* journalist Russell Baker describes a school experience we would all like to have.

Such an experiment is described in the *Journal of Educational Psychology,* Vol. 9: No 4, p. 453–460 1987.

From "Growing Up"
By Russell Baker

1 The notion of becoming a writer had flickered off and on in my head . . . but it wasn't until my third year in high school that the possibility took hold. Until then I'd been bored by everything associated with English courses. I found English grammar dull and baffling. I hated the assignments to turn out "compositions," and went at them like heavy labor, turning out laden, lackluster paragraphs that were agonies for teachers to read and for me to write. The classics thrust on me to read seemed as deadening as chloroform.

2 When our class was assigned to Mr. Fleagle for third-year English I anticipated another grim year in that dreariest of subjects. Mr. Fleagle was notorious among City students for dullness and inability to inspire. He was said to be stuffy, dull, and hopelessly out of date. To me he looked to be sixty or seventy and prim to a fault. He wore primly severe eyeglasses, his wavy hair was primly cut and primly combed. He wore prim vested suits with neckties blocked primly against the collar buttons of his primly starched white shirts. He had a primly jointed jaw, a primly straight nose, and prim manner of speaking that was so correct, so gentlemanly, that he seemed a comic antique.

3 I anticipated a listless, unfruitful year with Mr. Fleagle and for a long time was not disappointed. We read *Macbeth.* Mr. Fleagle loved *Macbeth* and wanted us to love it too, but he lacked the gift of infecting others with his own passion. He tried to convey the murderous ferocity of Lady Macbeth one day by reading aloud the passage that concludes

. . . I have given suck, and know
How tender 'tis to love the babe that milks me.
I would, while it was smiling in my face,
Have plucked my nipple from his boneless gums. . . .

The idea of prim Mr. Fleagle plucking his nipple from boneless gums was too much for the class. We burst into gasps of irrepressible snickering. Mr. Fleagle stopped.

4 "There is nothing funny, boys, about giving suck to a babe. It is the—the very essence of motherhood, don't you see."

5 He constantly sprinkled his sentences with "don't you see." It wasn't a question but an exclamation of mild surprise at our ignorance. "Your pronoun needs an antecedent, don't you see," he would say, very primly. "The purpose of the Porter's scene, boys, is to provide comic relief from the horror, don't you see."

6 Late in the year we tackled the informal essay. "The essay, don't you see, is the . . ." My mind went numb. Of all forms of writing, none seemed so boring as the essay. Naturally we would have to write informal essays. Mr. Fleagle distributed a homework sheet offering us a choice of topics. None was quite so simpleminded as "What I Did on My Summer Vacation," but most seemed to be almost as dull. I took the list home and dawdled until the night before the essay was due. Sprawled on the sofa, I finally faced up to the grim task, took the list out of my notebook, and scanned it. The topic on which my eye stopped was "The Art of Eating Spaghetti."

7 This title produced an extraordinary sequence of mental images. Surging up to the depths of memory came a vivid recollection of a night in Belleville when all of us were seated around the supper table—Uncle Allen, my mother, Uncle Charlie, Doris, Uncle Hal—and Aunt Pat served spaghetti for supper. Spaghetti was an exotic treat in those days. Neither Doris nor I had ever eaten spaghetti, and none of the adults had enough experience to be good at it. All the good humor of Uncle Allen's house reawoke in my mind as I recalled the laughing arguments we had that night about the socially respectable method for moving spaghetti from plate to mouth.

8 Suddenly I wanted to write about that, about the warmth and good feeling of it, but I wanted to put it down simply for my own joy, not for Mr. Fleagle. It was a moment I wanted to recapture and hold for myself. I wanted to relive the pleasure of an evening at New Street. To write it as I wanted, however, would violate all the rules of formal composition I'd learned in school, and Mr. Fleagle would surely give it a failing grade. Never mind. I would write something else for Mr. Fleagle after I had written this thing for myself.

9 When I finished it the night was half gone and there was no time left to compose a proper, respectable essay for Mr. Fleagle. There was no choice next morning but to turn in my private reminiscence of Belleville. Two days passed before Mr. Fleagle returned the graded papers, and he returned everyone's but mine. I was bracing myself for a command to report to Mr. Fleagle immediately after

school for discipline when I saw him lift my paper from his desk and rap for the class's attention.

10 "Now, boys," he said, "I want to read you an essay. This is titled 'The Art of Eating Spaghetti.'"

11 And he started to read. My words! He was reading *my words* out loud to the entire class. What's more, the entire class was listening. Listening attentively. Then somebody laughed, then the entire class was laughing, and not in contempt and ridicule, but with open-hearted enjoyment. Even Mr. Fleagle stopped two or three times to repress a small prim smile.

12 I did my best to avoid showing pleasure, but what I was feeling was pure ecstasy at this startling demonstration that my words had the power to make people laugh. In the eleventh grade, at the eleventh hour as it were, I had discovered a calling. It was the happiest moment of my entire school career. When Mr. Fleagle finished he put the final seal on my happiness by saying, "Now that, boys, is an essay, don't you see. It's—don't you see—it's of the very essence of the essay, don't you see. Congratulations, Mr. Baker."

13 For the first time, light shone on a possibility. It wasn't a very heartening possibility, to be sure. Writing couldn't lead to a job after high school, and it was hardly honest work, but Mr. Fleagle had opened a door for me. After that I ranked Mr. Fleagle among the finest teachers in the school.

Why were both student and teacher successful?

Topic for Composition

The reading selection "Pygmalion in the Classroom" is concerned with the effect on people of labels such as "bright" or "bad." Think of someone you know who was so labeled. Write a composition in which you relate the causes and consequences of the label.

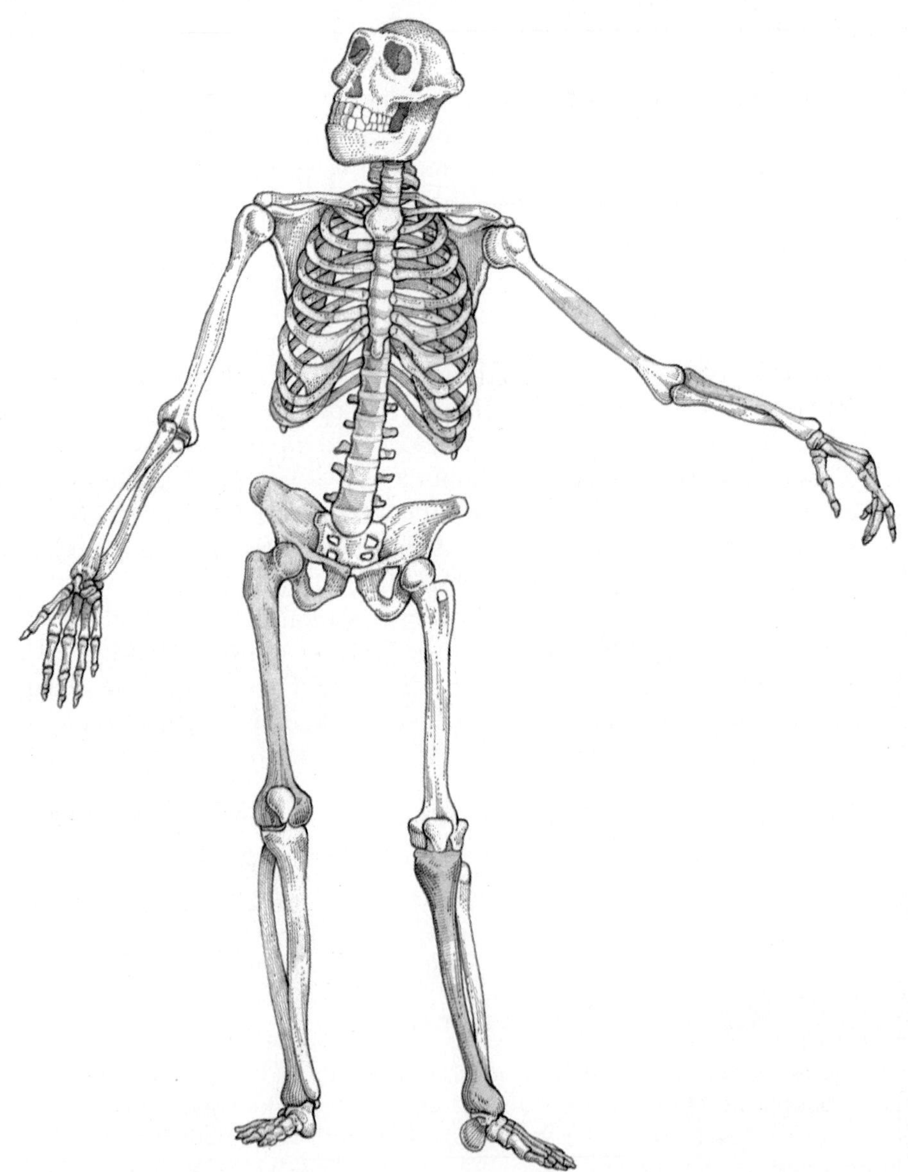

The skeleton of Lucy is over 40 percent complete, and with the use of information from other Hadar finds, almost all the skeleton can be reconstructed.

6

Lucy in the Sky

Making Notes in the Textbook

. . . the world displays
a lovely order . . .
And the most appealing
part of this harmony,
perhaps, is its
permanence—the
sense that we are part
of something with roots
stretching back nearly
forever, and branches
reaching forward just
as far.

—Bill McKibbon, The End of Nature

Before Reading

Man's* emergence from the apes is the subject of this chapter. Many sciences contribute to our knowledge of our human origins, our place in nature, and our relationship to the other animals with whom we share the earth. In the Study Activity, you will be taking notes from textbook passages in related fields including geology, anthropology, paleontology, archaeology, biology, and ecology. What is the subject matter of each of these disciplines?

This chapter's Reading Selection, "Lucy" is paleoanthropologist Donald Johanson's personal account of his discovery of a partial skeleton that had rested undisturbed for perhaps three and a half million years. His images of the living "Lucy" and of other long deceased members of our human family tree increase our understanding of the process of human evolution.

READING SELECTION

The following terms will assist your reading. The biological classification of human beings includes:

Kingdom	Animal
Class	Mammal
Order	Primate: humans, apes, monkeys and prosimians
Family	Hominid: erect, walking bi-pedal primate
Genus	Homo: man (includes males and females)
Species (a population that can interbreed):	sapiens
Subspecies	Homo sapiens sapiens: man of wisdom
Skeletal parts:	femur, sacrum, pelvis, scull, vertebrae

Lucy

By Donald Johanson and Maitland A. Edey

1 On the morning of November 30, 1974, I woke at daybreak. I was in Ethiopia, camped on the edge of a small muddy river, the Awash, at a place called Hadar, about a hundred miles northeast of Addis Ababa. I had been there for several weeks, acting as coleader of a group of scientists looking for fossils.

2 . . . Tom Gray joined me for coffee. Tom was an American graduate student who had come out to Hadar to study the fossil animals

* In this chapter, man refers to humanity—males and females of the genushomo.

and plants of the region, to reconstruct as accurately as possible what had lived there at various times in the remote past and what the climate had been like. My own target—the reason for our expedition—was hominid fossils: the bones of extinct human ancestors and their close relatives. I was interested in the evidence for human evolution. But to understand that, to interpret any hominid fossils we might find, we had to have the supporting work of other specialists like Tom.

3 As a paleoanthropologist—one who studies the fossils of human ancestors—I am superstitious. Many of us are, because the work we do depends a great deal on luck. . . . I know I am lucky, and I don't try to hide it. That is why I wrote "feel good" in my diary. When I got up that morning I felt it was one of those days when you should press your luck. One of those days when something terrific might happen.

4 Throughout most of that morning, nothing did. Gray and I got into one of the expeditions' four Land-Rovers and slowly jounced our way to Locality 162. This was one of several hundred **sites** that were in the process of being plotted on a master map of the Hadar area, with detailed information about geology and fossils being entered on it as fast as it was obtained. Although the spot we were headed for was only about four miles from camp, it took us half an hour to get there because of the rough **terrain**. When we arrived it was already beginning to get hot.

5 Tom and I surveyed for a couple of hours. It was now close to noon, and the temperature was approaching 110.

6 "I've had it," said Tom. "When do we head back to camp?"

7 "Right now. But let's go back this way and survey the bottom of that little gully over there."

8 The gully in question was just over the crest of the rise where we had been working all morning. It had been thoroughly checked out at least twice before by other workers, who had found nothing interesting. Nevertheless, conscious of the "lucky" feeling that had been with me since I woke, I decided to make that small final detour. There was **virtually** no bone in the gully. But as we turned to leave, I noticed something lying on the ground partway up the slope.

9 "There's a bit of a hominid arm," I said.

10 "Can't be. It's too small. Has to be a monkey of some kind."

11 We knelt to examine it.

12 "Much too small," said Gray again.

13 I shook my head. "Hominid."

14 "What makes you so sure?" he said.

15 "That piece right next to your hand. That's hominid too."

16 "Jesus Christ," said Gray. He picked it up. It was the back of a small skull. A few feet away was part of a femur: a thighbone. "Jesus Christ," he said again. We stood up, and began to see other bits of bone on the slope: a couple of vertebrae, part of a pelvis—all of them hominid. An unbelievable, impermissible thought flickered through my mind. Suppose all these fitted together? Could they be parts of a single, extremely primitive skeleton? No such skeleton had ever been found—anywhere.

17 "Look at that," said Gray. "Ribs."

18 *A single individual?*

19 "I can't believe it," I said. "I just can't believe it."

20 "By God, you'd better believe it!" shouted Gray. "Here it is. Right here!" His voice went up into a howl. I joined him. In that 110-degree heat we began jumping up and down. With nobody to share our feelings, we hugged each other, sweaty and smelly, howling and hugging in the heat-shimmering gravel, the small brown **remains** of what now seemed almost certain to be parts of a single hominid skeleton lying all around us.

21 "We've got to stop jumping around," I finally said. "We may step on something. Also, we've got to make sure."

22 "Aren't you sure, for Christ's sake?"

23 "I mean, suppose we find two left legs. There may be several individuals here, all mixed up. Let's play it cool until we can come back and make absolutely sure that it all fits together."

24 We collected a couple of pieces of jaw, marked the spot exactly and got into the blistering Land-Rover for the run back to camp. On the way we picked up two expedition geologists who were loaded down with rock samples they had been gathering.

25 "Something big," Gray kept saying to them. "Something big. Something *big.*"

26 "Cool it," I said.

27 But about a quarter of a mile from camp, Gray could not cool it. He pressed his thumb on the Land-Rover's horn, and the long blast brought a scurry of scientists who had been bathing in the river. "We've got it," he yelled. "Oh, Jesus, we've got it. We've got The Whole Thing!"

28 That afternoon everyone in camp was at the gully, sectioning off the site and preparing for a massive collecting job that ultimately took three weeks. When it was done, we had recovered several hundred pieces of bone (many of them fragments) representing about forty percent of the skeleton of a single individual. Tom's and my original hunch had been right. There was no bone **duplication**.

29 But a single individual of what? On preliminary examination it was very hard to say, for nothing quite like it had ever been discovered. The camp was rocking with excitement. That first night we never went to bed at all. We talked and talked. We drank beer after beer. There was a tape recorder in the camp, and a tape of the Beatles song "Lucy in the Sky with Diamonds" went belting out into the night sky, and was played at full volume over and over again out of sheer exuberance. At some point during that unforgettable evening—I no longer remember exactly when—the new fossil picked up the name of Lucy, and has been so known ever since, although its proper name—its **acquisition** number in the Hadar collection—is AL 288-1.

30 "Lucy?"

31 That is the question I always get from somebody who sees the fossil for the first time. I have to explain: "Yes, she was a female. And that Beatles song. We were sky-high, you must remember, from finding her."

32 Then comes the next question: "How did you know she was a female?"

33 "From her pelvis. We had one complete pelvic bone and her sacrum. Since the pelvic opening in hominids has to be proportionately larger in females than in males to allow for the birth of large-brained infants, you can tell a female."

34 And the next: "She was a hominid?"

35 "Oh, yes. She walked erect. She walked as well as you do."

36 "Hominids all walked erect?"

37 "Yes."

38 "Just exactly what is a hominid?"

39 That usually ends the questions, because that one has no simple answer. Science has had to leave the definition rather flexible because we do not yet know exactly when hominids first appeared. However, it is safe to say that a hominid is an erect-walking primate. That is, it is either an extinct ancestor to man,* a **collateral** relative

to man, or a true man. All human beings are hominids, but not all hominids are human beings.

40 We can picture human evolution as starting with a primitive apelike type that gradually, over a long period of time, began to be less and less apelike and more manlike. There was no abrupt crossover from ape to human, but probably a rather fuzzy time of in-between types that would be difficult to classify either way. We have no fossils yet that tell us what went on during that in-between time. Therefore, the handiest way of separating the newer types from their ape ancestors is to lump together all those that stood up on their hind legs. That group of men and near-men is called hominids.

41 I am a hominid. I am a human being. I belong to the genus *Homo* and to the species *sapiens;* thinking man. Perhaps I should say wise or knowing man—a man who is smart enough to recognize that he is a man. There have been other species of *Homo* who were not so smart, ancestors now extinct. *Homo sapiens* began to emerge a hundred thousand—perhaps two or three hundred thousand—years ago, depending on how one regards Neanderthal Man. He was another *Homo.* Some think he was the same species as ourselves. Others think he was an ancestor. There are a few who consider him a kind of cousin. That matter is unsettled because many of the best Neanderthal fossils were collected in Europe before anybody knew how to **excavate** sites properly or get good dates. Consequently, we do not have exact ages for most of the Neanderthal fossils in collections.

42 I consider Neanderthal **conspecific** with *sapiens,* with myself. One hears talk about putting him in a business suit and turning him loose in the subway. It is true; one could do it and he would never be noticed. He was just a little heavier-boned than people of today, more primitive in a few facial features. But he was a man. His brain was as big as a modern man's, but shaped in a slightly different way. Could he make change at the subway booth and recognize a token? He certainly could. He could do many things more complicated than that. He was doing them over much of Europe, Africa and Asia as long as sixty or a hundred thousand years ago.

43 Neanderthal Man had ancestors, human ones. Before him in time was a less advanced typed: *Homo erectus.* Put him on the subway and people would probably take a suspicious look at him. Before *Homo erectus* was a really primitive type, *Homo habilis;* put him on

the subway and people would probably move to the other end of the car. Before *Homo habilis* the human line may run out entirely. The next stop in the past, back of *Homo habilis,* might be something like Lucy.

44 All of the above are hominids. They are all erect walkers. Some were human, even though they were of exceedingly primitive types. Others were not human. Lucy was not. No matter what kind of clothes were put on Lucy, she would not look like a human being. She was too far back, out of the human range entirely. That is what happens going back along an evolutionary line. If one goes back far enough, one finds oneself dealing with a different kind of creature. On the hominid line the earliest ones are too primitive to be called humans. They must be given another name. Lucy is in that category.

45 For five years I kept Lucy in a safe in my office in the Cleveland Museum of Natural History. I had filled a wide shallow box with yellow foam padding, and had cut depressions in the foam so that each of her bones fitted into its own tailor-made nest. ***Everybody*** who came to the Museum—it seemed to me—wanted to see Lucy. What surprised people most was her small size.

46 Her head, on the evidence of the bits of her skull that had been recovered, was not much larger than a softball. Lucy herself stood only three and one-half feet tall, although she was fully grown. That could be deduced from her wisdom teeth, which had been exposed to several years of wear. My best guess was that she was between twenty-five and thirty years old when she died. She had already begun to show the onset of arthritis or some other bone ailment, on the evidence of **deformation** of her vertebrae. If she had lived much longer, it probably would have begun to bother her.

47 Her surprisingly good condition—her completeness—came from the fact that she had died quietly. There were no tooth marks on her bones. They had not been crunched and splintered, as they would have been if she had been killed by a lion or a saber-toothed cat. Her head had not been carried off in one direction and her legs in another, as hyenas might have done with her. She had simply settled down in one piece right where she was, in the sand of a long-vanished lake edge or stream—and died. Whether from illness or accidental drowning, it was impossible to say. The important thing was that she had not been found by a **predator** just after death and eaten. Her carcass had remained **inviolate**, slowly covered by sand or mud, buried deeper and deeper, the sand hardening into rock.

She had lain silently in her **adamant** grave for millenniums until the rains at Hadar had brought her to light again.

48 Lucy always managed to look interesting in her little yellow nest—but to a nonprofessional, not overly impressive. What was so special about Lucy? Why had she, as another member of the expedition put it, "blown us out of our little anthropological minds for months"?

49 "Three things," I always answered. "First: what she is—or isn't. She is different from anything that has been discovered and named before. She doesn't fit anywhere. She is just a very old, very primitive, very small hominid. Somehow we are going to have to fit her in, find a name for her.

50 "Second," I would say, "is her completeness. Until Lucy was found, there just weren't any very old skeletons. The oldest was one of those Neanderthalers I spoke of a little while ago. It is about seventy-five thousand years old. Yes, there are older hominid fossils, but they are all fragments. Everything that has been reconstructed from them has had to be done by matching up those little pieces—a tooth here, a bit of jaw there, maybe a complete skull from somewhere else, plus a leg bone from some other place. The fitting together has been done by scientists who know those bones as well as I know my own hand. And yet, when you consider that such a reconstruction may consist of pieces from a couple of dozen individuals who may have lived hundreds of miles apart and may have been separated from each other by a hundred thousand years in time—well, when you look at the complete individual you've just put together you have to say to yourself, 'Just how real is he?' With Lucy you know. It's all there. You don't have to guess. You don't have to imagine an arm bone you haven't got. You see it. You see it for the first time from something older than a Neanderthaler."

51 "How much older?"

52 "That's point number three. The Neanderthaler is seventy-five thousand years old. Lucy is approximately 3.5 million years old. She is the oldest, most complete, best-preserved skeleton of any erect-walking human ancestor that has ever been found."

53 That is the significance of Lucy: her completeness and her great age. They make her unique in the history of hominid fossil collecting. She is easy to describe, and she makes a number of anthropological problems easier to work out. But exactly what is she?

54 Unique Lucy may be, but she is incomprehensible outside the context of other fossils. She becomes meaningless unless she is

fitted into a scheme of hominid evolution and scientific logic. [The scheme] has been laboriously pieced together over more than a century by hundreds of specialists from four continents. Their fossil finds, their insights—sometimes inspired, sometimes silly—their application of techniques from such faraway disciplines as botany, nuclear physics and microbiology have combined to produce an increasingly clear and rich picture of man's emergence from the apes—a story that is finally, in the ninth **decade** of this century, beginning to make some sense.

Vocabulary

The following words are boldfaced in the text. Write a synonym or brief definition for each. Add other unfamiliar terms and their meanings to the list.

WORD OR PHRASE	SYNONYM OR BRIEF DEFINITION
site (4)	
terrain (4)	
extinct (5)	
virtually (8)	
remains (20)	
duplication (28)	
acquisition (29)	
collateral (39)	
excavate (41)	
conspecific (42)	
deformation (46)	
predator (47)	

WORD OR PHRASE	***SYNONYM OR BRIEF DEFINITION***
inviolate (47)	
adamant (47)	
decade (54)	

YOUR ADDITIONS

A. Select the synonym(s) for the italicized word(s).

1. This was one of several hundred *sites* that were being *plotted* on a master map.

    a. selected space — represented
    b. attractive scenes — buried
    c. plains — schemed
    d. disasters — indicated

2. I consider Neanderthal *conspecific* with sapiens, with myself.

    a. exactly like
    b. in the same category
    c. in contact
    d. conspicuous

3. There was *virtually* no bone in the gully.

    a. honorably
    b. exceptionally
    c. morally
    d. essentially

4. Remains indicated she had not been found by a *predator*.

    a. vegetarian
    b. priest
    c. hunter
    d. ancestor

5. Her carcass had remained *inviolate*.

    a. purple
    b. impure
    c. undisturbed
    d. mummified

6. There was no bone *duplication*.

    a. replication
    b. amputation
    c. implication
    d. reputation

7. A hominid is either an extinct ancestor, a *collateral* relative, or a true human being.

a. secure
b. having a common ancestor
c. living
d. upright and bi-pedal

8. She had lain silently in her *adamant* grave for *millenniums*.

a. cursed
b. coffin
c. shallow
d. stone

millions of years
hundreds of years
thousands of years
billions of years

Comprehension

SPECIFIC INFORMATION

A. Number in the correct order these stages in human evolution. Begin with Lucy.

__4__ Neanderthal

__2__ Homo Habilis

__3__ Homo erectus

__1__ Lucy

__5__ Homo sapiens, sapiens

B. Lucy's age at the time of her death was indicated by her

1. small size.
2. teeth.
3. skull.
4. musculature.

C. The excavators did not find

1. a hominid arm.
2. bits of a skull.
3. two left legs.
4. arthritic vertebrae.

D. The scientists on the expedition worked

1. competitively and aggressively.
2. casually, without discipline.
3. cooperatively yet autonomously.
4. in isolation from each other.

E. Lucy is important to research because she is

1. ancient, wise, and complete.
2. fragmented, old, and different.
3. charming, complete, and unique.
4. primitive, whole, and different.

F. The conflicting theories about Neanderthal result from

1. unsophisticated dating techniques.
2. limited discoveries over a small area.
3. overlapping disciplines.
4. the size of the Neanderthal brain.

ANALYSIS

G. This article most likely appeared in

1. *The National Enquirer*
2. *Readings in Anthropology an Introductory Text*
3. *Rolling Stone*
4. *Social Science Journal*

H. Johanson recreates the excitement of the discovery for his readers with

1. ancient curses.
2. statistics.
3. dialogue.
4. headlines.

I. The article appears to be unscientific because it

1. has an appealing subject.
2. is written in the first person.
3. is humorous and humane in tone.
4. all of the above.

J. The author uses the subway images in order to

1. illustrate stages in human evolution.
2. create distance and objectivity.
3. amuse and entertain.
4. avoid statistics.

Study Activity

MAKING NOTES IN THE TEXTBOOK

The subject of this chapter is fascinating to most students, but regardless of how intriguing any subject is, college reading assignments can create feelings of frustration and futility for several reasons: they are long, there is unfamiliar general and technical vocabulary, and the material is detailed and complete.

Making notes directly in the textbook helps to highlight for review a great deal of detailed information in a limited time.

WHY MARK THE TEXTBOOK?

The process of marking requires decision making, so it keeps you thinking. Consequently, comprehension usually improves. The process also brings to attention the terms and ideas that you don't fully understand. By scanning your notes, you can review quickly just prior to a lecture, lab, or class discussion. Notes also permit a more thorough review for quizzes, tests, and examinations. This can be your most valuable studying technique if you know what to note and how to do it.

ANNOTATING: DEVELOPING A SYSTEM OF SYMBOLS

Annotating is marking the text and writing comments in the margins that refer to the marked material.

Marks in textbooks should be coded. Here is a possible symbol system.

1. ________ and ✓ = central ideas
2. exp. or il. eg. = explanations and illustrations
3. ⬭ = vocabulary
4. [= ideas that go together
5. ▭ = signal expressions
6. 1, 2, 3 and/or a. b. c. = details that are part of a list
7. ——→ ←—— = cause-effect effect-cause
8. = = comparison (similarities)
9. x = contrast (differences)
10. c. p. = See page
11. What? or Yes! = reactions

The margins are used: top for vocabulary; sides for topics, notes of central ideas, reactions; bottom for questions.

In marking the text, you are responding in an organized but very personal way to what you are reading. You may change, and, or eliminate symbols, but you must be consistent. A note-taking system is illustrated in Figure 1. The first column indicates what to note; the second, how; the third presents an example.

Note	How?	Example
Unfamiliar vocabulary	Circle. Write word in upper margin. Add definition when you get it.	immutable unchanging Species were thought to be immutable

Note	How?	Example
Technical term and its definition	Circle. Underscore definition.	(Paleontology,) the systematic study of past life forms.
Key term and lengthy explanation	Circle. Bracket explanation in margin. Make note to aide comprehension.	Darwin called the process (natural selection.) [In the competition of life, those forms that are better adapted to their surroundings are at a considerable advantage and will tend to multiply. Similarly, those forms that are adaptable, change when their surroundings change, will also survive, while other less flexible creatures will perish. *(margin: adaptation → survival; inflexible → death)*
Central or unifying ideas in paragraphs and longer passages	Underscore in text; crossover lines of print when phrases or sentences interrupt; check and note the topic of the underscoring in the margin.	*(margin: cave art's purpose)* ✓ Cave art was most likely an instrument of magic, a visual prayer for fertility and a successful hunt.
Lengthy detailed passage	Bracket in text, but do not underscore; write major topics in the margin.	*(margin: cave art forms)* [Cave art took the form of engraving and painting either separately or in conjunction; [1] reliefs made by cutting away the rock to varying depths; [2] doodling on clay films on wall, ceiling, and floor; [3] and modeling clay figurines. *(margin: color)* [Coloring consisted of various kinds of ocher, manganese, and charcoal.
Good examples (clearly illustrate important points or show application of ideas)	Bracket in text; note your response in the margin.	*(margin: wow!)* [Venus of Willendorf, a fertility figurine with emphasis on torso, breasts, stomach, and buttocks to the near exclusion of the head]
Important names, dates, titles of publications, and documents	Underscore with a double line.	In the publication of Origin of the Species in 1859, Charles Darwin produced massive evidence to prove that species are capable of evolution, gradual change through time so that new species can arrive.

Note	How?	Example
Statement that you don't understand or one that requires more information	Bracket; write question mark in the margin.	? [Primates have kept a relatively unspecialized form of the hands and feet.
Statement you want to remember for future reference	Draw a double line in the margin; write "Yes!"	yes! ‖Man exploits the flight rather than the fight reaction toward an attack.
Statement that you don't understand or challenge.	Draw a double line in the margin; Write ? or What?	? what! ‖Neanderthal's brain was equal in size to modern man's.
Ideas that connect to other ideas (including visuals within the same chapter)	Draw double line in the margin; write topic; write book and "c. page reference" if you have one.	c. p87 ‖Primates on two legs escaped up trees carrying food.
Signal words in *important* contexts	Underscore the point. Box the expression. Write the topic in the margin, and use symbols to indicate the relationship between ideas.	
	List and Time Order: 1, 2, 3 a, b, c; write the total under topic in the margin. mammals' char : 4	Mammals—a class of vertebrate animals characterized by a [1] self-regulating body temperature, [2] hair, and in the [3] female, milk-producing [4] mammae or breasts, and two sets of teeth.
	Cause - Effect: cause → effect effect ← cause adaptation ↓ survival	Others because they could adapt to environmental changes have survived.
	Comparison (contrast) differences X man × others	Man differs from all other organisms, however, in . . .
	similarities = man = animals	When compared with animals, man shows striking resemblances.

Exercises

You will now have the opportunity to practice the skill on text material from different but closely related disciplines, and to anticipate questions based on your own annotations.

Preview the reading. Then work paragraph by paragraph; read first; think; then, write. Eventually you will be reading and writing almost simultaneously. Continually ask questions and look for the answers in the text. What is the key idea here? Which lines contain the best explanations or illustrations? What does this word mean? Where have I come across this idea?

A. The following passage is from the text *Invitation to Archaeology* by James Deetz. The first three paragraphs have been underscored and annotated. Underscore and annotate the remaining paragraphs. Answer the questions that follow.

The Site: Preparing to Excavate

archaeology

Archaeologists learn about past life from the fragmentary remains of the product of human activity. They pursue their investigations in all places where man lives or has lived at any time in the past.

site def.

2 types
domestic
non-dom.
(3)

The archaeologist's basic unit of study is the site. In the simplest terms, a site can be defined as that place where an archaeologist digs. A more specific definition is a spatial concentration of material evidence of human activity. While sites are frequently the remains of communities, they may also represent non-domestic activities. Examples include [1] cemeteries, frequently adjacent to communities, but at times separate; [2] hunt sites, often called kill sites, where animals were slaughtered by driving a herd over a cliff; [3] secret ceremonial grounds.

component def.

Archaeologists speak of sites as having components evidence of the use of the site by one or more groups of people. Each use accounts for one component.

The first step in an archaeological investigation is to conduct a survey. This involves going over the area on foot or by auto or horseback and inspecting aerial photographs. All sites discovered by this process are recorded. Test excavations, one or two small slashes, are made as the survey progresses to determine site depth and number of components. The sites are then given numbers, and a form is completed which provides information on the location, size, possible age, and state of preservation. When the survey has been completed, certain sites are singled out for investigation. Reasons for selection vary from size and depth to the possibility of impending destruction. Having selected a site, the archaeologist establishes a camp in the site's vicinity or houses his crew in a nearby town. In the United States, most archaeological fieldwork is done during the summer months and crews are made up of college students.

Prior to excavation the archaeologist draws a scale map of the site. A point is then located somewhere on or near the site and designated the datum point. The datum point is marked permanently with a cement post, steel pipe, or a natural feature such as a rock which will not be moved. The datum point indicates to future archaeological teams where previous excavations of the site were carried out.

The first excavation is usually not on the site at all, but at a point well away from the area thought to contain cultural remains. The pit is dug in order to learn the nature of the soils and deposits in an undisturbed state. Having prepared the map, established the datum point, and ascertained the normal condition of the deposits on the site, the archaeologist is ready to begin excavation of the cultural material.

1. What vocabulary should you know from this selection?

2. Write two information questions that the archaeology instructor might ask to test students' knowledge of this material.

B. Add marginal notations to the following passages from *Fossil Man* by Michael H. Day. Answer the questions.

Classification of Man

✓ When compared with many animals, man shows striking resemblances in the skull, the limbs, the senses, the brain, and the general arrangement of the internal organs. Indeed, it is possible to assign man to one of the major subdivisions of the animal kingdom, to a class of vertebrates, animals with backbones, known as mammals.

Mammals are animals which are characterized by their[1] self-regulating body temperature,[2] their milk-producing mammae or breasts, hair, and two sets of teeth, milk and permanent. Man is further assigned to an order of mammals called the primates, a group which includes tree shrews, tarsiers, lemurs, monkeys, and apes.

Classification is based upon structure and can be continued until individual species are recognized. A species can be defined as a group of animals, actually or potentially capable of interbreeding and producing fertile offspring which are like their parents. Man and the ape are two of more than fifteen thousand species of mammals.

1. List and define at least four terms that your instructor might require you to know from selection B:

2. List the characteristics of mammals:

3. Arrange the following terms beginning with the broadest classification and concluding with the most specific: primates; vertebrates; man and apes; mammals.

C. Underscore and annotate the following selection. Answer the question.

Primates

Nearly all primates live in trees or have had a near ancestor who lived in trees, and this means that to be successful they must have a structure that will allow them to move freely in a three-dimensional habitat. In general, they must be agile and able to grasp branches as well as have good stereoscopic vision, which will give them a good judgment of distance. Primates are generalized creatures that have kept a relatively unspecialized form of the hands and feet. Also they have retained the collar bone, or clavicle, which directs the shoulder to the side of the body and widens the range of the upper limb. Flat nails help to support the finger pads and improve the grip. The chief weapons of the primates are their long dagger-like canine teeth, but mostly they depend on their agility to survive, exploiting the "flight" rather than the "fight" reaction toward an attack.

1. What are the common features of primates?

D. Inferences about early hominid behavior are based on the evidence that currently exists. Both the inference and the evidence for it should be noted.

The Shanidar Discoveries

1 Archaeologist Ralph Soleki's discoveries in the Shanidar cave in the Zagras Mountains of Iraq have revealed important aspects of the Neanderthal that contradict the unattractive stereotype. 50 feet below the cave floor in a niche of stones, was the skeleton of a young man, and around the skeleton more than 2000 grams of fossil pollen. With the help of paleobotanist Arlette Leroi-Gourhan, Soleki concluded that one Spring day, 60,000 years ago people had lain the young man to rest on a bed of wild flowers. At least eight species of flowers mainly small brightly colored varieties were identified under the microscope. They were probably woven into the branches of a pine-like shrub, evidence of which was also found in the soil. Soleki suggests that ". . . no accident of nature could have deposited such remains so deep in the cave. Someone in the "Last Ice Age" must have ranged the mountainside in the mournful task of collecting flowers for the dead."

The skeleton of an elderly man found at Shanidar revealed that one forearm had been so severely damaged, it would have been almost useless during his lifetime. (His death had been the result of a rockslide and was unrelated to the injury.) He could not have hunted, but his age indicates that he had been helped to survive, perhaps through an early sense of humanity. Such nurturing would have been difficult in light of the harsh condition under which Neanderthal lived. Two skeletons were found to have artificially deformed skulls, apparently the result of strapping hard pads to the head during childhood. Neanderthal, like modern men and women, held concepts of aesthetics and acted to achieve them.

1. What inferences contradict the negative Neanderthal stereotype?

   a.

   b.

   c.

from *Human Evolution*

By Roger Lewin, 1984
W. H. Freeman

2 The anatomical changes in human development can be simply described. From an ape-like, tree-climbing ancestor, hominid became landed bipeds who acquired a substantially enlarged brain. However, the changes in behavior in the course of human evolution are complex and not so easily described. An important hypothesis advanced by Harvard University archaeologist Glynn Isaac is that food sharing among early hominid is a crucial key to the distinction between human and animal primates.

Isaac lists six key differences between modern humans and modern apes. First humans are bipedal and habitually carry around tools, food and other items. Second, while apes clearly communicate with each other none of them does so using a spoken language. Third, the acquisition of food among humans is a corporate responsibility, an activity involving exchange and sharing among adults and young; food acquisition among apes is a solitary affair. Fourth, humans typically postpone consumption of food until they return to a home base; apes eat the foot where they find it. Fifth, although chimpanzees occasionally hunt, their prey is usually small whereas human hunters can capture large animals. Sixth, primitive hunter-gatherers employ a small but effective collection of tools for their subsistence activities, such as stone flakes, digging sticks, spears, and crude containers; apes do occasionally use blades of grass or twigs while searching for termites, but they haven't been observed using tools while hunting or eating meat.

Collections of crude stone tools and bones concentrated in a small space indicate that as long ago as two million years, hominid had a home base to which whole or parts of animals were brought over a short period of time. Why were they behaving in such an unapelike manner? The assumption is that while adult hominid were out collecting food, the young were left in safety in a home base. Observations of modern hunter-gatherers indicate that males typically hunt while females, who are encumbered with young, typically gather plant food. Both sexes bring their spoils back to camp, where they are shared, among immediate families or among the camp.

Division of labor, tool making, hunting of large animals and food sharing are activities that require interdependence and spoken communication. The indications are that such a system, firmly underway a million years ago, made adaptation and survival possible.

1. What evidence for early hominid behavior currently exists?

   a.

   b.

   c.

2. What inferences have been made based on this evidence?

E. Read and make text notes on this passage from *Cultural Anthropology: Understanding Ourselves and Others* by Richly H. Crapo.

The Fossil Record

1 **Ancient *Homo sapiens sapiens*** Humans of completely modern biological type, *Homo sapiens sapiens,* existed by 40,000 years ago, according to the fossil record. These people with modern characteristics began to occur at that time throughout Africa, Europe, and Asia. The glacial period during which these early modern forms lived had its beginnings during the times of Neanderthal and began to terminate about 10,000 years ago.

2 This prehistoric period of human evolution was characterized by a greatly increased rate of change in technology, with more and more specialized tools and a tremendous number of local varieties and traditions within the tool kit. A major technological focus of this period was the manufacture of long, thin *blades* struck from a

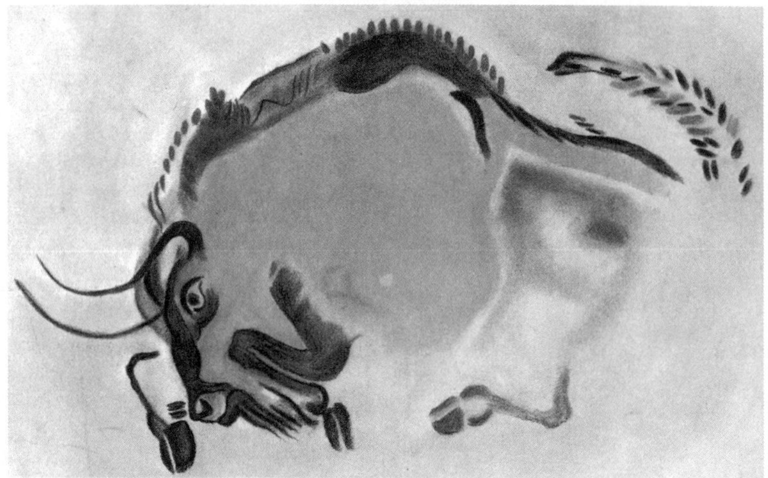

Why do scientists believe that the act rather than the object of creativity was of particular significance to early men and women?

prepared stone core. Such blades were used as both knives and scrapers. Another common type of blade was the *burin,* a chisel-like tool used for engraving bone, ivory, and similar materials. It seems to have originated in the plains areas of central and eastern Europe where wood suitable for making tools was lacking or at a premium. It was employed in the manufacture of the famous carved and engraved art works of this period and also made possible the carving of bone needles, wire pins, and detachable barbed harpoon heads.

3 The *spear-thrower* seems to have appeared toward the beginning of this period. It was a device for increasing the leverage of the human arm to propel a spear or dart to a greater distance and at a greater speed. The bow and arrow, an even more efficient device for use in hunting, came into being in this early Ice Age period. It was invented about 30,000 years ago, possibly in the Sahara—which was not a desert but a grassland region occupied by human hunters during the peak of the last glacial period. The new and highly efficient bow and arrow device was borrowed gradually and spread throughout most of the inhabited world, reaching the Western Hemisphere about 2,000 years ago.

4 The final outstanding trait of this period of early modern *Homo sapiens* was their now-famous art works, which included stone and bone carvings and modeled clay figures, engravings, and paintings found in caves like those at Altamira, Spain, and Lascaux, France. The central theme of this cave art was the portrayal of animals. The artistic tradition of these people emphasized the animals they hunted, which were generally portrayed in a realistic style. Often they were depicted as pregnant or with darts aimed at or entering their bodies. These two traits suggest that the pictures had magical functions for the early hunters: increasing the fertility of the animals that served as the basis for their survival and insuring the success of the hunt. This interpretation is supported by other indications that it was the act of creating the image itself, rather than the pure aesthetic value of portrayals, that was most valued. For one thing, vegetation and other aspects of the background were not portrayed. Second, individual animals were portrayed at different scales; they were generally not arranged in any mural depiction as a group. Third, individual portrayals were created at very different angles to each other, often overlapping earlier—apparently no longer important—ones. Finally, the paintings and wall reliefs were generally located in the darker, less accessible, recesses of the caves, rather than in

the inhabited cave entrances where they might have been mere decorations. These facts make sense if the creation of each portrayal were part of a religious ritual in which it was the creative act itself, rather than the aesthetic value of the end product, that was most valued.

Humans were rarely depicted and then only in a highly stylized manner that almost never seemed to attempt to capture the unique traits of an individual person. That is, this art work was not portraiture but seems to have served other purposes. The most outstanding examples of human representations are small figurines of modeled clay, stone, or ivory, known commonly as "Venus" figurines. These female figurines were found in the Northern Hemisphere from France to Siberia. Most are found in eastern Europe and all date from 20,000 to 27,000 years ago. They are generally fat and have exaggerated sexual features with large, pendulous breasts, protruding abdomens—sometimes suggesting pregnancy—and large hips and buttocks. The legs, on the other hand, tend to dwindle to a point, with no apparent feet. Similarly, the hands and arms are underemphasized, often being portrayed as mere lines on the body. The head may display hair but never has facial abstract representations of femininity in general. Like the cave painting, these figurines may have had a religious significance in magic rituals intended to insure fertility.

1. What terms might you be quizzed on in this reading?

2. What information questions (where, why) might the instructor ask?

3. What essay questions (explain, describe) might the instructor ask?

Critical Thinking

QUESTIONS FOR INDEPENDENT AND GROUP WORK

Exchange and answer the questions that you and your classmates have developed to accompany the note-taking.

Topic for Composition

Readings in this chapter stress the important link between adaptation and survival. As human beings, we know something about our past life forms, but what can we anticipate? Use your imagination to describe the individual who will have evolved through adaptation to survive many millenium from now.

Sculpture of Frederick Douglass by John Rhoden.

"To those who have suffered in slavery I can say, I too have suffered . . . to those who have battled for liberty, brotherhood and citizenship I can say, I too have battled" (Douglass).

What symbols of Douglass's victory are evident in this sculpture?

7

Liberty Looked From Every Star

Doing Library Research

"Learning would spoil the best [slave] in the world"; . . . "if you teach [him]—speaking of myself—how to read the bible, there will be no keeping him"; . . . "If you learn him [the slave] how to read, he'll want to know how to write; and this accomplished, he'll be running away with himself." . . . Very well thought I; knowledge unfits a child to be a slave. . . . and from that moment I understood the direct pathway from slavery to freedom.

—Frederick Douglass, My Bondage and My Freedom

Before Reading

Is it possible for a slave to have autonomy? The reading selections in this chapter are from primary sources, the actual letters, journals, and autobiographical works of slaves or former slaves written between 1821 and 1865. The accompanying study skill is library research. These selections were compiled by a student who was researching the topic "autonomy and slavery in North America."

You probably have an impression of the practice of slavery in the United States. What are your sources of information? What books have you read on the subject? What films or television programs have you seen? Have you ever interviewed anyone on the subject? From what you know, do you think it was possible for slaves to be autonomous?

READING SELECTION

This letter was written by Jourdan Anderson to his former owner. Anderson presents a list of demands which must be met before he and his family will return to the plantation. The letter was printed in The Freedman's Book, which was edited by abolitionist Lydia Maria Child.

To My Old Master . . .

By Jourdan Anderson

To my old Master, Colonel P. H. Anderson
Big Spring, Tennessee

1 Sir: I got your letter, and was glad to find that you had not forgotten Jourdan, and that you wanted me to come back and live with you again, promising to do better for me than anybody else can. I have often felt uneasy about you. I thought the Yankees would have hung you long before this, for harboring Rebs they found at your house. I suppose they never heard about your going to Colonel Martin's to kill the Union soldier that was left by his company in their stable. Although you shot at me twice before I left you, I did not want to hear of your being hurt, and am glad you are still living. It would do me good to go back to the dear old home again, and see Miss Mary and Miss Martha and Allen, Esther, Green and Lee. Give my love to them all, and tell them I hope we will meet in the better world, if not in this. I would have gone back to see you all when I was working in the Nashville Hospital, but one of the neighbors told me that Henry intended to shoot me if he ever got a chance.

2 I want to know particularly what the good chance is you propose to give me. I am doing tolerably well here. I get twenty five dollars a month, with victuals and clothing; have a comfortable home for Mandy—the folks call her Mrs. Anderson—and the children—Milly, Jane, and Grundy—go to school and are learning well. The teacher says Grundy has a head for a preacher. They go to Sunday school and Mandy and me attend church regularly. We are kindly treated. Sometimes we over-hear others saying, "Them colored people were slaves down in Tennessee." The children feel hurt when they hear such remarks; but I tell them it was no disgrace in Tennessee to belong to Colonel Anderson. Many darkeys would have been proud, as I used to be, to call you master. Now if you will write and say what back wages you will give me, I will be better able to decide whether it would be to my advantage to move back again.

3 As to my freedom, which you say I can have, there is nothing to be gained on that account, as I got my free papers in 1864 from the Provost-Marshal-General of the Department of Nashville. Mandy says she would be afraid to go back without some proof that you were disposed to treat us justly and kindly; and we have concluded to test your sincerity by asking you to send us our wages for the time we served you. This will make us forget and forgive old scores, and rely on your justice and friendship in the future. I served you faithfully for thirty-two years, and Mandy twenty years. At twenty-five dollars a month for me, and two dollars a week for Mandy, our earnings would amount to eleven thousand six hundred and eighty dollars. Add to this the interest for the time our wages have been kept back, and deduct what you paid for our clothing, and three doctor's visits to me, and pulling a tooth for Mandy, and the balance will show what we are in justice entitled to. Please send the money by Adam's Express, in care of V. Winters, Esq., Dayton, Ohio. If you fail to pay us for faithful labors in the past, we can have little faith in your promises in the future. We trust the good Maker has opened your eyes to the wrongs which you and your fathers have done to me and my fathers, in making us toil for you for generations without recompense. Here I draw my wages every Saturday night; but in Tennessee there was never any pay-day for the Negroes any more than for the horses and the cows. Surely there will be a day of reckoning for those who defraud the laborer of his hire.

4 In answering this letter, please state if there would be any safety for my Milly and Jane, who are now grown up, and are both good

looking girls. You know how it was with poor Matilda and Catherine. I would rather stay here and starve—and die, if it come to that—than have my girls brought to shame by the violence and wickedness of their young masters. You will also please state if there has been any schools opened for the colored children in your neighborhood. The great desire of my life now is to give my children an education, and have them form virtuous habits.

5 Say howdy to George Carter, and thank him for taking the pistol from you when you were shooting at me.

From your old servant,
JOURDAN ANDERSON

Given Jourdan Anderson's demands, what inferences can you make about life in slavery?

A. specific forms of exploitation under which slaves lived?

B. deprivations and indignities of slave life?

C. perceptions master and slave had of one another?

D. Jourdan Anderson's "real" expectations?

E. Jourdan Anderson's autonomous response?

There is additional reading on this topic from primary sources, biographies, diaries, and letters, on pages 150–159 of this chapter and in Connections.

Study Activity

DOING LIBRARY RESEARCH

The library research assignment requires you to write several pages based on in-depth examination of published material on a specific topic. Research writing assignments can have long-range rewards because the skills developed serve you both during and after college. These skills are, in fact, recognized in many careers as essential for ascending the professional hierarchy beyond entry level positions. Your more immediate reward is the joy of discovery, the intellectual excitement that comes from unearthing material that confirms or expands ideas on a thoughtfully selected topic.

This section will help you to become familiar with the term paper process and the resources available to you. It will also give you an opportunity to practice several steps that library research requires.

The research process encompasses the following activities:

1. Selecting a topic (a question that research will answer)
2. Locating sources of information
3. Recording sources
4. Evaluating sources
5. Formulating a thesis (an answer to the question)
6. Outlining the paper
7. Abstracting information (summarizing, quoting, and paraphrasing) that supports the thesis
8. Drafting the paper
9. Giving formal documentation or recognition to all sources of information
10. Redrafting, editing, and proofreading

The discussion will focus on steps 1 through 7 (see Chapter 12 for instruction in formal note outlining). The actual drafting of a complete paper is not covered in this text. Your instructor and your librarian can refer you to writing manuals that provide detailed instruction in this exacting endeavor.

Selecting a Topic

The topic of your research may be assigned by your instructor. Otherwise, it will be up to you to determine a topic within fairly broad guidelines. The research assignment has two objectives which you should keep in mind when selecting a topic. The first is to take you beyond what your course has covered in homework, lecture, and class discussion. The second is to individualize your course by encouraging you to investigate some aspect of particular interest to you. Therefore, the topic that you select must have both relevance to the course and real meaning for you.

The student who discovered the reading material for this chapter had been directed to research some aspect of the very broad concept of autonomy. Like you, she had spent time reading about and discussing the idea of autonomy from a number of perspectives. Now she began to concentrate on a personal meaning of the term. Essentially, she did some "before reading." First, she looked for words with similar meanings and then words with opposite meanings. The notion that the opposite of "autonomy" was a kind of slavery struck a responsive chord in this student, who, in fact, was a descendant of individuals who had been slaves. Through her exploration, the concept evolved into the general topic "Autonomy and Slavery."

Using Questions to Narrow a Topic

Posing the topic in the form of a question gives your research a focus. Consider the following questions on autonomy and slavery which the student asked:

Who were the autonomous slaves?

Who were the literate slaves?

What conditions fostered autonomy?

What conditions discouraged autonomy?

What were the results of autonomous behavior? for the slave? for the master?

How do we know about autonomy or its absence in the lives of slaves?

A. Using the following question words, add to the list:

Where?

When?

Why?

Eventually the student expressed her topic as the following question: "To what extent could slaves be autonomous in the years preceding the Civil War?" She decided to confine her research to the actual documents of slaves—their journals, diaries, letters, and autobiographies.

A Final Note on Selecting a Topic

If you have concerns about any aspect of the research assignment—its scope, focus, or approach—request an appointment with your instructor. You will probably come away with a clearer understanding of what is expected of you, as well as the titles of books and articles which will prove valuable.

Locating Sources

You will do most of your research in the library. Librarians can assist you to find books, journals, and other sources of information; however, familiarity with the library resources described here, their functions, and their locations in your college library will certainly increase your efficiency.

HIGH TECH/LOW TECH: THE COMPUTER DATABASE/THE CARD CATALOGUE

Traditionally, the card catalogue has been the key to all that the library has to offer, including books, indexes, magazines, records, tapes, and films. Today, however, in most libraries a computer database is replacing the card catalogue as the most efficient means for searching the collection. It takes a very short time to learn how to run the program and usually there is staff assistance to orient you to any new technology.

The computer search and the card catalogue search utilize a similar approach. Books, for example, are listed under the author, the title, and sometimes the subject.

FINDING BOOKS IN THE STACKS

Both the computer screen and the index card provide you with a call number that indicates the book's location. Study the cards in Figure 1 for *My Bondage and My Freedom,* by Frederick Douglass.

There are three steps in locating the book in the stacks. We will use the call number for *My Bondage and My Freedom* to trace the steps;

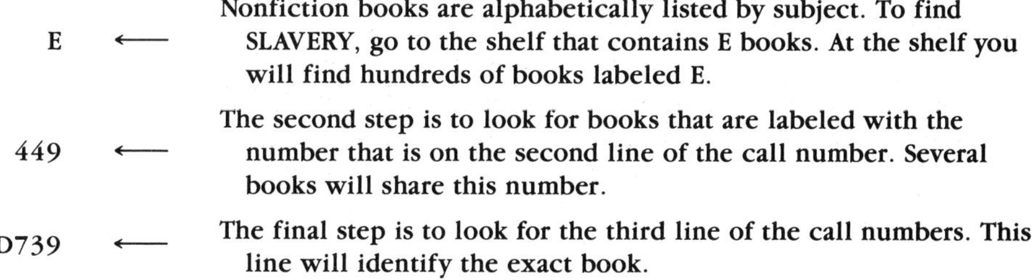

E ⟵ Nonfiction books are alphabetically listed by subject. To find SLAVERY, go to the shelf that contains E books. At the shelf you will find hundreds of books labeled E.

449 ⟵ The second step is to look for books that are labeled with the number that is on the second line of the call number. Several books will share this number.

.D739 ⟵ The final step is to look for the third line of the call numbers. This line will identify the exact book.

If the call number includes the abbreviation *Ref.,* the book will be found in the reference room and cannot be removed from the library. The vast majority of books are, of course, on the shelves or stacks and are available for loan. They are arranged according to subject, so that while you are searching for a specific book, you will probably come across other intriguing titles. Take the time to "sample" these books also by previewing the contents page and index and reading a few lines in the body of the text. They may prove to be worthwhile for your paper.

author card

E
449
.D739

Douglass, Frederick, 1817?–1895.
My bondage and my freedom. With a new introd. by Philip S. Foner. New York, Dover Publications, [1969]

xiii, 464 p. illus., port. 21 cm. (Black rediscovery) 3.50

"Unabridged and unaltered republication of the work first published in 1855."

1. Slavery in the United States—Anti-slavery movements. 2. Slavery in the United States—Maryland. I. Title.

E449.D739 ~~1969~~ 301.45'22'0924 73–92688
SBN 486-22457-0 MARC

Library of Congress 70 [12]

title card

My bondage and my freedom

E
449
.D739

Douglass, Frederick, 1817?–1895.
My bondage and my freedom. With a new introd. by Philip S. Foner. New York, Dover Publications, [1969]

xiii, 464 p. illus., port. 21 cm. (Black rediscovery) 3.50

"Unabridged and unaltered republication of the work first published in 1855."

1. Slavery in the United States—Anti-slavery movements. 2. Slavery in the United States—Maryland. I. Title.

E449.D739 ~~1969~~ 301.45'22'0924 73–92688
SBN 486-22457-0 MARC

Library of Congress 70 [12]

subject card

SLAVERY IN THE UNITED STATES - ANTI-SLAVERY MOVEMENTS.

E
449
.D739

Douglass, Frederick, 1817?–1895.
My bondage and my freedom. With a new introd. by Philip S. Foner. New York, Dover Publications, [1969]

xiii, 464 p. illus., port. 21 cm. (Black rediscovery) 3.50

"Unabridged and unaltered republication of the work first published in 1855."

1. Slavery in the United States—Anti-slavery movements. 2. Slavery in the United States—Maryland. I. Title.

E449.D739 ~~1969~~ 301.45'22'0924 73–92688
SBN 486-22457-0 MARC

Library of Congress 70 [12]

Figure 1 *Library Catolog Cards*

IN THE REFERENCE ROOM

In the reference section of a library numerous works offer general, detailed, historical, and current information.

Encyclopedias

If you are seeking an established noncontroversial body of knowledge on a topic, you may consult an encyclopedia. The *American Encyclopedia* and the *Encyclopedia Brittanica* cover topics in sufficient depth and use vocabulary considered appropriate to introductory level college instruction. There are specialized encyclopedias for specific fields including religion, education, music, painting, engineering, and technology. Biographical encyclopedias such as *Who's Who?* give information about persons who have distinguished themselves in various fields.

Bibliographies

For a list of books and articles on a particular subject, period, or author, request a bibliography from the librarian. Many bibliographies are annotated; that is, specific items are briefly discussed in terms of their uniqueness or usefulness. Bibliographies may be indexed in the card catalogue or the computer database. See Figure 2 for an example of a bibliography in a card catalogue.

Study Figure 3 for an example of an annotated entry in a specialized Afro-American history bibliography.

Indexes to Periodicals

Journals, magazines, and newspapers are called "periodicals" because they are issued periodically on a quarterly, monthly, weekly, daily, or other basis. Indexes to periodicals are available in the reference room. An index refers to an alphabetical listing of names and topics. The index itself does not supply information, but

Miller, Elizabeth W., ed. THE NEGRO IN AMERICA: A BIBLIOGRAPHY. 2d ed. Cambridge, Mass., Harvard University Press, 1970. 351 p.

A thorough bibliography of materials published between 1954 and 1970. Emphasis is on social, political and economic issues, but art and history are included. This is one of the best sources for students doing serious study on the black man in America. The final chapter, "A Guide to Further Research," is an excellent listing of important materials to use when studying a specific subject.

Figure 2 *Example of bibliography in the card catalog.*

Frazier, Thomas R. ed. AFRO-AMERICAN HISTORY: PRIMARY SOURCES. New York, Harcourt, Brace and World Inc., 1970. 514 p.
While not an anthology of articles on Afro-American studies, its importance justifies its inclusion in this bibliography. Essays, poetry, speeches, interviews and many other kinds of primary sources are included which relate to the central topics of Afro-American studies.

Figure 3 *Example of annotated entry in a specialized bibliography.*

indicates where information can be found. The card catalogue, for example, is an index to everything that can be found in the library. Information in periodicals must be indexed; otherwise, you would have to spend hours going through copies of publications to find data relevant to your topics.

Readers' Guide

The most generally useful index is *The Readers' Guide to Periodical Literature.* It is published twice monthly from September through June, once in July and once in August in paperback form. At the end of the year, a bound volume of the year's issues, which is called a cumulation, is distributed to libraries. Published since 1900, the *Readers' Guide* indexes more than 100 magazines. In the front material to each volume, you will find the names of the periodicals indexed and a key to the many abbreviations used. Indexing is alphabetical under author, subject, and occasionally title. Subjects may be broken down into subheadings, which interrupt the alphabetical organization.

EXERCISES

A. Examine the excerpt in Figure 4 from the *Readers' Guide,* Volume 40. Check the articles you think might be relevant to the topic "Autonomy and Slavery."

B. Study the following basic form of the subject listing from the *Readers' Guide* and the explanation that follows:

SLAVERY
Slaves freed. S. B. Oates. il pors Am Heritage 32:74–83 D '80

The subject (slavery) is in capital boldface letters on the first line. The second line, which is indented, begins with the title (Slaves freed). The title is followed by the author's name, (S. B. Oates) unless a staff writer wrote

SLAUGHTER, Paul
Morocco. il Peter Phot Mag 9:26-30+ My '80
SLAVE labor camps. See Concentration camps
SLAVERY
Conspiracy and revivalism in 1802: a direful symbiosis. T. C. Parramore. bibl Negro Hist Bull 43:28-31 Ap/My/Je '80
Emerson and the anti-slave. L. D. Mitchell and L. Gougeon. bibl f Negro Hist Bull 42:16 Ja/F/Mr '79
Experiment at Nashoba Plantation [1825] P. Robbins. il por Am Hist Illus 15:12-19 Ap '80
Final arbiter: a history of the decisions rendered by the Supreme Court of the United States relative to the Negro prior to the Civil War. O. Taylor. bibl f Negro Hist Bull 43:8-10 Ja/F/Mr '80
Moynihan Report: black history seduced and abandoned [black family life] H. G. Gutman. Nation 229:232-6 S 22 '79; Discussion. 230:98+ F 2 '80
Negro governors [slaves electing slave governors in New England] M. O'Dea. il Am Hist Illus 15:22-5+ Jl '80
White indentured servitude and the Atlantic slave trade. R. A. Chee-Mooke. bibl f Negro Hist Bull 43:20-2 Ja/F/Mr '80

Emancipation

Slaves freed. S. B. Oates. il pors Am Heritage 32:74-83 D '80

Historiography

But the cat himself knows: slavery in the Ante-Bellum South—a historiographical survey. H. Tulloch. bibl il Hist Today 30:57-60 My '80

International aspects

Slavery declining, but not dead. P. M. Jones. il map Sr Schol 113:21 O 31 '80

Pamphlets

David Walker: An Appeal to whom? [analysis of pamphlet Appeal to the coloured citizens of the world] P. Buckingham. bibl f il Negro Hist Bull 42:24-6 Ja/F/Mr '79

Figure 4 *Excerpt from* The Reader's Guide to Periodical Literature, *Volume 40.*

the article, in which case no author's name may appear. The abbreviation *il* indicates illustration, *pors* indicates portraits. The title of the periodical follows *(American Heritage)*. Following this is the volume number (32) and after the colon the page numbers (74–83). The abbreviated date of the issue (December 1980) concludes the reference.

C. Study the following subject listing and answer the questions that follow:

SLAVERY
But the cat himself knows: slavery in the Ante-Bellum South—a historiographical survey. H. Tulloch. bibl il Hist Today 30:57–60 My '80

1. What is the subject of the article?

2. What is the title?

3. In what periodical does the article appear?

4. What volume includes the issue?

5. What is the exact date of publication?

6. On what page does the article begin?

D. Study the following author reference in the *Readers' Guide* and complete the periodical loan slip that follows. Note that the author's name appears on the first line. The remainder of the reference contains the same information in the same order as the subject reference.

MILLER, Randall M.
Man in the Middle: the black slave driver, excerpt from
Dear Master: letters of a slave. il Am Heritage 30:40–9
O '79

PERIODICAL LOAN SLIP

Periodical Name ____________

Periodical Date ____________

Vol. ________ Pages ________

CHECK ONE:

BOUND ✓ (Stacks)

RESERVE ________ (Circ. Desk)

MICROFILM ________ (AV Room)

PERIODICALS RM.____(Info. Desk)

Your Name ____________

Soc. Sec. #____________

Today's Date____________

DO NOT WRITE BELOW THIS LINE

WHERE ARE PERIODICALS LOCATED?

When you have identified a promising article by using an index or the *Readers' Guide,* you must find out whether the periodical in which the article appears is part of the library's collection. A list of the library's periodicals and their dates is usually available at the central information desk or in the reference room. Periodicals on the list can generally be found in one of four places:

1. Bound volumes of past issues may be organized alphabetically by title in a separate section of the stacks.
2. Periodicals on microfilm are filed in an audiovisual room.
3. Individual recent issues may be organized alphabetically in a periodicals room.
4. A periodical which is on reserve must be requested from a librarian.

NEWSPAPER INDEXES

Major newspapers, including the *London Times, New York Times,* and *The Wall Street Journal,* publish indexes. The *New York Times Index* is published twice a year, with annual cumulations. Articles are indexed alphabetically according to the subject. The date of the issue, the page, and the column are given. Many libraries have transferred their bound copies of newspapers to microfilm, which is easy to use.

E. Study the excerpt in Figure 5 from the *New York Times Index, 1863.* Check the articles that might be worth perusing for a paper on autonomy and slavery.

OTHER VALUABLE INDEXES

Of particular value to college students are the periodical indexes for special subjects. A partial listing follows:

1. For short stories or essays included in anthologies, see *Short Story Index and General Guide to Essays and Literature.*
2. For illustrations, songs, and speeches, see the *Index to Illustrations, Index to Songs,* and *Index to Speeches.*
3. There are numerous indexes to current information in specific disciplines and fields, including *Applied Science and Technology Index, The Social Science and Humanities Index, The Business Periodicals Index.*

Sherman, Gen., Sanguinary Failure of at Vicksburgh.......... ....Jan. 19—4-5
Sherman, Gen., Movement to join Grant..Nov. 13—4-5
Shipbuilding in the East.... ....July 30—4-4
Shipments, Proposals to Change to English Steamers........................ Feb. 28—4-3
Sickles, Major-Gen.—His Value to the Army.......................... ....June 17—4-4
Sickles. Major-Gen., Wounded at Gettysburgh.. ....July 6—4-3
Sickles, Gen., Speech at New-York.....Nov. 2—4-3
Sismondi on the Dangers to Free Governments..................................March 12—4-3

Slavery; President Lincoln's Proclamation Emancipating Slaves in Southern States........................Jan. 3—4-3
Does the War Promote Pro-Slavery Reaction?................ ....Jan. 31—4-2
Southern and English Apostles of Slavery............. ....June 3—4-4
As a Revolutionary Force...............June 16—4-5
Defenders in the Confederacy ....July 12—4-2
And the Union...... ....July 29—4-4
The True Policy Toward................Nov. 27—4-2
As a War Force.......... ....Dec. 7—4-4
The Rebel Loss of ....May 6—4-5
Slidell on Davis as a Repudiator............April 13—4-4
Smith, Gerrit, on the Duty of Suppressing the Rebellion..... ....March 12—4-4
Smith, Gerrit, on the Preservation of the Union.................... ... .May 28—4-2
Social Evils in Great Cities............. ...Nov. 22—4-2
Social Theories and their Exponents. ......Aug. 8—4-5
Soldiers' Families and Delayed Back Pay..... ....Jan. 8—4-5
Pay and Mail Robbers..................Jan. 25—4-4
And the Copperheads............. ...March 12—4-2
Robbery of Sick and Disabled.........March 22—4-5
Vote and the New-York Legislature... .April 18—4-2
And the Rioters.........................July 18—4-4
Vote Against Copperheads..............Oct. 21—4-2

South, the, Effect of the War on the....Jan. 11—4-4
Opinions of the North at............... Jan. 18—4-3
The Demands of the......................March 2—4-3
Trade of—the New Circular on..........April 7—4-4
The, Jeff. Davis on the Scarcity in......April 17—4-2
The Bread Riots at the..................April 20—1-4
Bread Riots; the Ladies the Leaders at Atlanta........ ....April 21—4-3
Trade of its, the Future........ ....May 22—4-2
Development of the Strength of the...June 1—4-2
The, Retributions for Crime.... ....Aug. 9—4-4
The, Never for Disunion............... Aug. 11—4-3
Southwest Territory Clear of Rebels.......Feb. 18—4-5
Southwestern Campaign—a Splendid Record..................................July 25—4-4
South Carolina and the Food Question.....April 18—4-3
South Carolina, the Reckoning with.......Aug. 25—4-2
South Carolina—Position of in Regard to Chattanooga............................Oct. 4—4-3
Spalding, Hon. E. G., on the Finances of the Country....................... ....Jan. 14—4-3
Speculations on Unforeseen Causes of Great Failures....................... ..March 2?—4-4
Spies, the Execution of; T. M. Campbell Case.......................................May 1—4-3
Springfield, Mo., the Scare in Over.........Jan. 13—4-5
Stanton, Secretary, Abuse of and Services.Aug. 3—4-4
State Defence, the Duty of..................June 27—4-4
State Sovereignty—Shall We Go to Pieces?.Feb. 15—4-2
State Sovereignty—its Relations to the Army.......................................Aug. 23—4-2
Statistical Bureau, the Necessity for a. ...Jan. 24—4-4
Steamboat Burning at the West..... ......Oct. 4—4-6
Stephens, A. H.; What he Said on Slavery the Corner-stone of the Confederacy ....March 29—4-2
Stephens, A. H., and Robert Ould's Mission to Hampton Roads...............July 8—4-4

Figure 5 *Excerpt from the* New York Times Index, *1863*.

4. For articles published in the nineteenth century, see *Poole's Index.*

F. The Reference Room Librarian directed the student who was researching autonomy and slavery to a specialized periodical index, *Index to Black Periodicals.* Study the excerpt in Figure 6 and check off articles that appear relevant to the topic.

Recording Sources

PREPARING A WORKING BIBLIOGRAPHY

Once you have your sources of information, it is important to prepare a working bibliography, a list of the books and periodicals that you will use as you progress

Slavery—Anti-Slavery Movements

The Black Voice in Eighteenth-Century Britain: African Writers Against Slavery and the Slave Trade. Notes. Victor C. D. Mtubani. *Phylon* 45, No.2 (Summer 1984):85–97

Building an Antislavery Wall: Black Americans in the Atlantic Abolitionist Movement, 1830–1860. By R. J. M. Blackett. Reviewed by Marcellus C. Barksdale. *Phylon* 45, No.2 (Summer 1984):158

Slave Revolt, Slave Debate: A Comparison. Notes. John Herbert Roper and Lolita G. Brockington. *Phylon* 45, No.2 (Summer 1984):98–110

Slavery, War, and Revolution: The British Occupation of Saint Dominique, 1793–1798. By David Geggus. Reviewed by Roger N. Buckley. *Caribbean Review* 13, No.4 (Fall 1984):50

Testing the Chains: Resistance to Slavery in the British West Indies. By Michael Craton. Reviewed by Roger N. Buckley. *Caribbean Review* 13, No.4 (Fall 1984):50

Slavery—Narratives

The Odyssey of an Ex-Slave: Robert Ball Anderson's Pursuit of the American Dream. Notes. Darold D. Wax. *Phylon* 45, No.1 (Spring 1984):67–79

The Slave Narrative: Its Place in American History. By Marion Wilson Starling. Reviewed by Beryle Banfield. *Interracial Books for Children* 15, Nos. 7–8 (1984):35

Slavery and Religion

"A Home in Dat Rock": Afro-American Folk Sources and Slave Visions of Heaven and Hell. Lewis V. Baldwin. *Journal of Religious Thought* 41 (Spring/Summer 1984):38–57

The Rise of African Churches in America (1786–1822): Re-Examining the Contexts. Will B. Gravely. *Journal of Religious Thought* 41 (Spring/Summer 1984):58–73

Slavery—Slave Culture

Candomblé: A Spiritual Microcosm of Africa. Sheila Walker. *Black Art* 5, No. 4 (1984):10–22

Sleet, Moneta (Jr.)

Reverend James Cleveland: His Church and Home Are His Greatest Joys. *Ebony* 40 (December 1984):148–152

Sloan, Lester

The Long Hike. *Black Enterprise* 14 (June 1984):266

Small Business Administration

Changing the Rules. Sheila Spence. *Black Enterprise* 15 (December 1984):24

Small Claims Courts

So Sue Me! Sandra Jackson-Opoku. *Black Enterprise* 15 (September 1984):57–58

Smikle, Ken

Wired for Success. *Essence* 14 (January 1984):22

Smith, Alan M. (joint editor)

See Glasrud, Bruce A.

Smith, Alonzo N.

Afro-Americans and the Presidential Elections of 1948. *Western Journal of Black Studies* 8, No. 2 (Summer 1984):101–110

Smith, Annette (joint author)

See Eshleman, Clayton

Smith, Annette (joint translator)

See Eshleman, Clayton

Smith, Barbara

Home Girls: A Black Feminist Anthology. Book review. C. Lynn Munro. *Black American Literature Forum* 18 (Winter 1984):175–177

Smith, Charles U.

The Role of the NAACP in Public Education of Children in the United States. *Negro Educational Review* 35, Nos. 3–4 (July-October 1984):92–101

Smith, Dorothy H. (about)

How I Made a Million. Lloyd Gite. *Essence* 15 (June 1984):70–72

Smith, Dorset L. (about)

A Not So Ordinary Man. Maxine Childress Brown. *About Time* 12, No. 11 (November 1984):18

Smith, Ervin

The Ethics of Martin Luther King, Jr. Reviewed by Howard Ross. *Phylon* 45, No.1 (Spring 1984):81–82

Smith, Frederick F. (Jr.)

Are America's Law Firms Willing to Make Blacks Partners? *Black Enterprise* 15 (November 1984):63–66

Smith, Howard (about)

High Tech: Winning Success in Silicon Valley. *Ebony* 40 (November 1984):37–38

Smith, J. Clay

Review: Affirmative Action. *Howard Law Journal* 27, No. 2 (1984):495–522

Smith, Joshua I. (about)

Black Pioneers in the Computer Industry. *Black Collegian* 15 (November/December 1984):97

Smith, Kristina (about)

Smith Maintains Crown as 1st Black Rose Bowl Queen. *Jet* 67 (November 12, 1984):51

Figure 6 *Excerpt from* Index to Black Periodicals.

through your research project. The following index card system works well for this purpose.

1. Make a separate card for each source.
2. For books, turn to the copyright page (the reverse side of the title page). Record the author(s) or editor(s) name(s), the entire title, the place of publication, the publisher, the date, and the call number so that you will not have to return to the card catalogue. Study the following basic form:

> Escott, Paul D. *Slavery Remembered: A Record of Twentieth-Century Slave Narratives* Chapel Hill: The University of North Carolina Press, 1979.

Working bibliography: book (basic form).

3. For articles, record information directly from the periodicals' index, include author (if given), title of the article, name of publication, volume (unless it is a weekly publication, in which case the date is sufficient), page numbers, and library location. Study the following basic form:

> Mohr, C. L. "Slavery in Oglethorpe County, Georgia 1773–1865." *Phylon* 33 (Spring 72): 4–21.
>
> stacks

Working bibliography: article in a periodical (basic form).

4. For an article from a newspaper, the title and the issue are sufficient; however, for large metropolitan dailies, title of article and page number should also be included.

> *New York Times* "Slavery as a Revolutionary Force," June 18, 1863, p. 4.
>
> microfilm

Working bibliography: newspaper article (basic form).

5. For encyclopedia articles, record the name of the encyclopedia, the edition, the abbreviation *s.v.,* (for ***sub verbo,*** or "under the word," and the title of the article. Add the author's name if the article is signed. Study the following basic form:

> *Encyclopaedia Brittanica* 1972 ed., s.v. "Modern (or plantation) Slavery and the Slave Trade."
>
> reference room

Working bibliography: encyclopedia article (basic form).

PREPARING FOR FINAL DOCUMENTATION

Documentation is the method by which writers acknowledge their sources. It has several purposes: It gives credit to the originator of an idea; it reveals how current the material is; and it permits interested readers to pursue the topic by guiding them to worthwhile articles and books. Different disciplines, departments in a university, and instructors have their preferred style of documentation. It is important to check with your instructor regarding the desired format.

Documentation is achieved through citation.

1. Bibliographic citations describe the whole document the researcher has used, whether a book, pamphlet, essay in a book, or periodical article. These citations appear in an alphabetical list at the end of the paper.

2. Footnote citations refer to the specific page on which a fact or opinion is found. Cited material within the text is numbered sequentially. The numbers refer to footnote citations, which appear at the bottom of each page or on a separate page right before the bibliography.

3. Another kind of in text citation requires the author's last name and the date of publication in parenthesis (just the date if the author's name is given in the narrative). Here titles are found in an alphabetical list of sources called the reference list. It appears at the end of the paper just before a bibliography that includes background materials and works for further reading.

A. Although final form is not required for working bibliography cards, it is very helpful *to use from the beginning* the standard format that is required in the final bibliography.

Read the following cards and indicate the information needed to make each entry complete: author(s) or editor(s) names, title, place of publication, publisher, date of publication, pages.

Example:

> *My Bondage and My Freedom*. New York: Dover Publications Inc., 1855, 1969.

Missing: ____________________

> Grant, Joanne. *Black Protest History Documents and Analyses 1619 to the Present*. New York: 1968.

Missing: ____________________

> *New York Times* December 7, 1863, p. 4.

Missing: ____________________

> Cassell, F. A. "Slaves of the Chesapeake Bay Area and the War of 1812" 57 (April 72) 144–155.

Missing: ____________________

B. Revise the order and punctuation of these entries:

The Atlantic Slave Trade "Negro History Bulletin" 35 (Feb. 1972) 44–47. R. L. J. Harris	
Frazier, Thomas R. ed., Harcourt Brace and World Inc., New York. *Afro-American History: Primary Sources.* 1970	
Randall M. Miller *American Heritage* Man in the Middle 30:40–9 (October '79)	
1969, Freedman, Francis S. ed: *The Black American Experience,* N.Y. Random House.	

EVALUATING SOURCES

Preliminary Reading

Once the working bibliography has been compiled, you can begin to examine books and articles more thoroughly. The object of your preliminary reading is to single out the best sources and to move toward formulating a thesis, a controlling idea and point of view for your paper.

Study the following criteria for selection:

Date	Is the date appropriate? For current social science theory on slavery, for example, recent dates are desirable; for firsthand accounts of slavery by slaves, earlier dates are, of course, anticipated.
Author	Is the author recognized as an authority in the field? Has your instructor mentioned the author's work? Is the author's background apparent in the material on the book jacket? You may wish to check a biographical resource such as *Who's Who?*
Objectivity and Authenticity	Is there more fact than opinion? Are sources of information documented? That is, are facts, statistics, quotations, and theories (that are not the author's) given footnotes which refer to sources in the bibliography?
Level of Material	Is the vocabulary and amount of detail at an acceptable level for a college paper? The scholarly or professional journal is preferred to a popular magazine. The fully documented book published by a university press is preferred to a mass-market publication.
Relevance to the Topic	Does the material address your topic?

Applying the Criteria for Selection

The student with the topic "Possibilities for Autonomy in Slavery," came across *Slavery Remembered* by Paul D. Escott and decided to use it in her paper. Read the index card and excerpts from sections of the book to see why it met the criteria for selection.

> Escott, Paul D. *Slavery Remembered: A Record of Twentieth-Century Slave Narratives*
> Chapel Hill: The University of North Carolina Press, 1979.

Working bibliography card.

Contents

Preface xiii

Introduction: The Narratives as a Source 3

1. Two Peoples and Two Worlds 18
2. The Slaves' Experiences on the Plantation 36
3. Forms of Slave Resistance 71
4. Bases of a Black Culture 95
5. "Seeing How the Land Lay" in Freedom 119
6. "Starting Uphill, den Going Back" 143
7. Life Patterns of the Freedom Generation 159

Afterword 177

Appendix A: Methods of Recording and Coding Information 183
Appendix B: Race of Interviewers 188
Appendix C: Additional Tables 192

Notes 201
Bibliography 213
Index 217

Slavery Remembered

(continued from front flap)

including diet, physical treatment, working conditions, housing, forms of resistance, and black overseers; slave cultural institutions;

status distinctions among slaves; experience during the Civil War and Reconstruction; and the subsequent life histories of the former slaves. Escott has taken pains to let the slaves speak for themselves, which some of them do with eloquence, through direct quotation, and he provides numerous tables to summarize and illuminate controversial areas of slave life.

The sweep of *Slavery Remembered* is much greater than that of the few competing works, and it will prove enlightening reading for all who are interested in slavery and the black experience.

Paul D. Escott, assistant professor of history at The University of North Carolina at Charlotte, is author of *After Secession: Jefferson Davis and the Failure of Confederate Nationalism.*

Table 3.8 *Sex of Reported Resisters—Selected Types of Resistance*

	Percentage			
Type of Resistance	Male	Female	Both Involved	Number
Ran away (including Civil War)	80.9	11.6	7.4	215
Ran away (excluding Civil War)	63.6	21.6	14.8	88
Hid in woods	69.6	24.3	6.1	115
Killed overseer or other white	61.1	27.8	11.1	18
Stole	53.3	26.7	20.0	30
Verbal confrontation	48.5	51.5	0.0	33
Struck master, stayed	35.3	62.7	2.0	51

from *Slavery Remembered,* Chapter 3

Improving the Conditions of Life: Forms of Slave Resistance

1 North America's slaves did not passively accept treatment dictated by their masters. In the narratives, along with descriptions of the slaves' treatment and their feelings about it, there is a wealth of information testifying to a continual battle over the ground rules of plantation life. The slaves challenged some of the master's standards openly, struggled to subvert those that they could not overturn, and seized any opportunity that offered a means to improve their lives. In a thousand ways, ranging from subtle deception to bold defiance, they fought their owners. Many options, including successful revolution, were beyond the limits of possibility in the South; so the slaves used what tools they had in the arena closest at hand. Their

resistance helped to shape the conditions of life on the plantation, and their wills often forced an improvement in those conditions.

2 Too often historians tend to define resistance by its extremes. The question, How did the slaves resist bondage? sometimes becomes, When did they stage violent revolutions? or worse, Why did they not revolt more often? To understand the slaves' resistance and assess its scope, one must accurately judge the possibilities open to them. Most former slaves interviewed for the narratives revealed that they had exhibited both a stubborn predisposition to resist and a sensible rejection of daring but hopeless action.

3 The slaves built a defiant mentality upon a sober appraisal of their situation. For example, one form of resistance which the former slaves often mentioned was running away; yet, the narratives make clear that for the great majority of slaves this course of action seemed totally impractical. "We knew we could run away, but what then?" asked a former slave. "[We] couldn't git away," explained another. Once caught, the runaway "was subjected to very harsh punishment." The odds did indeed weigh heavily against a slave fugitive. Held in ignorance, he had to travel great distances, usually at night, through rugged, unfamiliar territory guarded by patrollers and inhabited by the suspicious white majority. As one man said, the whites "had a 'greement"—both as a matter of law and custom—"to be on the watch for runaway niggers." They had dogs that "would track you and all you got was a beating." Consequently, many slaves concluded that there was "no use tryin' run off because they catch you an' bring you back." Speaking for countless others, John White said, "I never tried it. . . . I had whippings enough already."

BIBLIOGRAPHY, *SLAVERY REMEMBERED*

Andrews, Sidney. *The South Since the War, as Shown by Fourteen Weeks of Travel and Observation in Georgia and the Carolinas.* Boston: Ticknor and Fields, 1866.

Blassingame, John W. *The Slave Community: Plantation Life in the Antebellum South.* New York: Oxford University Press, 1972.

———. "Using the Testimony of Ex-Slaves: Approaches and Problems." *Journal of Southern History* 41 (1975):473–92.

———, ed. *Slave Testimony: Two Centuries of Letters, Speeches, Interviews, and Autobiographies.* Baton Rouge: Louisiana State University Press, 1977.

FORMULATING A THESIS

Critical Reading for Writing

The thesis of a research paper is often based on the ideas discovered in a preliminary reading of source material. It is helpful, therefore, to annotate the working bibliography card. You do this by noting your initial response to the material on the back. Your comments should include a statement of the central idea and an indication of how well the material addresses the topic. This is also the point at which to quote a vivid statement to make a brief summary of a key idea.

Here is the back of the student's working bibliography card for Paul Escott's *Slavery Remembered:*

> Slave narratives indicate slaves rebelled intelligently; succeeded in improving their conditions and avoided punishment.
>
> ch 3 p 1
>
> on target and well documented

A. Following are three selections identified by the student researching slavery and autonomy. Read each selection and record your response in the space provided on the index card that follows the selection.

1. Anthony Chase belonged to a Baltimore widow who refused to permit him to purchase his freedom. Instead, she hired him out to Jeremiah Hoffman, to whom Chase wrote the following letter of explanation after his escape. (Spelling and grammar are the original.)

"Letter of 'explanation'" August 8th, 1827

Sir

I know that you will be astonished and surprised when you become acquainted with the unexspected course that I am now about to take, a step that I never had the most distant idea of taking, but what can a man do who has his hands bound and his feet fettered He will certainly try to get them loosened by fair and Honorable means and if not so he will ceartainly get them loosened in any way that he may think the most adviseable. I hope Sir that you will not think that I had any faoult to find of you or your family no sir I have none and I could of lived with you all the days of my life if my conditions could of been in any way bettered which I intreated with my mistress to do but it was all in vain She would not consent to any thing that would melorate my condition in any shape of measure So I shall go to sea in the first vesel that may offer an oppertunity and as soon as I can acumulate a sum of money suficent I will Remit it to my mistress to prove to her and to the world that I dont mean to be dishonest but wish to pay her every cent that I think my servaces is worth I have served her 11 years faithfully and think it hard that I offerred $5.00 what I was valued at 4 years ago and also to pay 4 per cent until the whole sum was payed which I believe I could of done in 2 years and a half or 3 years at any rate but now as I have to Runaway like a criminal I will pay her when I can Though I am truly sorry that I must leave you in the situation that I do, but I will Recommend to you as a Servant Samuel Brown that I think a good & honest man and one that is acquainted well with his business that you can Refer to Mrs Snyder who is well acquainted with him and has lived in the hous with him. as my mistress is not in Town I have taken the Last months wages to defray my exspenses but that money and the five dollars that you lent me the day before I left you I shall ceartainly Return before I ship for the sea. I dont supose that I shall ever be forgiven for this act but I hope to find forgiveness in that world that is to com. I dont take this step mearly because I wish to be free but because I want to do justice to myself and to others and also to procure a liveing for a family a thing that my mistress would not let me do though I humblely Requested her to let me do so

Before I was married I was Promised my freedom then after finding this Peace of writeing which you will find incloesed I was then confident that I was free at Mr Williams Death, and so I married I must now beg for your forgiveness and at the same time pray to god for your helth and happyness as well as that of your family

I am Sir your most Obedient Servt &c
Anthony Chase

PS. People will say that my wife has persuaided me to this but I so declare that she is inocent of any thing of the kind and was always oppoesed to any thing of the kind. AC.

1.

central idea:
relevant/irrelevant to the topic:

Working bibliography (reverse side).

2. Solomon Northup's autobiography presents a remarkably detailed picture of slave life and plantation society in the Deep South. His description of a slave auction follows:

from *Twelve Years a Slave*

In the first place we were required to wash thoroughly, and those with beards, to shave. We were then furnished with a new suit each, cheap, but clean. The men had hat, coat, shirt, pants and shoes; the women frocks of calico, and handkerchiefs to bind about their heads. We were now conducted into a large room in the front part of the building to which the yard was attached, in order to be properly trained, before the admission of customers. The men were arranged on one side of the room, the women on the other. The tallest was placed at the head of the row, then the next tallest and so on in the order of their respective heights. Emily was at the foot of the line of women. Freeman charged us to remember our places; exhorted us to appear smart and lively,—sometimes threatening, and again, holding out various inducements. During the day he exercised us in the art of "looking smart," and of moving to our places with exact precision.

After being fed, in the afternoon, we were again paraded and made to dance. Bob, a colored boy, who had some time belonged to Freeman, played on the violin. Standing near him, I made bold to inquire if he could play the "Virginia Reel." He answered he could not, and asked me if I could play. Replying in the affirmative he handed me the violin. I struck up a tune, and finished it.

Freeman ordered me to continue playing, and seemed well pleased, telling Bob that I far excelled him—a remark that seemed to grieve my musical companion very much.

Next day many customers called to examine Freeman's "new lot." The latter gentleman was very loquacious, dwelling at much length upon our several good points and qualities. He would make us hold up our heads, walk briskly back and forth, while customers would feel of our hands and arms and bodies, turn us about, ask us what we could do, make us open our mouths and show our teeth, precisely as a jockey examines a horse which he is about to barter for or purchase. Sometimes a man or woman was taken back to the small house in the yard, stripped, and inspected more minutely. Scars upon a slave's back were considered evidence of a rebellious or unruly spirit, and hurt his sale.

One old gentleman, who said he wanted a coachman, appeared to take a fancy to me. From his conversation with Burch, I learned he was a resident in the city. I very much desired that he would buy me, because I conceived it would not be difficult to make my escape from New Orleans on some northern vessel. Freeman asked him fifteen hundred dollars for me. The old gentleman insisted it was too much as times were very hard. . . . During the day, however, a number of sales were made. David and Caroline were purchased together by a Natchez planter. They left us, grinning broadly, and in the most happy state of mind, caused by the fact of their not being separated. Lethe was sold to a planter of Baton Rouge, her eyes flashing as she was led away.

The same man also purchased Randall. The little fellow was made to jump, and run across the floor, and perform many other feats, exhibiting his activity and condition. All the time the trade was going on, Eliza was crying aloud, and wringing her hands. She besought the man not to buy him, unless he also bought herself and Emily. She promised, in that case, to be the most faithful slave that ever lived. The man answered that he could not afford it, and then Eliza burst into a paroxysm of grief, weeping plaintively. Freeman turned round to her, savagely with his whip in his uplifted hand, ordering her to stop her noise, or he would flog her. He would not have such work—such sniveling; and unless she ceased that minute, he would take her to the yard and give her a hundred lashes. Yes, he could take the nonsense out of her pretty quick—if he didn't, might he be d—d. Eliza shrunk before him, and tried to wipe away her tears, but it was all in vain. She wanted to be with her children, she said, the little time she had to live. All the frowns and threats of Freeman could not wholly silence the afflicted mother. She kept on begging and beseeching them, most piteously, not to separate the three. Over and over again she told them how she loved her boy. A great many times she repeated her former promises—how very faithful and obedient she would be; how hard she would labor day and night, to the last moment of her life, if he would only buy them all together. But it was of no avail; the man could not afford it. The bargain was agreed upon, and Randall must go alone. Then Eliza ran to him; embraced him passionately; kissed him again and again; told him to remember her—all the while her tears falling in the boy's face like rain.

Freeman damned her, calling her a blubbering, bawling wench, and ordered her to go to her place, and behave herself, and be somebody. He swore he wouldn't stand such stuff but a little longer. He would soon give her something to cry about, if she was not mighty careful, and that she might depend upon.

The planter from Baton Rouge, with his new purchases was ready to depart.

"Don't cry, mama. I will be a good boy. Don't cry," said Randall, looking back, as they passed out of the door.

What has become of the lad, God knows. It was a mournful scene indeed. I would have cried myself if I had dared.

2.

central idea:
relevant/irrelevant to the topic:

Working bibliography (reverse side).

3. *The Life of Josiah Henson* was published in 1849. Eventually Henson escaped to Canada, where he became a Methodist minister and established a school. He returned twice to the South to lead slaves out. Note the struggle between autonomy and agency depicted in the following passage.

"A Slave's Dilemma"

. . . My master, at the age of forty-five or upwards, married a young woman of eighteen, who had some little property, and more thrift.

. . . After a time, however, continual dissipation was more than a match for domestic saving. My master fell into difficulty, and from difficulty into a lawsuit with a brother-in-law, who charged him with dishonesty in the management of the property confided to him in trust.

. . . Harsh and tyrannical as my master had been, I really pitied him in his present distress. At times he was dreadfully dejected, at others, crazy with drink and rage. Day after day he would ride over to Montgomery Court House about his business, and every day his affairs grew more desperate. He would come into my cabin to tell me how things were going, but spent the time chiefly in lamenting his misfortunes and cursing his brother-in-law. I tried to comfort him as best I could. He had confidence in my fidelity and judgment, and partly through pride, partly through that divine spirit of love I had learned to worship in Jesus, I entered with interest into all his perplexities. The poor, furious, moaning creature was utterly incapable of managing his affairs. . . .

One night in the month of January, long after I had fallen asleep, he came into my cabin and waked me up. I thought it strange, but for a time he said nothing and sat moodily warming himself at the fire. Then he began to groan and wring his hands. "Sick, massa?" said I. He made no reply but kept on moaning. "Can't I help you any way, massa?" I spoke tenderly, for my heart was full of compassion at his wretched appearance. At last, collecting himself, he cried, "Oh, Sie! I'm ruined, ruined, ruined!" "How so, massa?" "They've got judgment against me, and in less than two weeks every [slave] I've got will be put up and sold." Then he burst into a storm of curses at his brother-in-law. I sat silent, powerless to utter a word. Pity for him and terror at the anticipation of my own family's future fate filled my heart. "And now, Sie," he continued, "there's only one way I can save anything. You can do it; won't you, won't you?" In his distress he rose and actually threw his arms around me. Misery had leveled all distinctions. "If I can do it, massa, I will. What is it?" Without replying he went on, "Won't you, won't you? I raised you, Sie; I made you overseer; I know I've abused you, Sie, but I didn't mean it." Still he avoided telling me what he wanted. "Promise me you'll do it, boy." He seemed resolutely bent on having my promise first, well-knowing from past experience that what I agreed to do I spared no pains to accomplish. Solicited in this way, with urgency and tears, by the man whom I had so zealously served for over thirty years, and who now seemed absolutely dependent upon his slave—impelled, too, by the fear which he skilfully awakened, that the sheriff would seize every one who belonged to him, and that all would be separated, or perhaps sold to go to Georgia or Louisiana—an object of perpetual dread to the slave of the more northern states—I consented, and promised faithfully to do all I could to save him from the fate impending over him.

At last the proposition came. "I want you to run away, Sie, to your master Amos in Kentucky, and take all the servants along with you." I could not have been more startled had he asked me to go to the moon. Master Amos was his brother. "Kentucky, massa? Kentucky? I don't know the way." "O, it's easy enough for a smart fellow like you to find it. I'll give you a pass and tell you just what to do." Perceiving that I hesitated, he endeavored to frighten me by again referring to the terrors of being sold to Georgia.

For two to three hours he continued to urge the undertaking; appealing to my pride, my sympathies, and my fears, and at last, appalling as it seemed, I told him I would do my best. There were eighteen Negroes, besides my wife, two children and myself, to transport nearly a thousand miles, through a country about which I knew nothing, and in mid-winter—for it was the month of February, 1825. My master proposed to follow me in a few months and establish himself in Kentucky.

My mind once made up, I set earnestly about the needful preparations. They were few and easily made. A one horse wagon well stocked with oats, meal, bacon, for our own and the horse's support, was soon made ready. My pride was aroused in view of the importance of my responsibility, and heart and soul I became identified with my master's project of running off his Negroes. The second night after the scheme was formed we were under way. Fortunately for the success of the undertaking, these people had long been under my direction, and were devotedly attached to me in return for the many alleviations I had afforded to their miserable condition, the comforts I had procured them, and the consideration I had always manifested for them. Under these circumstances no difficulty arose from want of submission to my authority. The dread of being separated and sold away down South, should they remain on the old estate, united them as one man, and kept them patient and alert.

We started from home about eleven o'clock at night, and till the following noon made no permanent halt. The men trudged on foot, the children were put into the wagon, and now and then my wife rode for a while. On we went through Alexandria, Culpepper, Fauquier, Harpers Ferry, Cumberland, over the mountains on the National Turnpike, to Wheeling. In all the taverns along the road were regular places for the droves of Negroes continually passing along under the system of the internal slave trade. In these we lodged, and our lodging constituted our only expense, for our food we carried with us. To all who asked questions I showed my master's pass, authorizing me to conduct his Negroes to Kentucky.

Arriving in Wheeling, in pursuance of the plan laid down by my master, I sold the horse and wagon and purchased a large boat called, in that region, a yawl. Our mode of locomotion was now decidedly more agreeable than tramping along day after day, at the rate we had kept up ever since leaving home. Very little labor at the oars was necessary. The tide floated us steadily along, and we had ample leisure to sleep and recruit our strength.

A new and unexpected trouble now assailed me. On passing along the Ohio shore, we were repeatedly told by persons conversing with us, that we were no longer slaves, but free men, if we chose to be so. At Cincinnati especially, crowds of colored people gathered around us, and insisted on our remaining with them. They told us we were fools to think of going on and surrendering ourselves up to a new owner; that now we could be our own master, and put ourselves out of all reach of pursuit. I saw the people under me were getting much excited. There were divided counsels and signs of disobedience. . . . I began, too, to feel my own resolution giving away. Freedom had ever been an object of my ambition, though no other means of obtaining it had occurred to me but by purchasing it myself. I had never dreamed of running away. I had a sentiment of honor on the subject. The duties of the slave to his master as appointed over him in the Lord, I had ever heard urged by ministers and religious men. It seemed like outright stealing. And now I felt the devil was getting the upper hand of me. Strange as all this may seem, I really felt it then. Entrancing as the idea was, that the coast was clear for a run for freedom, that I might liberate my companions, might carry off my wife and children, and some day own a house and land, and be no longer despised and abused—still my notions of right were against it. I had promised my master to take his property to Kentucky, and deposit it with his brother Amos. Pride, too, came in to confirm me. I had undertaken a great thing; my vanity had been flattered all along the road by hearing myself praised. I thought it would be a feather in my cap to carry it through thoroughly; and had often painted the scene in my imagination of the final surrender of my charge to master Amos, and the immense admiration and respect with which he would regard me.

Under the influence of these impressions, and seeing that the allurements of the crowd were producing a manifest effect, I sternly . . . ordered the boat to be pushed off into the stream. A shower of curses followed me from the shore but the Negroes under me, accustomed to obey, and, alas, too degraded and ignorant of the advantages of liberty to know what they were forfeiting, offered no resistance to my command.

Often since that day has my soul been pierced with bitter anguish at the thought of having been thus instrumental in consigning to the infernal bondage of slavery so many of my fellow-beings. I have wrestled in prayer with God for forgiveness. . . . But I console myself with the thought that I acted according to my best light, though the light that was in me was darkness. Those were my days of ignorance. I knew not the glory of free manhood. I knew not that the title-deed of the slaveowner is robbery and outrage.

What advantages I may have personally lost by thus throwing away an opportunity of obtaining freedom I know not; but the perception of my own strength of character, the feeling of integrity, the sentiment of high honor I thus gained by obedience to what I believed right—these advantages I do know and prize. He that is faithful over a little, will alone be faithful over much. Before God, I tried to do my best, and the error of judgment lies at the door of the degrading system under which I had been nurtured.

3.

central idea:
relevant/irrelevant to the topic:

Working bibliography (reverse side).

B. Formulate your thesis. Based on what you have read in this chapter's letters and narratives of slaves and former slaves, what is your tentative answer to the topic question "To what extent was autonomy possible for North American slaves?"

OUTLINING THE PAPER

Once you have determined a thesis, the next step in the research writing process is to develop a tentative outline for your paper. Study the following sample:

Thesis: Limited autonomy was possible for slaves in the years preceding the Civil War.

Intro: Approach—the use of slave narratives and letters

I. Autonomy defined

II. Factors that mitigated against outright autonomy
   - A. Close supervision
   - B. Dehumanization
   - C. Religious training (enculturation)

III. Factors enhancing possibilities for autonomy
   - A. Education
   - B. Special skills
   - C. Self-esteem

IV. Forms which slaves' limited autonomy took
   - A. Escape
   - B. Hiding
   - C. Making demands
   - D. Controlling plantation life

ABSTRACTING INFORMATION

Points in the tentative outline are now fleshed out with information that the student abstracts, paraphrases, and in some cases quotes from sources.

A. Practice this most important research reading skill by quoting or paraphrasing from the reading material in this chapter to support specific points in the sample outline on page 000. The following example is based on the passage from *Slavery Remembered* which appears on page 000 of this text.

Point in outline	IV. Forms which slaves' limited autonomy took

Quotation in support of the point	In the opinion of Paul Escott, The slaves challenged some of the master's standards openly, struggled to subvert those that they could not overturn, and seized any opportunity that offered a means to improve their lives. In a thousand ways, ranging from subtle deception to bold defiance, they fought their owners."
Paraphrase in support of the point	According to Paul Escott, the narratives of North American slaves reveal that they were not passive objects of their masters' dictatorial treatment. On the contrary, slaves challenged their masters openly when possible and quietly when opposition was dangerous. They used the tools that they possessed.

Note that it is inadvisable to drop either a quotation or a paraphrase into your narrative. Rather, introduce them with such phrases as "according to" or "in the opinion of."

1. Point in outline	Factors that mitigated against autonomy dehumanization
Paraphrase or quotation in support	
2. Point in outline	Factors that mitigated against autonomy religious training (enculturation)
Paraphrase or quotation in support	
3. Point in outline	Factors that enhanced possibilities for autonomy education
Paraphrase or quotation in support	

Connections

Frederick Douglass, the author of *My Bondage and My Freedom,* was born into slavery. After escaping to freedom, he devoted his talents as writer and speaker to the abolitionist cause. Today, he is counted among the great journalists and statespersons of the United States.

My Bondage and My Freedom

By Frederick Douglass

1 I lived in the family of Master Hugh, at Baltimore, seven years, during which time—as the almanac makers say of the weather—my condition was variable. The most interesting feature of my history here, was my learning to read and write, under somewhat marked disadvantages. In attaining this knowledge, I was compelled to resort to indirections by no means congenial to my nature, and which were really humiliating to me. My mistress who, as the reader has already seen, had begun to teach me—was suddenly checked in her benevolent design, by the strong advice of her husband.

2 . . . Seized with a determination to learn to read, at any cost, I hit upon many expedients to accomplish the desired end. The plea which I mainly adopted, and the one by which I was most successful, was that of using my young white playmates, with whom I met in the street, as teachers. I used to carry, almost constantly a copy of Webster's spelling book in my pocket; and, when sent of errands, or when play time was allowed me, I would step, with my young friends, aside, and take a lesson in spelling. I generally paid my tuition fee to the boys, with bread, which I also carried in my pocket. For a single biscuit, any of my hungry little comrades would give me a lesson more valuable to me than bread. Not every one, however, demanded this consideration, for there were those who took pleasure in teaching me, whenever I had a chance to be taught by them. I am strongly tempted to give the names of two or three of those little boys, as a slight testimonial of the gratitude and affection I bear them, but prudence forbids; not that it would injure me, but it might, possibly, embarrass them; for it is almost an unpardonable offense to do any thing, directly or indirectly, to promote a slave's freedom, in a slave state. It is enough to say, of my warm-hearted little play fellows, that they lived on Philpot Street, very near Durgin & Bailey's shipyard.

3 Although slavery was a delicate subject, and very cautiously talked about among grown-up people in Maryland, I frequently talked about it—and that very freely—with the white boys. I would, sometimes, say to them, while seated on a curb stone or a

cellar door, "I wish I too could be free, as you will be when you get to be men. You will be free, you know, as soon as you are twenty-one, and can go where you like, but I am a slave for life. Have I not as good a right to be free as you have?" Words like these, I observed, always troubled them; and I had no small satisfaction in wringing from the boys, occasionally, that fresh and bitter condemnation of slavery, that springs from nature, unseared and unperverted. . . . I do not remember ever to have met with a boy, while I was in slavery, who defended the slave system; but I have often had boys to console me, with the hope that something would yet occur, by which I might be made free. Over and over again, they have told me, that "they believed I had as good a right to be free as they had"; and that "they did not believe God ever made any one to be a slave." The reader will easily see, that such little conversation with my play fellows, had no tendency to weaken my love of liberty, nor to render me contented with my condition as a slave.

4 When I was about thirteen years old, and had succeeded in learning to read, every increase of knowledge, especially respecting the FREE STATES, added something to the almost intolerable burden of the thought—"I AM A SLAVE FOR LIFE." To my bondage I saw no end. It was a terrible reality, and I shall never be able to tell how sadly that thought chafed my young spirit. Fortunately, or unfortunately, about this time in my life, I had made enough money to buy what was then a very popular school book, viz: the *Columbian Orator*. I bought this addition to my library, of Mr. Knight, on Thames Street, Fell's Point, Baltimore, and paid him fifty cents for it. I was first led to buy this book, by hearing some little boys say that they were going to learn some little pieces out of it for the Exhibition. This volume was, indeed, a rich treasure, and every opportunity afforded me, for a time, was spent in diligently perusing it.

5 Among much other interesting matter, that which I had perused and reperused with unflagging satisfaction, was a short dialogue between a master and his slave. The slave is represented as having been recaptured, in a second attempt to run away; and the master opens the dialogue with an upbraiding speech, charging the slave with ingratitude, and demanding to know what he has to say in his own defense. Thus upbraided, and thus called upon to reply, the slave rejoins, that he knows how little anything that he can say will avail, seeing that he is completely in the hands of his owner; and with noble resolution, calmly says, "I submit to my fate." Touched

by the slave's answer, the master insists upon his further speaking, and recapitulates the many acts of kindness which he has performed toward the slave, and tells him he is permitted to speak for himself. Thus invited to the debate, the quondam slave made a spirited defense of himself, and thereafter the whole argument, for and against slavery, was brought out. The master was vanquished at every turn in the argument; and seeing himself to be thus vanquished, he generously and meekly emancipates the slave, with his best wishes for his prosperity.

6 It is scarcely necessary to say, that a dialogue, with such an origin, and such an ending—read when the fact of my being a slave was a constant burden of grief—powerfully affected me; and I could not help feeling that the day might come, when the well-directed answers made by the slave to the master, in this instance, would find their counterpart in myself.

7 This, however, was not all the [zeal] which I found in this *Columbian Orator.* I met there one of Sheridan's might speeches, on the subject of Catholic Emancipation, Lord Chatham's speech on the American war, and speeches by the great William Pitt and by Fox. These were all choice documents to me, and I read them, over and over again, with an interest that was ever increasing, because it was ever gaining in intelligence; for the more I read them, the better I understood them. The reading of these speeches added much to my limited stock of language, and enabled me to give tongue to many interesting thoughts, which had frequently flashed through my soul, and died away. . . . The mighty power and heart-searching directness of truth, penetrating even the heart of a slaveholder, compelling him to yield up his earthly interests to the claims of eternal justice, were finely illustrated in the dialogue just referred to; and from the speeches of Sheridan, I got a bold and powerful denunciation of oppression, and a most brilliant vindication of the rights of man. Here was, indeed, a noble acquisition. If I ever wavered under the consideration, that the Almighty, in some way, ordained slavery, and willed my enslavement for his own glory, I wavered no longer. I had now penetrated the secret of all slavery and oppression, and had ascertained their true foundation to be in the pride, the power and the avarice of man. The dialogue and the speeches were all redolent of the principles of liberty, and poured floods of light on the nature and character of slavery. With a book of this kind in my hand, my own human nature, and the facts of my experience, to help me, I

was equal to a contest with the religious advocates of slavery, whether among the whites or among the colored people, for blindness, in this matter, is not confined to the former. I have met many religious colored people, at the south, who are under the delusion that God requires them to submit to slavery, and to wear their chains with meekness and humility. I could entertain no such nonsense as this; and I almost lost my patience when I found any colored man weak enough to believe such stuff.

8 Nevertheless, the increase of knowledge was attended with bitter, as well as sweet, results. The more I read, the more I was led to abhor and detest slavery, and my enslavers. "Slaveholders," thought I, "are only a band of successful robbers, who left their homes and went into Africa for the purpose of stealing and reducing my people to slavery." I loathed them as the meanest and the most wicked of men. As I read, behold! the very discontent so graphically predicted by Master Hugh, had already come upon me. I was no longer the light-hearted, gleesome boy, full of mirth and play, as when I landed first at Baltimore. Knowledge had come; light had penetrated the moral dungeon where I dwelt; and, behold! there lay the bloody whip, for my back, and here was the iron chain; and my good, kind master, he was the author of my situation. The revelation haunted me, stung me, and made me gloomy and miserable. As I writhed under the sting and torment of this knowledge, I almost envied my fellow slaves their stupid contentment. This knowledge opened my eyes to the horrible pit, and revealed the teeth of the frightful dragon that was ready to pounce upon me, but it opened no way for my escape.

9 I have often wished myself a beast, or a bird—anything, rather than a slave. I was wretched and gloomy, beyond my ability to describe. I was too thoughtful to be happy. It was this everlasting thinking which distressed and tormented me; and yet there was not getting rid of the subject of my thoughts. All nature was redolent of it. Once awakened by the silver trump of knowledge, my spirit was roused to eternal wakefulness. Liberty! the inestimable birthright of every man, had, for me, converted every object into an asserter of this great right. It was heard in every sound, and beheld in every object. It was ever present, to torment me with a sense of my wretched condition. The more beautiful and charming were the smiles of nature, the more horrible and desolate was my condition. I saw nothing without seeing it, and I heard nothing without hearing

it. I do not exaggerate, when I say, that it looked from every star, smiled in every calm, breathed in every wind, and moved in every storm.

10 I have no doubt that my state of mind had something to do with the change in the treatment adopted by my once kind mistress toward me. I can easily believe that my leaden, downcast, and discontented look was very offensive to her. Poor lady! She did not know my trouble, and I dared not tell her. Could I have freely made her acquainted with the real state of my mind, and given her the reasons therefor, it might have been well for both of us. Her abuse of me fell upon me like the blows of the false prophet upon his ass; she did not know that an angel stood in the way; and—such is the relation of master and slave—I could not tell her.

11 Nature had made us friends; slavery made us enemies. My interests were in a direction opposite to hers, and we both had our private thoughts and plans. She aimed to keep me ignorant; and I resolved to know, although knowledge only increased my discontent. My feelings were not the result of any marked cruelty in the treatment I received; they sprung from the consideration of my being a slave at all. It was slavery—not its mere incidents—that I hated. I had been cheated. I saw through the attempts to keep me in ignorance; I saw that slaveholders would have gladly made me believe that they were merely acting under the authority of God in making a slave of me, and in making slaves of others; and I treated them as robbers and deceivers. Their feeding and clothing me well could not atone for taking my liberty from me. The smiles of my mistress could not remove the deep sorrow that dwelt in my young bosom. Indeed, these, in time, came only to deepen my sorrow. She had changed; and the reader will see that I had changed, too. We were both victims to the same overshadowing evil—she, as mistress, I, as slave. I will not censure her harshly; she cannot censure me, for she knows I speak but the truth, and have acted in my opposition to slavery, just as she herself would have acted, in a reverse of circumstances.

In the "hot and stony neighborhood" suggested by Bernard Malamud's short story, adolescents informally socialize each other into adulthood. What may be the consequences?

8

Rites of Passage

Analyzing and Summarizing the Short Story

Conscience is, in most,
an anticipation of the
opinion of others.

—Sir Henry Taylor: The Statesman

Before Reading

In this chapter, the reading selections are two short stories. The imagined world of a story can give us profound insights into the real world and the human condition. The first story, "A Summer's Reading" by Bernard Malamud depicts a lonely, aimless young person's terrible and touching need for acceptance, recognition, and respect; the second, "Distance" by Raymond Carver is a love story that makes us feel the special intensity of teenage marriage.

Reading literature is pleasurable reading. For students, it must also be careful, active reading that requires defining unfamiliar words, marking off meaningful passages, and following the development of relationships.

Before you read, think about the quotation that introduces this chapter. Who provides a child's conscience? At what age should a person have acquired a conscience and be held responsible for "doing the right thing."

READING SELECTION

A Summer's Reading

By Bernard Malamud

1 George Stoyonovich was a neighborhood boy who had quit high school on an **impulse** when he was sixteen, run out of patience, and though he was ashamed every time he went looking for a job, when people asked him if he had finished and he had to say no, he never went back to school. This summer was a hard time for jobs and he had none. Having so much time on his hands, George thought of going to summer school, but the kids in his classes would be too young. He also considered registering in a night high school, only he didn't like the idea of teachers always telling him what to do. He felt they had not respected him. The result was he stayed off the street and in his room most of the day. He was close to twenty and had needs with the neighborhood girls, but no money to spend, and he couldn't get more than an occasional few cents because his father was poor, and his sister Sophie, who resembled George, a tall bony girl of twenty-three, earned very little and what she had she kept for herself. Their mother was dead, and Sophie had to take care of the house.

2 Very early in the morning George's father got up to go to work in a fish market. Sophie left at about eight for her long ride in the subway to a cafeteria in the Bronx. George had his coffee by himself, then hung around in the house. When the house, a five-room railroad flat

above a butcher store, got on his nerves he cleaned it up—mopped the floors with a wet mop and put things away. But most of the time he sat in his room. In the afternoons he listened to the ball game. Otherwise he had a couple of old copies of the *World Almanac* he had bought long ago, and he liked to read in them and also the magazines and newspapers that Sophie brought home, that had been left on the tables in the cafeteria. They were mostly picture magazines about movie stars and sports figures, also usually the *News* and *Mirror*. Sophie herself read whatever fell into her hands, although she sometimes read good books.

3 She once asked George what he did in his room all day and he said he read a lot too.

4 "Of what besides what I bring home? Do you ever read any worthwhile books?"

5 "Some," George answered, although he really didn't. He had tried to read a book or two that Sophie had in the house but found he was in no mood for them. Lately he couldn't stand made-up stories, they got on his nerves. He wished he had some hobby to work at—as a kid he was good in carpentry, but where could he work at it? Sometimes during the day he went for walks, but mostly he did his walking after the hot sun had gone down and it was cooler in the street.

6 In the evening after supper George left the house and wandered in the neighborhood. During the sultry days some of the storekeepers and their wives sat in chairs on the thick, broken sidewalks in front of their shops, fanning themselves, and George walked past them and the guys hanging out on the candy store corner. A couple of them he had known his whole life, but nobody recognized each other. He had no place special to go, but generally, saving it till the last, he left the neighborhood and walked for blocks till he came to a darkly lit little park with benches and trees and an iron railing, giving it a feeling of privacy. He sat on a bench here, watching the leafy trees and the flowers blooming on the inside of the railing, thinking of a better life for himself. He thought of the jobs he had had since he had quit school—delivery boy, stock clerk, runner, lately working in a factory—and he was dissatisfied with all of them. He felt he would someday like to have a good job and live in a private house with a porch, on a street with trees. He wanted to have some dough in his pocket to buy things with and a girl to go with, so as not to be so lonely, especially on Saturday nights. He wanted people to like him and respect him. He thought about these

things often but mostly when he was alone at night. Around midnight he got up and drifted back to his hot and stony neighborhood.

7 One time while on his walk George met Mr. Cattanzara coming home very late from work. He wondered if he was drunk but then could tell he wasn't. Mr. Cattanzara, a stocky, bald-headed man who worked in a change booth on an IRT station, lived on the next block after George's, above a shoe repair store. Nights, during the hot weather, he sat on his stoop in an undershirt, reading the *New York Times* in the light of the shoemaker's window. He read it from the first page to the last, then went up to sleep. And all the time he was reading the paper, his wife, a fat woman with a white face, leaned out of the window, gazing into the street, her thick white arms folded under her loose breast, on the window ledge.

8 Once in a while Mr. Cattanzara came home drunk, but it was a quiet drunk. He never made any trouble, only walked stiffly up the street and slowly climbed the stairs into the hall. Though drunk he looked the same as always, except for his tight walk, the quietness, and that his eyes were wet. George liked Mr. Cattanzara because he remembered him giving him nickels to buy lemon ice with when he was a **squirt**. Mr. Cattanzara was a different type than those in the neighborhood. He asked different questions than the others when he met you, and he seemed to know what went on in all the newspapers. He read them, as his fat sick wife watched from the window.

9 "What are you doing with yourself this summer, George?" Mr. Cattanzara asked. "I see you walkin' around at nights."

10 George felt embarrassed. "I like to walk."

11 "What are you doin' in the day now?"

12 "Nothing much just now. I'm waiting for a job." Since it shamed him to admit that he wasn't working, George said, "I'm reading a lot to pick up my education."

13 "What are you readin'?"

14 George hesitated, then said, "I got a list of books in the library once and now I'm gonna read them this summer." He felt strange and a little unhappy saying this, but he wanted Mr. Cattanzara to respect him.

15 "How many books are there on it?"

16 "I never counted them. Maybe around a hundred."

17 Mr. Cattanzara whistled through his teeth.

18 "I figure if I did that," George went on earnestly, "it would help me in my education. I don't mean the kind they give you in high

school. I want to know different things than they learn there, if you know what I mean."

19 The change maker nodded. "Still and all, one hundred books is a pretty big load for one summer."

20 "It might take longer."

21 "After you're finished with some, maybe you and I can shoot the breeze about them?" said Mr. Cattanzara.

22 "When I'm finished," George answered.

23 Mr. Cattanzara went home and George continued on his walk. After that, though he had the urge to, George did nothing different from usual. He still took his walks at night, ending up in the little park. But one evening the shoemaker on the next block stopped George to say he was a good boy, and George figured that Mr. Cattanzara had told him all about the books he was reading. From the shoemaker it must have gone down the street, because George saw a couple of people smiling kindly at him, though nobody spoke to him personally. He felt a little better around the neighborhood and liked it more, though not so much he would want to live in it forever. He had never exactly disliked the people in it, yet he had never liked them very much either. It was the fault of the neighborhood. To his surprise, George found out that his father and Sophie knew about his reading too. His father was too shy to say anything about it—he was never much of a talker in his whole life—but Sophie was softer to George, and she showed him in other ways she was proud of him.

24 As the summer went on George felt in a good mood about things. He cleaned the house every day, as a favor to Sophie, and he enjoyed the ball games more. Sophie gave him a buck a week allowance, and though it still wasn't enough and he had to use it carefully, it was a helluva lot better than just having **two bits** now and then. What he bought with the money—cigarettes mostly, an occasional beer or movie ticket—he got a big kick out of. Life wasn't so bad if you knew how to appreciate it. Occasionally he bought a paperback book from the newsstand, but he never got around to reading it, though he was glad to have a couple of books in his room. But he read thoroughly Sophie's magazines and newspapers. And at night was the most enjoyable time, because when he passed the storekeepers sitting outside their stores, he could tell they regarded him highly. He walked erect, and though he did not say much to them, or they to him, he could feel approval on all sides. A couple of

nights he felt so good that he skipped the park at the end of the evening. He just wandered in the neighborhood, where people had known him from the time he was a kid playing punchball whenever there was a game of it going; he wandered there, then came home and got undressed for bed, feeling fine.

25 For a few weeks he had talked only once with Mr. Cattanzara, and though the change maker had said nothing more about the books, asked no questions, his silence made George a little uneasy. For a while George didn't pass in front of Mr. Cattanzara's house anymore, until one night, forgetting himself, he approached it from a different direction than he usually did when he did. It was already past midnight. The street, except for one or two people, was deserted, and George was surprised when he saw Mr. Cattanzara still reading his newspaper by the light of the street lamp overhead. His impulse was to stop at the stoop and talk to him. He wasn't sure what he wanted to say, though he felt the words would come when he began to talk; but the more he thought about it, the more the idea scared him, and he decided he'd better not. He even considered beating it home by another street, but he was too near Mr. Cattanzara, and the change maker might see him as he ran, and get annoyed. So George **unobtrusively** crossed the street, trying to make it seem as if he had to look in a store window on the other side, which he did, and then went on, uncomfortable at what he was doing. He feared Mr. Cattanzara would glance up from his paper and call him a dirty rat for walking on the other side of the street, but all he did was sit there, sweating through his undershirt, his bald head shining in the dim light as he read his *Times,* and upstairs his fat wife leaning out of the window, seeming to read the paper along with him. George thought she would spy him and yell out to Mr. Cattanzara, but she never moved her eyes off her husband.

26 George made up his mind to stay away from the change maker until he had got some of his softback books read, but when he started them and saw they were mostly story books, he lost his interest and didn't bother to finish them. He lost his interest in reading other things too. Sophie's magazines and newspapers went unread. She saw them piling up on a chair in his room and asked why he was no longer looking at them, and George told her it was because of all the other reading he had to do. Sophie said she had guessed that was it. So for the rest of the day, George had the radio on, turning to music when he was sick of the human voice. He kept the house

fairly neat, and Sophie said nothing on the days when he neglected it. She was still kind and gave him his extra buck, though things weren't so good for him as they had been before.

27 But they were good enough, considering. Also his night walks invariably picked him up, no matter how bad the day was. Then one night George saw Mr. Cattanzara coming down the street toward him. George was about to turn and run but he recognized from Mr. Cattanzara's walk that he was drunk, and if so, probably he would not even bother to notice him. So George kept on walking straight ahead until he came **abreast** of Mr. Cattanzara and though he felt wound up enough to pop into the sky, he was not surprised when Mr. Cattanzara passed him without a word, walking slowly, his face and body stiff. George drew in a breath of relief at his narrow escape, when he heard his name called, and there stood Mr. Cattanzara at his elbow, smelling like the inside of a beer barrel. His eyes were sad as he gazed at George, and George felt so intensely uncomfortable he was tempted to shove the drunk aside and continue on his walk.

28 But he couldn't act that way to him, and, besides, Mr. Cattanzara took a nickel out of his pants pocket and handed it to him.

29 "Go buy yourself a lemon ice, Georgie."

30 "It's not that time anymore, Mr. Cattanzara," Georgie said, "I am a big guy now."

31 "No, you ain't," said Mr. Cattanzara, to which George made no reply he could think of.

32 "How are all your books comin' along now?" Mr. Cattanzara asked. Though he tried to stand steady, he swayed a little.

33 "Fine, I guess," said George, feeing the red crawling up his face.

34 "You ain't sure?" The change maker smiled slyly, a way George had never seen him smile.

35 "Sure I'm sure. They're fine."

36 Though his head swayed in little arcs, Mr. Cattanzara's eyes were steady. He had small blue eyes which could hurt if you looked at them too long.

37 "George," he said, "name me one book on that list that you read this summer, and I will drink to your health."

38 "I don't want anybody drinking to me."

39 "Name me one so I can ask you a question on it. Who can tell, if it's a good book maybe I might wanna read it myself."

40 George knew he looked passable on the outside, but inside, he was crumbling apart.

41 Unable to reply, he shut his eyes, but when—years later—he opened them, he saw Mr. Cattanzara had, out of pity, gone away, but in his ears he still heard the words he had said when he left: "George, don't do what I did."

42 The next night he was afraid to leave his room, and though Sophie argued with him he wouldn't open the door.

43 "What are you doing in there?" she asked.

44 "Nothing."

45 "Aren't you reading?"

46 "No."

47 She was silent a minute, then asked, "Where do you keep the books you read? I never see any in your room outside of a few cheap trashy ones."

48 He wouldn't tell her.

49 "In that case you're not worth a buck of my hard-earned money. Why should I break my back for you? Go on out, you bum, and get a job."

50 He stayed in his room for almost a week, except to sneak into the kitchen when nobody was home. Sophie **railed** at him, then begged him to come out, and his old father wept, but George wouldn't budge, though the weather was terrible and his small room **stifling**. He found it very hard to breathe; each breath was like drawing a flame into his lungs.

51 One night, unable to stand the heat anymore, he burst into the street at one A.M., a shadow of himself. He hoped to sneak to the park without being seen, but there were people all over the block, wilted and listless, waiting for a breeze. George lowered his eyes and walked, in disgrace, away from them, but before long he discovered they were still friendly to him. He figured Mr. Cattanzara hadn't told on him. Maybe when he woke up out of his drunk the next morning, he had forgotten all about meeting George. George felt his confidence slowly come back to him.

52 That night a man on a street corner asked him if it was true that he had finished reading so many books, and George admitted he had. The man said it was a wonderful thing for a boy his age to read so much.

53 "Yeah," George said, but he felt relieved. He hoped nobody would mention the books anymore, and when, after a couple of days, he accidentally met Mr. Cattanzara again, *he* didn't, though George had the idea he was the one who had started the rumor that he had finished all the books.

54 One evening in the fall, George ran out of his house to the library, where he hadn't been in years. There were books all over the place, wherever he looked, and though he was struggling to control an inward trembling, he easily counted off a hundred, then sat down at a table to read.

Vocabulary

The following words are boldfaced in the text. Write a synonym or brief definition for each. Add other unfamiliar terms and their meanings to the list.

WORD OR PHRASE	SYNONYM OR BRIEF DEFINITION
impulse (1)	
squirt (8)	
two bits (24)	
unobtrusively (25)	
abreast (27)	
railed (50)	
stifling (50)	

YOUR ADDITIONS

INTRODUCING FIGURATIVE LANGUAGE

Textbook authors seek primarily to communicate factual information to readers. In textbooks, the *denotative,* that is the *literal* or exact meanings of words nd phrases is important. Authors of fiction, on the other hand, seek not simply to communicate information but to evoke, that is, to call forth from their readers specific associations and emotions. Therefore, they select words and phrases that will arouse feelings and memories.

Language of this kind is *figurative* rather than literal. It connotes or suggests meanings that go beyond the literal and denotative. For example, the word "rat" has the denotative meaning of long-tailed rodent, but it suggests (connotes) far more. Sensory words such as "stifling," "sultry," "wilted and listless" are selected not merely to describe a place but also to capture its atmosphere. Finally in fiction, the names of people and places and even occupations may have figurative meanings. Mr. Cattanzara is the change maker in the subway. Literally, he makes change in bills and coins; figuratively, he makes a great change in George.

Give both a literal and a figurative explanation for the italicized words in the following lines from the story.

Example "George knew he looked passable on the outside, but *inside he was crumbling apart.*"

Literally: his body parts were decomposing

Figuratively: he was out of control

Example: "Around midnight he got up and drifted back to his hot and *stony* neighborhood."

Literally: made of cement and brick

Figuratively: unfeeling and unfriendly

1. "Though his head swayed in little arcs, Mr. Cattanzara's eyes were steady. He had small blue eyes which could *hurt* if you looked at them too long."

   Literally: cause physical harm

   Figuratively: cause embarrassment

2. "Unable to reply he shut his eyes, but when—*years later*—he opened them, he saw that Mr. Cattanzara had, out of pity, gone away . . ."

   Literally: many years-periods of 365 days

   Figuratively: what seemed a long time

3. "He hoped to sneak to the park without being seen, but there were people all over the block, wilted and listless, waiting for a *breeze.*"

   Literally: some periods of wind

   Figuratively: very hot-wishing for cooler temperatures

4. ". . . George walked past them and the guys hanging out on the candy store corner. A couple of them he had known his whole life, but *nobody recognized each other.*"

Literally: do not Know the other person

Figuratively: act as if you don't know

Comprehension

SPECIFIC INFORMATION

A. Rearrange the following plot incidents by numbering them in the order in which they occur in the story:

1. __4__ George locked himself into his stifling room.
2. __1__ George told Mr. Cattanzara he was reading one hundred books.
3. __3__ Mr. Cattanzara questioned George about his reading.
4. __5__ George ran to the library.
5. __2__ George crossed the street to avoid Mr. Cattanzara.

CHARACTER ANALYSIS

B. George's behavior is motivated by his need for

1. food and clothing.
2. esteem and prestige.
3. fame and money.
4. responsibility and cooperation.

C. Mr. Cattanzara is motivated by

1. pride in his own accomplishments.
2. an intense interest in current events.
3. a belief in George's potential for success.
4. his wife's encouragement.

D. The most significant conflict in this story is between George and

1. his family.
2. the neighborhood.
3. himself.
4. Mr. Cattanzara.

E. The narrator describes the action from ________ point of view.

1. Sophie's
2. Mr. Cattanzara's
3. each character's
4. George's

F. Select the answer you prefer and explain your choice by completing the statement in the space provided.

George's mood throughout the story

1. remains constant.
2. changes.
3. is one of depression.

in response to how people treat him.

INFERENCES AND INTERPRETATIONS

G. The image of Mr. Cattanzara's wife suggests Mr. Cattanzara's

1. free spirit.
2. disappointing life.
3. only happiness.
4. generous nature.

H. The narrator calls attention to Mr. Cattanzara's daily reading of the *New York Times*. This is to illustrate

1. how empty his life is of real interest.
2. how different he is from the others.
3. the real reason for his alcoholism.
4. his keen interest in stocks and sports.

I. By not revealing George to be a fraud, the change maker helps George to

1. ruin his young life.
2. face community disapproval.
3. unite his family.
4. save his self-respect.

J. The central idea, or theme, most clearly dramatized by the story is that

1. youth is wasted on the young.
2. self-respect is a necessary step toward autonomy.
3. the strength of the family is the strength of the individual.
4. participation and responsibility bring maturity.

Critical Thinking

QUESTIONS FOR INDEPENDENT AND GROUP WORK

A. Predict George's future and explain your prediction. In the story he is 20. At 30, he may very well be

1. a carpenter with a family living in a free-standing house.
2. a teacher and guidance counselor.
3. still taking handouts from Sophie.
4. (your idea)

B. (To answer the following question, you may have to review your notes from preceding chapters.) Which of the following concepts help you to understand George's behavior in "A Summer's Reading"? Explain your choices.

1. cultural discontinuity

2. self-fulfilling prophecy

3. hierarchy of needs

4. rite of passage

C. Is the conclusion of the story—George sitting down to read—strong, or weak? Explain your choice.

Study Activity

SUMMARIZING THE SHORT STORY

In college composition and literature classes, students are required to read, think about, discuss, and respond in writing to fictional works such as the short story "A Summer's Reading." A summary of a short story is a brief but comprehensive restatement of its important features, including title; author; theme, or central idea; major character; setting; and plot incidents or action. The student's purpose for including a summary of a fictional work in a writing assignment on literature is to establish a factual basis for emotional response and intelligent interpretation. Summarizing is also an excellent note-taking technique in preparation for class discussion and examination.

Your awareness of the basic story elements, which are briefly discussed in the following list, will give form and clarity to your summary. These terms assist students to analyze—that is, to isolate and examine elements of a fictional work—so they can gain an understanding of that work as a complex, integrated whole.

Short Story A long or short written or spoken narrative. The short story is organized according to its author's plan to achieve a particular emotional effect and to dramatize and communicate a particular idea.

Theme or **Central Idea** The story gives concrete representation to the central idea, or theme. A stated theme for "A Summer's Reading," should reflect the idea that self-respect is a necessary step toward autonomy.

Setting The imagined world of the story, including time, place, and material objects. Taken together, these evoke *atmosphere*. The setting of "A Summer's Reading" is a working-class New York neighborhood in the 1950s. The atmosphere is, for the most part, tense and oppressive.

Character A person in a fictional work. Characters are often classified as either *flat* or *round*. Flat characters, sometimes called *stereotyped* characters, do not change or grow in the course of a story. They are all good or all bad, and their behavior is predictable. Round characters, on the other hand, have depth. They are complex personalities with strengths and weaknesses who can't be "typed." George, in "A Summer's Reading," is a round character. We learn about character in the same way that we learn about people—from what we hear them say and observe them do, from what others say and do to and about them, from what the narrator tells us. When Sophie "rails" at George, calls him a "bum," and then "begs" him to come out of his room—and when his old father "weeps"—we get a sense of the complexity of George's character.

protagonist The leading character or center of interest in a narrative. George is the protagonist in this story.

antagonist The character or force that represents the opposition to the protagonist. From George's point of view, Mr. Cattanzara is the antagonist in "A Summer's Reading."

conflict Opposition. Conflict motivates action and also sustains the reader's interest. Conflict generally exists between characters; it can also exist between characters and their environment and between characters and themselves. George is in conflict with his family, his neighborhood, the change maker, and, most significantly, himself.

Plot The pattern in which the author arranges the parts of the story. Plot includes *exposition, action, climax,* and the *denouement.*

exposition Introductory background information about characters which sets the stage for action. Paragraphs 1 through 8 provide exposition in "A Summer's Reading."

action The events that take place; what happens. The action in "A Summer's Reading" begins when George meets Mr. Cattanzara; it ends when George sits down to read.

climax The event in the story which marks a change in the fortunes of the hero, or protagonist. George's painful confrontation with Mr. Cattanzara is the climax of the story, although George has a delayed reaction to it.

denouement The final unraveling of plot; the falling action which follows the climax.

Scene Dramatized, rather than described, incident in which characters speak and interact.

Point of View The angle from which the narrator tells the story. The most common points of view are *first* person and *third* person. In the first-person point of view, the story is told by one of the characters, who refers to himself or herself as "I." In the third-person point of view, the story is told by an outsider who reveals the characters' words, actions, appearances, and mental activities. The third-person narrator of "A Summer's Reading" tells the story by focusing on George's observations, actions, and emotions.

PATTERNS OF ORGANIZATION

The thought patterns of cause-effect, contrast, time-order, and simple listing are useful for examining and summarizing story elements. Characters' behavior, for example, can be analyzed in terms of cause (motivation) and effect (consequence). We know that George is motivated by a need for esteem; therefore, in the first plot incident he lies to Mr. Cattanzara. We know that Mr. Cattanzara is motivated by a desire to help George to acquire a sense of pride and self-respect; therefore, he doesn't reveal George to be a fraud. The consequence of both characters' behavior is apparent in the last incident—George's running to the library to read.

Character can be measured in terms of contrast. How different is a character at the conclusion of a story? How has he or she grown or changed? How do characters contrast with each other?

The time-order thought pattern suggests an approach to following and summarizing action (plot incidents). Do incidents occur in chronological order? Do flashbacks temporarily interrupt the time sequence? Do separate incidents occur at the same point in time? In your summary, you will list these incidents using appropriate directional words in the order in which they occur in the story.

USING STORY ELEMENTS AS A FOUNDATION FOR SUMMARIZING

A. You may apply the following questions to any short story as a basis for writing a summary. Practice the skill by using "A Summer's Reading" as your text.

Theme

What aspect of the human condition does the story dramatize? (for example, growing up? finding love? suffering rejection?)

What is the author saying about this aspect of the human condition?

Setting

Where and when does the story take place?

Characters

Name the major characters and discuss their motivation.

Conflict

Determine its source by elaborating upon your "yes" answers to the following questions.

Does conflict exist between characters?

Does conflict exist between character and environment (setting)?

Does conflict exist between a character and himself or herself?

Action

List the plot incidents in the order in which they occur. Be sure to indicate the climax, the incident that marks a change in the fortunes of the protagonist. (Generally, short stories contain very few incidents. The first incident in "A Summer's Reading" is not introduced until paragraph 7.)

Language

Is there a particularly meaningful visual image or figurative expression? Describe or quote it here:

GUIDED SUMMARY

B. Use your notes on "A Summer's Reading" to complete this guide.

"A Summer's Reading" by Bernard Malamud is from the short story collection, "The Magic Barrel," published in 1956. The theme, or central idea, that the story elements dramatize is

The setting is

The atmosphere

The major character(s) is (are)

The source of conflict in the story is

Action begins when

The turning point, or climax, occurs

In the final incident

A STUDENT'S SUMMARY OF "A SUMMER'S READING"

You may compare your own work to this draft of a student's summary. The instructor's comments and revision suggestions are indicated.

This story's elements dramatize a boy's inward growing up, the story elements [also] dramatize this aspect of the human condition—self respect is a necessary step toward autonomy.

The story [took place] ~~happened~~ in [the] ~~a~~ summer; the setting was in a working class neighborhood. The major character [George] was a teenage boy who had quit high school. He didn't have anything he thought he need[ed] to have: money, a girl, a respectable job, but deep down he unknowingly needed esteem and respect. His action in the story was motivated by [this] ~~a~~ (aimless) need of esteem.

Another major character was Mr. Cattanzara, a man who worked in a change booth in a subway station. He lived on the next block after George's. He drank very often, worked late, and lived a very dis[ap]pointed life. His only hobby [was] ~~is~~ reading [The] *New York Times*, page by page, every night. His action in the story was motivated by a "desire to help George to acquire a sense of pride and self-respect."

Conflict existed between the characters: George lied to Mr. Cattanzara for he was too embarrassed to say he was actually doing nothing. Later, George had to face Mr. Cattanzara's challenge.

Conflict also existed between George and his environment. At the beginning of the story, the stony neighborhood made him feel he was not expected, worthless, even [nonexistent] ~~unexisted~~. After his lie—"going to read one hundred books in the summer"—spread throughout the neighborhood, he noticed people paid attention to him, smiled [at] ~~to~~ him, and showed [him] ~~their~~ respect ~~to him~~. ~~They made~~

George taste the ~~fine~~ feeling of being respected. After Mr. Cattanzara exposed George's lie face to face, ~~He~~ hid in his room for a week, ashamed to come out to face not being respected again.

The main conflict existed between George and himself. He had no patience to do what he should, but he suffered by ~~being~~ nothing. He told Mr. Cattanzara he was going to read a hundred books because he wanted Mr. Cattanzara (who was only one in the neighborhood kind to him) to respect him and at that moment be believed himself ~~too~~. But he didn't have the strenght to keep his word; his weakness made him ~~become~~ a liar. Mr. Cattanzara's challenge stimulated his sense of shame. Real shame has destructive and redemptive power. Shame can destroy someone by breaking him down and making him feel small and worthless. But shame can also be redemptive by giving a motivation for change. In the story, when George realized Mr. Cattanzara didn't rell the neighbors anything about his lie, the neighbors still thought he was a good boy who was reading that "one hundred books." The fear of the greater shame, the desire to keep people's respect~~ation~~ and maybe higher motivation ~~was~~ to restore his reputation to Mr. Cattanzara, ~~he~~ ran to the library to read.

I think the most important thing in this stor is the actions that happened inside of ~~the~~ character.

Connections

Titles, like names, places, and occupations may have [illegible] on several levels in a work of fiction. Before you begin to read this story, consider the different kinds of distance that exist in our lives.

The story teller describes his characters as ". . . kids themselves . . . crazy in love, this eighteen-year-old boy and his seventeen-year-old girl friend when they married. Not all that long afterwards they had a daughter." The story of these three echoes a question asked earlier: Can people love deeply and be autonomous at the same time?

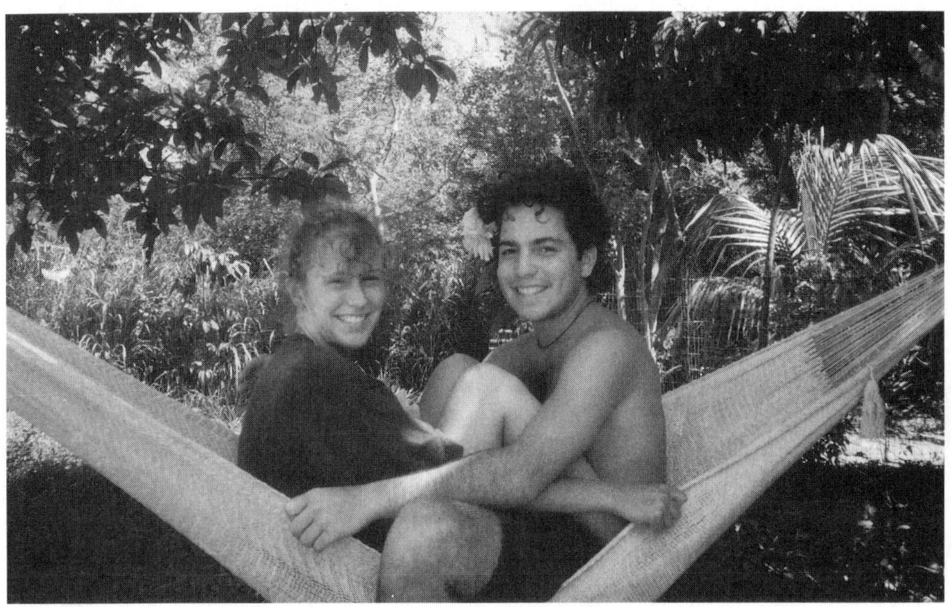

Can people love deeply, yet remain autonomous?

Distance*

By Raymond Carver
(1938–1988)

1 She's in Milan for Christmas and wants to know what it was like when she was a kid. Always that on the rare occasions when he sees her.

* From *Fires,* copyright © 1983 by Raymond Carver Estate. Reprinted by permission of Capra Press, Santa Barbara.

2 Tell me, she says. Tell me what it was like then. She sips Strega, waits, eyes him closely.

3 She is a cool, slim, attractive girl, a survivor from top to bottom.

4 That was a long time ago. That was twenty years ago, he says. They're in his apartment on the Via Fabroni near the Cascina Gardens.

5 You can remember, she says. Go on, tell me.

6 What do you want to hear? he asks. What can I tell you? I could tell you about something that happened when you were a baby. It involves you, he says. But only in a minor way.

7 Tell me, she says. But first get us another drink, so you won't have to interrupt half way through.

8 He comes back from the kitchen with drinks, settles into his chair, begins.

9 They were kids themselves, but they were crazy in love, this eighteen-year-old boy and his seventeen-year-old girl friend when they married. Not all that long afterwards they had a daughter.

10 The baby came along in late November during a severe cold spell that just happened to coincide with the peak of the waterfowl season in that part of the country. The boy loved to hunt, you see, that's part of it.

11 The boy and girl, husband and wife now, father and mother, lived in a three-room apartment under a dentist's office. Each night they cleaned the upstairs office in exchange for their rent and utilities. In the summer they were expected to maintain the lawn and the flowers, and in winter the boy shoveled snow from the walks and spread rock salt on the pavement. The two kids, I'm telling you, were very much in love. On top of this they had great ambitions and they were wild dreamers. They were always talking about the things they were going to do and the places they were going to go.

12 He gets up from his chair and looks out the window for a minute over the tile rooftops at the snow that falls steadily through the late afternoon light.

13 Tell the story, she says.

14 The boy and girl slept in the bedroom, and the baby slept in a crib in the living room. You see, the baby was about three weeks old at this time and had only just begun to sleep through the night.

15 One Saturday night, after finishing his work upstairs, the boy went into the dentist's private office, put his feet up on the desk,

and called Carl Sutherland, an old hunting and fishing friend of his father's.

16 Carl, he said when the man picked up the receiver. I'm a father. We had a baby girl.

17 Congratulations, boy, Carl said. How is the wife?

18 She's fine, Carl. The baby's fine, too, the boy said. Everybody's fine.

19 That's good, Carl said. I'm glad to hear it. Well, you give my regards to the wife. If you called about going hunting, I'll tell you something. The geese are flying down there to beat the band. I don't think I've ever seen so many of them and I've been going for years. I shot five today. Two this morning and three this afternoon. I'm going back in the morning and you come along if you want to.

20 I want to, the boy said. That's why I called.

21 You be here at five-thirty sharp then and we'll go, Carl said. Bring lots of shells. We'll get some shooting in all right. I'll see you in the morning.

22 The boy liked Carl Sutherland. He's been a friend of the boy's father, who was dead now. After the father's death, maybe trying to replace a loss they both felt, the boy and Sutherland had started hunting together.

23 The boy hung up the telephone and went downstairs to tell the girl. She watched while he laid out his things. Hunting coat, shell bag, boots, socks, hunting cap, long underwear, pump gun.

24 What time will you be back? the girl asked.

25 Probably around noon, he said. But maybe not until after five or six o'clock. Is that too late?

26 It's fine, she said. We'll get along just fine. You go and have some fun. You deserve it. Maybe tomorrow evening we'll dress Catherine up and go visit Sally.

27 Sure, that sounds like a good idea, he said. Let's plan on that.

28 Sally was the girl's sister. She was ten years older. The boy was a little in love with her, just as he was a little in love with Betsy, who was another sister the girl had. He'd said to the girl, If we weren't married I could go for Sally.

29 What about Betsy? the girl said. I hate to admit it but I truly feel she's better looking than Sally or me. What about her?

30 Betsy too, the boy said and laughed. But not in the same way I could go for Sally. There's something about Sally you could fall for. No, I believe I'd prefer Sally over Betsy, if I had to make a choice.

31 But who do you really love? the girl asked. Who do you love most in all the world? Who's your wife?

32 You're my wife, the boy said.

33 And will we always love each other? the girl asked, enormously enjoying this conversation he could tell.

34 Always, the boy said. And we'll always be together. We're like the Canada geese, he said, taking the first comparison that came to mind, for they were often on his mind in those days. They only marry once. They choose a mate early in life, and they stay together always. If one of them dies or something, the other one will never remarry. It will live off by itself somewhere, or even continue to live with the flock, but it will stay single and alone amongst all the other geese.

35 That's sad, the girl said. It's sadder for it to live that way, I think, alone but with all the others, than just to live off by itself somewhere.

36 It is sad, the boy said. But it's Nature.

37 Have you ever killed one of those marriage? she asked. You know what I mean.

38 He nodded. He said, Two or three times I've shot a goose, then a minute or two later I'd see another goose turn back from the rest and begin to circle and call over the goose that lay on the ground.

39 Did you shoot it too? she asked with concern.

40 If I could, he answered. Sometimes I missed.

41 And it didn't bother you? she said.

42 Never, he said. You can't think about it when you're doing it. You see, I love everything there is about geese. I love to just watch them even when I'm not hunting them. But there are all kinds of contradictions in life. You can't think about the contradictions.

43 After dinner he turned up the furnace and helped her bathe the baby. He marveled again at the infant who had half his features, the eyes and mouth, and half the girl's, the chin and nose. He powdered the tiny body and then powdered in between the fingers and toes. He watched the girl put the baby into its diaper and pajamas.

44 He emptied the bath into the shower basin and then he went upstairs. It was cold and overcast outside. His breath streamed in the air. The grass, what there was of it, looked like canvas, stiff and gray under the street light. Snow lay in piles beside the walk. A car went

by and he heard sand grinding under the tires. He let himself imagine what it might be like tomorrow, geese milling in the air over his head, the gun plunging against his shoulder.

45 Then he locked the door and went downstairs.

46 In bed they tried to read but both of them fell asleep, she first, letting the magazine sink to the quilt. His eyes closed, but he roused himself, checked the alarm, and turned off the lamp.

47 He woke to the baby's cries. The light was on out in the living room. He could see the girl standing beside the crib rocking the baby in her arms. In a minute she put the baby down, turned out the light and came back to bed.

48 It was two o'clock in the morning and the boy fell asleep once more.

49 The baby's cries woke him again. This time the girl continued to sleep. The baby cried fitfully for a few minutes and stopped. The boy listened, then began to doze.

50 He opened his eyes. The living room light was burning. He sat up and turned on the lamp.

51 I don't know what's wrong, the girl said, walking back and forth with the baby. I've changed her and given her something more to eat. But she keeps crying. She won't stop crying. I'm so tired I'm afraid I might drop her.

52 You come back to bed, the boy said. I'll hold her for a while.

53 He got up and took the baby while the girl went to lie down.

54 Just rock her for a few minutes, the girl said from the bathroom. Maybe she'll go back to sleep.

55 The boy sat on the sofa and held the baby. He jiggled it in his lap until its eyes closed. His own eyes were near closing. He rose carefully and put the baby back in the crib.

56 It was fifteen minutes to four and he still had forty-five minutes that he could sleep. He crawled into bed.

57 But a few minutes later the baby began to cry once more. This time they both got up, and the boy swore.

58 For God's sake what's the matter with you? the girl said to him. Maybe she's sick or something. Maybe we shouldn't have given her the bath.

59 The boy picked up the baby. The baby kicked its feet and was quiet. Look, the boy said, I really don't think there's anything wrong with her.

60 How do you know that? the girl said. Here, let me have her. I know that I ought to give her something, but I don't know what I should give her.

61 After a few minutes had passed and the baby had not cried, the girl put the baby down again. The boy and girl looked at the baby, and then they looked at each other as the baby opened its eyes and began to cry.

62 The girl took the baby. Baby, baby, she said with tears in her eyes.

63 Probably it's something on her stomach, the boy said.

64 The girl didn't answer. She went on rocking the baby in her arms, paying no attention now to the boy.

65 The boy waited a minute longer then went to the kitchen and put on water for coffee. He drew on his woolen underwear and buttoned up. Then he got into his clothes.

66 What are you doing? the girl said to him.

67 Going hunting, he said.

68 I don't think you should, she said. Maybe you could go later on in the day if the baby is all right then. But I don't think you should go hunting this morning. I don't want to be left alone with the baby crying like this.

69 Carl's planning on me going, the boy said. We've planned it.

70 I don't give a damn about what you and Carl have planned, she said. And I don't give a damn about Carl, either. I don't even know the man. I don't want you to go is all. I don't think you should even consider wanting to go under the circumstances.

71 You've met Carl before, you know him, the boy said. What do you mean you don't know him?

72 That's not the point and you know it, the girl said. The point is I don't intend to be left alone with a sick baby.

73 Wait a minute, the boy said. You don't understand.

74 No, you don't understand, she said. I'm your wife. This is your baby. She's sick or something. Look at her. Why is she crying? You can't leave us to go hunting.

75 Don't get hysterical, he said.

76 I'm saying you can go hunting any time, she said. Something's wrong with this baby and you want to leave us to go hunting.

77 She began to cry. She put the baby back in the crib, but the baby started up again. The girl dried her eyes hastily on the sleeve of her nightgown and picked the baby up once more.

78 The boy laced his boots slowly, put on his shirt, sweater, and his coat. The kettle whistled on the stove in the kitchen.

79 You're going to have to choose, the girl said. Carl or us. I mean it, you've got to choose.

80 What do you mean? the boy said.

81 You heard what I said, the girl answered. If you want a family you're going to have to choose.

82 They stared at each other. Then the boy took his hunting gear and went upstairs. He started the car, went around to the windows and, making a job of it, scraped away the ice.

83 The temperature had dropped during the night, but the weather had cleared so that the stars had come out. The stars gleamed in the sky over his head. Driving, the boy looked out at the stars and was moved when he considered their distance.

84 Carl's porchlight was on, his station wagon parked in the drive with the motor idling. Carl came outside as the boy pulled to the curb. The boy had decided.

85 You might want to park off the street, Carl said as the boy came up the walk. I'm ready, just let me hit the lights. I feel like hell, I really do, he went on. I thought maybe you had overslept so I just this minute called your place. Your wife said you had left. I feel like hell.

86 It's okay,the boy said, trying to pick his words. He leaned his weight on one leg and turned up his collar. He put his hands in his coat pockets. She was already up, Carl. We've both been up for a while. I guess there's something wrong with the baby. I don't know. The baby keeps crying, I mean. The thing is, I guess I can't go this time, Carl.

87 You should have just stepped to the phone and called me, boy, Carl said. It's okay. You know you didn't have to come over here to tell me. What the hell, this hunting business you can take it or leave it. It's not important. You want a cup of coffee?

88 I'd better get back, the boy said.

89 Well, I expect I'll go ahead then, Carl said. He looked at the boy.

90 The boy kept standing on the porch, not saying anything.

91 It's cleared up, Carl said. I don't look for much action this morning. Probably you won't have missed anything anyway.

92 The boy nodded. I'll see you, Carl, he said.

93 So long, Carl said. Hey, don't let anybody ever tell you otherwise, Carl said. You're a lucky boy and I mean that.

94 The boy started his car and waited. He watched Carl go through the house and turn off all the lights. Then the boy put the car in gear and pulled away from the curb.

95 The living room light was on, but the girl was asleep on the bed and the baby was asleep beside her.

96 The boy took off his boots, pants and shirt. He was quiet about it. In his socks and woolen underwear, he sat on the sofa and read the morning paper.

97 Soon it began to turn light outside. The girl and the baby slept on. After a while the boy went to the kitchen and began to fry bacon.

98 The girl came out in her robe a few minutes later and put her arms around him without saying anything.

99 Hey, don't catch your robe on fire, the boy said. She was leaning against him but touching the stove, too.

100 I'm sorry about earlier, she said. I don't know what got into me. I don't know why I said those things.

101 It's all right, he said. Here, let me get this bacon.

102 I didn't mean to snap like that, she said. It was awful.

103 It was my fault, he said. How's Catherine?

104 She's fine now. I don't know what was the matter with her earlier. I changed her again after you left, and then she was fine. She was just fine and she went right off to sleep. I don't know what it was. Don't be mad with us.

105 The boy laughed. I'm not made with you. Don't be silly, he said. Here, let me do something with this pan.

106 You sit down, the girl said. I'll fix this breakfast. How does a waffle sound with this bacon?

107 Sounds great, he said. I'm starved.

108 She took the bacon out of the pan and then she made waffle batter. He sat at the table, relaxed now, and watched her move around the kitchen.

109 She left to close their bedroom door. In the living room she put on a record that they both liked.

110 We don't want to wake that one up again, the girl said.

111 That's for sure, the boy said and laughed.

112 She put a plate in front of him with bacon, a fried egg, and a waffle. She put another plate on the table for herself. It's ready, she said.

113 It looks swell, he said. He spread butter and poured syrup over the waffle. But as he started to cut into the waffle, he turned the plate into his lap.

114 I don't believe it, he said, jumping up from the table.

115 The girl looked at him and then at the expression on his face. She began to laugh.

116 If you could see yourself in the mirror, she said. She kept laughing.

117 He looked down at the syrup that covered the front of his woolen underwear, at the pieces of waffle, bacon, and egg that clung to the syrup. He began to laugh.

118 I was starved, he said, shaking his head.

119 You were starved, she said, laughing.

120 He peeled off the woolen underwear and threw it at the bathroom door. Then he opened his arms and she moved into them.

121 We won't fight any more, she said. It's not worth it, is it?

122 That's right, he said.

123 We won't fight any more, she said.

124 The boy said, We won't. Then he kissed her.

125 He gets up from his chair and refills their glasses.

126 That's it, he says. End of story. I admit it's not much of one.

127 I was interested, she says. It was very interesting if you want to know. But what happened? she says. I mean later.

128 He shrugs and carries his drink over to the window. It's dark now but still snowing.

129 Things change, he says. I don't know how they do. But they do without your realizing it or wanting them to.

130 Yes, that's true, only—but she does not finish what she started.

131 She drops the subject then. In the window's reflection he sees her study her nails. Then she raises her head. Speaking brightly, she asks if he is going to show her the city, after all.

132 He says, Put your boots on and let's go.

133 But he stays by the window, remembering that life. They had laughed. They had leaned on each other and laughed until the tears had come, while everything else—the cold and where he'd go in it—was outside, for a while anyway.

Comprehension

SPECIFIC INFORMATION

A. The two relationships in this story are between

1. father and grown daughter.
2. three sisters.
3. teenage parents.
4. father and son.

B. The setting in "Distance" switches from ______ and back.

1. modern Strega
2. modern Milan
3. a small rural town in the U.S. twenty years ago
4. a small town in Italy twenty years ago

C. In both the past and the present, the weather is significantly

1. changeable.
2. cold.
3. sultry.
4. temperate.

D. The baby in the story is

1. hyperactive.
2. spoiled.
3. three weeks old.
4. sick and hysterical.

E. Catherine is the name of the

1. prettier sister.
2. wife and daughter.
3. daughter.
4. father's friend.

F. The infant is cared for

1. mechanically as though she were an object.
2. by only the mother.
3. with tenderness and love.
4. primarily by the father.

G. The boy says to the girl, "We're like the Canada geese" because for him the geese symbolize

1. passion.
2. rebellion.
3. independence.
4. loyalty.

H. The relationship between father and daughter appears

1. hostile.
2. indifferent.
3. companionable but strained.
4. open and affectionate.

I. The "stories" are told from the point of view of

1. the wife/mother.
2. a narrator/friend.
3. the daughter.
4. the boy.

J. "Distance" can best be classified as

1. adventure.
2. fantasy.
3. romance.
4. realism.

K. The language is

1. simple and clear.
2. poetic and musical.
3. technical.
4. harsh.

INFERENCES AND INTERPRETATIONS

Reading fiction often releases our imaginations and allows us to become creative thinkers, seeing the characters in our minds, hypothesizing new plot incidents, and devising conflicts that they must struggle to resolve.

A. The father describes his daughter as "a cool, slim attractive girl, a survivor from top to bottom." If you were casting the girl and the other characters in a film version of the story, who would play their parts?

B. Use your understanding of the characters and your imagination to answer these questions.

The girl has an appointment, perhaps to see one of her sisters, Does she leave the crying baby? Explain.

The girl leaves to keep the appointment with her sister. When does she return?

What does she find when she returns to the apartment?

Who makes breakfast?

C. Names and places have significance in fiction. We don't learn the names of the boy or girl or the place where they live. What effect does this have?

D. What motivates the daughter to ask for a memory of the past?

Describe her emotions after she hears the story.

Describe how the father feels after telling the story.

E. How does the chapter's opening quotation apply to the boy? How does it apply to the man the boy becomes?

F. The boy recognizes the contradiction in loving the geese and hunting them. He states, ". . . There are all kinds of contradictions in life. You can't think about the contradictions."

Can you recognize contradictions in your own life? Which do you confront? Which do you ignore?

Study Activity

Write a summary of "Distance" using the story elements questions and the guide on pages 184–185.

Topics for Composition

A. Think of a story from your childhood that you like to hear or that someone likes to tell. Retell it in short story form. Use the third person point of view.

B. Is it wise or a mistake to have children when you are very young? Refer to the short story "Distance" to support your position on this question.

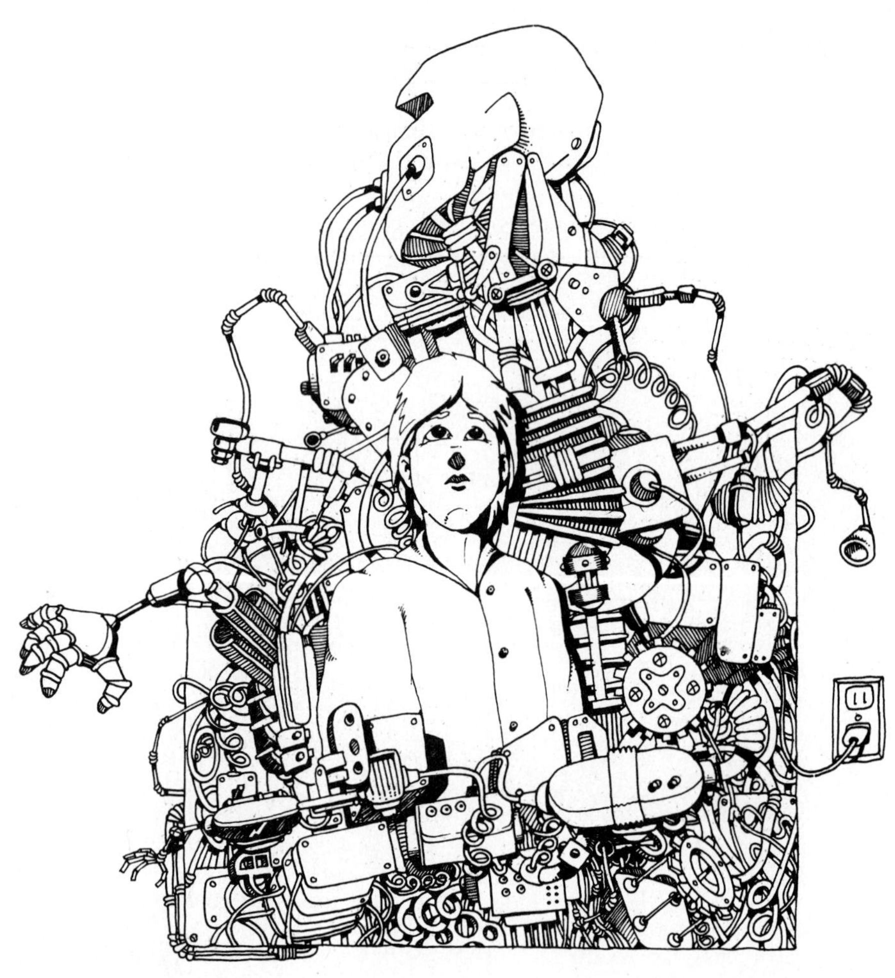

Humanity and technology are at war in this autistic child's struggle for autonomy. Is he a symbol for our times?

9

Joey: "A Mechanical Boy"

Summarizing the Case Study

Feelings are more
important than
anything under the sun.
—Joey

Before Reading

The reading selection in this chapter, the case study of an emotionally ill child, was written by Bruno Bettelheim, a world-famous child psychologist. Bettelheim tells the life story of Joey, his patient at the Orthogenic Institute in Chicago. Joey believed that he was a mechanical boy. He was convinced and could almost convince others that he was run by machine. His obsession prevented others from reaching out to him. In the selection, Bettelheim recounts the struggles of the staff to help Joey, and he also suggests an explanation for why Joey's illness took its strange form.

We know that many children enjoy playing superhero and in that role have superhuman, machinelike powers. Eventually, their pretending ends. Joey, on the other hand, chose not to return to reality. Before you read the selection, reflect for a moment on why a child might reject his own humanity: How do machines surpass human abilities? Who, in literature and films, are our most familiar machine-like heroes? What do we admire in them? What, to you, is the greatest difference between a human being and the most sophisticated machine?

An understanding of the following technical terms will assist your comprehension:

Acting Out Delusions Dramatizing fantasies that are held as a result of mental illness.

Schizophrenia Mental disorder characterized by withdrawal from reality and accompanied by disturbed emotional behavior.

Case Study Detailed analysis of a person or group that typifies a condition, situation, or life way.

Autism A form of childhood schizophrenia characterized by complete self-involvement and the ability to establish contact with others.

Compulsive Defenses Rigid, inflexible patterns of behaving for self-protection.

Integration Emotional harmony.

Pathological Sick or diseased.

READING SELECTION

This is the case history of a schizophrenic child who converted himself into a "machine" because he did not dare to be human. His story sheds light on emotional development in a mechanized society.

Joey: "A Mechanical Boy"

By Bruno Bettelheim

1 Joey, when we began our work with him, was a mechanical boy. He functioned as if by remote control, run by machines of his own powerfully creative fantasy. Not only did he himself believe that he was a machine but, more remarkably, he created this impression in others. Even while he performed actions that are **intrinsically** human, they never appeared to be other than machine-started and executed. On the other hand, when the machine was not working we had to concentrate on recollecting his presence, for he seemed not to exist. A human body that functions as if it were a machine and a machine that duplicates human functions are equally fascinating and frightening. Perhaps they are **so uncanny** because they remind us that the human body can operate without a human spirit, that body can exist without soul. And Joey was a child who had been robbed of his humanity.

2 Not every child who possesses a fantasy world is possessed by it. Normal children may retreat into **realms** of imaginary glory or magic powers, but they are easily recalled from these excursions. Disturbed children, however, are not always able to make the trip; they remain withdrawn, prisoners of the inner world of delusion and fantasy.

3 In any age, when the individual has escaped into a delusional world, he has usually fashioned it from bits and pieces of the world at hand. Joey, in his time and world, chose the machine and froze himself in its image. His story has a general relevance to the understanding of emotional development in a machine age.

4 During Joey's first weeks with us we would watch absorbedly as this at once fragile-looking and **imperious** nine-year-old went about his mechanical existence. Entering the dining room, for example, he would string an imaginary wire from his "energy source"—an imaginary electric outlet—to the table. There he "insulated" himself with paper napkins and finally plugged himself in. Only then could Joey eat, for he firmly believed that the "current" ran his ingestive system. So skillful was the pantomime that one had to look twice to be sure there was neither wire nor outlet nor plug. Children and members of our staff spontaneously avoided stepping on the "wires" for fear of interrupting what seemed the source of his very life.

5 For long periods of time, when his "machinery" was **idle** he would sit so quietly that he would disappear from our focus. Yet in the next moment he might be "working" and the center of our captivated attention. Many times a day he would turn himself on and shift noisily through a sequence of higher and higher gears until he "exploded," screaming "crash, crash!" and hurling items from his ever-present apparatus—radio tubes, light bulbs, even motors, or lacking these, any handy breakable object. (Joey had an astonishing knack for snatching bulbs and tubes unobserved.) As soon as the object thrown had shattered, he would cease his screaming and wild jumping and retire to mute, motionless nonexistence.

6 Our maids, **inured to** difficult children, were exceptionally attentive to Joey. They were apparently moved by his extreme infantile fragility, so strangely combined with maniacal superiority. Occasionally some of the apparatus he fixed to his bed to "live him" during his sleep would fall down in disarray. This machinery he contrived from masking tape, cardboard, wire, and other paraphernalia. Usually the maids would pick up such things and leave them on a table for the children to find, or disregard them entirely. But Joey's machine they carefully restored: "Joey must have the carburetor so he can breathe." Similarly, they were on the alert to pick up and preserve the motors that ran him during the day and the exhaust pipes through which he exhaled.

7 How had Joey become a human machine? From intensive interviews with his parents we learned that the process had begun even before birth. Schizophrenia often results from parental rejection, sometimes combined **ambivalently with** love. Joey, on the other hand, had been completely ignored. "I never knew I was pregnant," his mother said, meaning that she had already excluded Joey from her consciousness. His birth, she said, "did not make any difference." Joey's father, a rootless draftee in the wartime civilian army, was equally unready for parenthood. So, of course, are many young couples. Fortunately, most such parents lose their indifference upon the baby's birth. But not Joey's parents. "I did not want to see or nurse him," his mother declared. "I had no feeling of actual dislike—I simply didn't want to take care of him." For the first three months of his life Joey "cried most of the time." A colicky baby, he was kept on a rigid four-hour feeding schedule, was not touched unless necessary, and was never cuddled or played with. The

mother, preoccupied with herself, usually left Joey alone in the crib or playpen during the day. The father discharged his frustrations by punishing Joey when the child cried at night.

8 Soon the father left for overseas duty, and the mother took Joey, now a year and a half old, to live with her at her parents' home. On his arrival the grandparents noticed that **ominous** changes had occurred in the child. Strong and healthy at birth, he had become frail and irritable; a responsive baby, he had become remote and inaccessible. When he began to master speech, he talked only to himself. At an early date he became preoccupied with machinery, including an old electric fan which he could take apart and put together again with surprising skill.

9 Joey's mother impressed us with a **fey** quality that expressed her insecurity, her detachment from the world and her low physical vitality. We were struck especially by her total indifference as she talked about Joey. This seemed much more remarkable than the actual mistakes she made in handling him. Certainly he was left to cry for hours when hungry, because she fed him on a rigid schedule; he was toilet-trained with great rigidity so that he would give no trouble. These things happen to many children. But Joey's existence never registered with his mother. When she told us about his birth and infancy, it was as if she were talking about some vague acquaintance, and soon her thoughts would wander off to another person or to herself.

10 When Joey was not yet four, his nursery school suggested that he enter a special school for disturbed children. At the new school his autism was immediately recognized. During his three years there he experienced a slow improvement. Unfortunately a subsequent two years in a parochial school destroyed this progress. He began to develop compulsive defenses, which he called his "preventions." He could not drink, for example, except through an elaborate piping system built of straws. Liquids had to be "pumped" into him, in his fantasy, or he could not suck. Eventually his behavior became so upsetting that he could not be kept in the parochial school. At home things did not improve. Three months before entering the Orthogenic School he made a serious attempt at suicide.

11 To us Joey's pathological behavior seemed the expression of an overwhelming effort to remain almost nonexistent as a person. For weeks Joey's only reply when addressed was "Bam." Unless he thus

neutralized whatever we said, there would be an explosion, for Joey plainly wished to close off every form of contact not **mediated by** machinery. Even when he was bathed he rocked back and forth with mute, engine-like regularity, flooding the bathroom. If he stopped rocking, he did this like a machine too; suddenly he went completely rigid. Only once, after months of being lifted from his bath and carried to bed did a small expression of puzzled pleasure appear on his face as he said very softly: "They even carry you to your bed here."

12 For a long time after he began to talk he would never refer to anyone by name, but only as "that person" or "the little person" or "the big person." He was unable to designate by its true name anything to which he attached feelings. Nor could he name his anxieties except through neologisms or word contaminations. One of his machines, the "criticizer," prevented him from "saying words which have unpleasant feelings." Yet he gave personal names to the tubes and motors in his collection of machinery. Moreover, these dead things had feelings; the tubes bled when hurt and sometimes got sick. He consistently maintained this reversal between **animate and** inanimate objects.

13 Joey's preoccupation with machinery made it difficult to establish even practical contacts with him. If he wanted to do something with a counselor, such as play with a toy that had caught his vague attention, he could not do so: "I'd like this very much, but first I have to turn off the machine." But by the time he had fulfilled all requirements of his preventions, he had lost interest. When a toy was offered to him, he could not touch it because his motors and his tubes did not leave him a hand free. Even certain colors were dangerous and had to be strictly avoided in toys and clothing, because "some colors turn off the current, and I can't touch them because I can't live without the current."

14 Joey was convinced that machines were better than people. Once when he bumped into one of the pipes on our jungle gym he kicked it so violently that his teacher had to restrain him to keep him from injuring himself. When she explained that the pipe was much harder than his foot, Joey replied: "That proves it. Machines are better than the body. They don't break; they're much harder and stronger." If he lost or forgot something, it merely proved that his brain ought to be thrown away and replaced by machinery. If he

spilled something his arm should be broken and twisted off because it did not work properly. When his head or arm failed to work as it should, he tried to punish it by hitting it. Even Joey's feelings were mechanical. Much later in his therapy, when he had formed a timid attachment to another child and had been rebuffed, Joey cried: "He broke my feelings."

15 Gradually we began to understand what had seemed to be contradictory in Joey's behavior—why he held on to the motors and tubes, then suddenly destroyed them in a fury, then set out immediately and urgently to equip himself with new and larger tubes. Joey had created these machines to run his body and mind because it was too painful to be human. But again and again he became dissatisfied with their failure to meet his need and rebellious at the way they frustrated his will. In a recurrent frenzy he "exploded" his light bulbs and tubes, and for a moment became a human being—for one crowning instant he came alive. But as soon as he had asserted his dominance through the self-created explosion, he felt his life ebbing away. To keep on existing he had immediately to restore his machines and replenish the electricity that supplied his life energy.

16 What deep-seated fears and needs underlay Joey's delusional system? We were long in finding out, for Joey's preventions effectively concealed the secret of his autistic behavior. In the meantime we dealt with his **peripheral** problems one by one.

17 During his first year with us Joey's most trying problem was toilet behavior. This surprised us; his original personality damage had antedated the period of his toilet-training. Rigid and early toilet-training, however, had certainly contributed to his anxieties. It was our effort to help Joey with this problem that led to his first recognition of us as human beings.

18 Going to the toilet, like everything else in Joey's life, was surrounded by elaborate preventions. We had to accompany him; he had to take off all his clothes; he could only squat, not sit, on the toilet seat; he had to touch the wall with one hand, in which he also clutched frantically the vacuum tubes that powered his elimination. He was terrified lest his whole body be sucked down.

19 To counteract this fear we gave him a metal wastebasket in lieu of a toilet. Eventually, when eliminating into the wastebasket, he no longer needed to take off his clothes, or to hold on to the wall. He still needed the tubes and motors which, he believed, moved his

bowels for him. But here again the all-important machinery was itself a source of new terrors. In Joey's world the gadgets had to move their bowels, too. He was terribly concerned that they should, but since they were so much more powerful than men, he was also terrified that if his tubes moved their bowels, their feces would fill all of space and leave him no room to live. He was thus always caught in some fearful contradiction.

20 Our readiness to accept his toilet habits, which obviously entailed some hardship for his counselors, gave Joey the confidence to express his obsessions in drawings. Drawing these fantasies was a first step toward letting us in, however distantly, to what concerned him most deeply. It was the first step in a year-long process of expressing his anal preoccupations. As a result he began seeing feces everywhere; the whole world became to him a mire of excrement. At the same time he began to eliminate freely wherever he happened to be. But with this release from his infantile imprisonment in compulsive rules, the toilet and the whole process of elimination became less dangerous. Thus, Joey took a further step forward; defecation became the first physiological process he could perform without the help of vacuum tubes.

21 It must not be thought that he was proud of this ability. Taking pride in an achievement presupposes that one accomplished it of one's own free will. He still did not feel himself an autonomous person who could do things on his own. To Joey defecation still seemed enslaved to some incomprehensible but utterly binding cosmic law, perhaps the law his parents had imposed on him when he was being toilet-trained.

22 It was not simply that his parents had subjected him to rigid, early training. Many children are so trained. But in most cases the parents have a deep emotional investment in the child's performance. The child's response in turn makes training an occasion for interaction between them and for the building of genuine relationships. Joey's parents had no emotional investment in him. His obedience gave them no satisfaction and won him no affection or approval. As a toilet-trained child he saved his mother labor, just as household machines saved her labor. As a machine he was not loved for his performance, nor could he love himself.

23 So it had been with all other aspects of Joey's existence with his parents. Their reactions to his eating or noneating, sleeping or wakening, urinating or defecating, being dressed or undressed, washed

or bathed did not flow from a unitary interest in him, deeply embedded in their personalities. By treating him mechanically, his parents made him a machine.

24 The various functions of life—even the parts of his body—bore no integrating relationship to one another and to any sense of self that was acknowledged and confirmed by others. Toilet-training had not gained him a pleasant feeling of body master; speech had not led to communication of thought or feeling. On the contrary, each achievement only steered him away from self-mastery and integration. Toilet training had enslaved him. Speech left him talking in neologisms that obstructed his and our ability to relate to each other. In Joey's development, therefore, the normal process of growth had been made to run backward. Whatever he had learned put him not at the end of his infantile development toward integration but, on the contrary, farther behind than he was at its very beginning. Had we understood this sooner, his first years with us would have been less baffling.

25 It is unlikely that Joey's calamity could befall a child in any time and culture but our own. He suffered no physical deprivation; he starved for human contact. Just to be taken care of is not enough for relating. It is a necessary but not a sufficient condition. At the extreme where utter scarcity reigns, the forming of relationships is certainly **hampered**. But our society of mechanized plenty often makes for equal difficulties in a child's learning to relate. Where parents can provide the simple creature comforts for their children only at the cost of significant effort, it is likely that they will feel pleasure in being able to provide for them; it is this, the parents' pleasure, that gives children a sense of personal worth and sets the process of relating in motion. But if comfort is so readily available that the parents feel no particular pleasure in winning it for their children, then the children cannot develop the feeling of being worthwhile around the satisfaction of their basic needs. The child must be on the receiving end of care and concern given with pleasure, and without the demand for repayment, if he is to feel loved and worthy of respect and consideration. This feeling gives him the ability to trust; he can entrust his well-being to persons to whom he is so important. Out of such trust the child learns to form close and stable relationships.

26 When Joey could finally trust us enough to let himself become more infantile, he began to play at being a papoose. There was a

corresponding change in his fantasies. He drew endless pictures of himself as an electrical papoose. Totally enclosed, suspended in empty space, he is run by unknown, unseen powers through wireless electricity.

27 As we eventually came to understand, Joey had created a mechanical womb. In his papoose fantasies lay the wish to be entirely reborn. His new experiences in the school suggested that life, after all, might be worth living. Now he was searching for a way to be reborn in a better way. Since machines were better than men, what was more natural than to try rebirth through them? This was the deeper meaning of his electrical papoose.

28 As Joey made progress, his pictures of himself became more dominant in his drawings. Though still machine-operated, he has grown in self-importance. Another great step forward is represented in a picture in which he has acquired hands that do something, and he has had the courage to make a picture of the machine that runs him. Later still the papoose became a person, rather than a robot encased in glass.

29 Eventually Joey began to create an imaginary family at the school: the "Carr" family? Why the Carr family? In the car he was enclosed as he had been in his papoose, but at least the car was not stationary; it could drive. The Carr family was Joey's way of exploring the possibility of leaving the school, of living with a good family in a safe, protecting car [see Figure 6].

30 Joey at last broke through his prison. In this brief account it has not been possible to trace the painfully slow process of his first true relations with other human beings. Suffice it to say that he ceased to be a mechanical boy and became a human child. This newborn child was, however, nearly 12 years old. To recover the lost time is a tremendous task. That work has occupied Joey and us ever since. Sometimes he sets to it with a will, at other times the difficulty of real life makes him regret that he ever came out of his shell. But he has never wanted to return to his mechanical life.

31 One last detail, and this fragment of Joey's story has been told. When Joey was 12, he made a float for our Memorial Day parade. It carried the slogan; "Feelings are more important than anything under the sun." Feelings, Joey had learned, are what make for humanity; their absence, for a mechanical existence. With this knowledge Joey entered the human condition.

Figure 7 *A growing autonomy is shown in Joey's drawings of the imaginary "Carr" (car) family. Top drawing shows a machine which can move but is unoccupied. Machine in center is occupied, but by a passive figure. In bottom drawing figure has gained control of machine.*

Vocabulary

The following words are bold faced in the reading selection. Write a synonym or brief definition for each. Add other unfamiliar terms and their meanings to the list.

WORD OR PHRASE	SYNONYM OR BRIEF DEFINITION
intrinsically (1)	
uncanny (1)	
realm (2)	
imperious (4)	
idle (5)	
inured (6)	
ambivalently (7)	
ominous (8)	
fey (9)	
mediated (11)	
animate (12)	
neologism (12)	
peripheral (16)	
hampered (25)	

YOUR ADDITIONS

A. From the list, select the synonym for the underscored words in the following sentences.

1. confusingly
2. negotiated
3. threatening
4. weird
5. more obvious
6. inflexible
7. come before
8. naturally

Example ______ Joey pondered the compulsive rules of his private universe.

______ a. In the first months ominous changes had occurred in the child.

______ b. He wished to close off contact not mediated by machine.

______ c. We dealt with peripheral problems one by one.

______ d. His original personality damage had antedated his toilet training.

______ e. Schizophrenia develops from parental rejection, sometimes combined ambivalently with love.

______ f. It is uncanny that the human body can exist without spirit.

______ g. The staff spontaneously avoided stepping on the "wires."

B. The following sentences are paraphrased from the selection. Fill in the blanks with an appropriate synonym for the word(s) in parentheses. You may use more than one word.

Example We began to understand the (contradiction) ______ in Joey's behavior.

1. He performed actions which are (intrinsically) ______ human, yet seemed machine generated.

2. Our maids, (inured to) ______ difficult children, were especially attentive to Joey.

3. We were struck by Joey's mother's total (indifference) _____ she talked about him.

4. Joey's (pathological) _____ behavior seemed the expression of his effort to remain nonexistent as a person.

5. He still did not feel himself an (autonomous) _____ person, who could do things on his own.

6. He expressed his (obsessions) _____ in drawings.

7. Joey wished to close off contact not (mediated) _____ by machine.

8. He reversed (animate) _____ and inanimate objects.

9. Where scarcity reigns, relationships are (hampered) _____.

10. Joey played at being a (papoose) _____.

Comprehension

SPECIFIC INFORMATION

A. The major obstacle to working with Joey was

1. his mother's refusal to cooperate with Bruno Bettelheim.
2. the staff's inability to make contact with him.
3. his extremely complex toilet ritual.
4. time lost tripping over wires and replacing light bulbs.

B. Which of Joey's needs did his parents meet?

1. love and belonging
2. safety
3. self-esteem
4. physiological

C. Joey frequently "exploded," throwing his machine parts all over the place. This was because he

1. was afraid to be human.
2. wanted the nurses to pick up the pieces.
3. wasn't pleased with his treatment.
4. found being a machine frustrating.

D. Joey's progress was reflected in his

1. language skills
2. compulsive toilet rituals
3. drawing and painting
4. intelligence

ANALYSIS

E. Which of the following statements is not Joey's point of view?

1. "If he lost or forgot something, it merely proved that his brain ought to be thrown away and replaced by machinery."
2. "Feelings are more important than anything under the sun."
3. "By treating him mechanically his parents made him a machine."
4. "Since machines were better than men, what was more natural than to try rebirth through them?"

F. Which of the following information is not included in the selection?

1. a summary of Bettelheim's interviews with Joey's parents
2. an analysis and explanation of Joey's behavior
3. records of staff meetings at the Orthogenic Institute
4. description of stages in Joey's progress

G. The dominant patterns of organization in this case study are

1. comparison (contrast) and simple list.
2. cause-effect and comparison (contrast).
3. time order and cause-effect.
4. simple list and time order.

H. The reading selection doesn't contain subtopics. Where in the text is the appropriate position for the following subtopics?

Example: Medical and Family History above paragraph 7

1. Why Joey "explodes" above paragraph ____
2. Progress in Pictures above paragraph ____
3. Prognosis above paragraph ____
4. Diagnosis: Making a Human Machine above paragraph ____

5. Reaching Joey — above paragraph ______

6. A Symbol for Modern Times — above paragraph ______

Bruno Bettelheim's thesis is

1. Joey was reborn at the age of twelve.
2. Machines are better than the human body.
3. Schizophrenia often results from parental rejection sometimes combined ambivalently with love.
4. A "mechanical boy" gives us insight into emotional development in our own time and culture.

Critical Thinking

QUESTIONS FOR INDEPENDENT AND GROUP WORK

Select the best answers to the following questions and *explain* your choices in the spaces provided.

A. The following abilities did not help Joey to achieve autonomy

1. toilet training and speech
2. drawing and painting
3. taking apart and reassembling objects

B. Bettelheim suggests that Joey chose to be a machine because

1. he had been rigidly toilet-trained.
2. his parents had no emotional investment in him.
3. he didn't want to feel.
4. he had mechanical skills.

C. Select and explain one answer to the following question: Based on what you have read and discussed, a "mechanical boy" can exist

1. in another solar system.
2. before the Industrial Revolution.
3. here and now.
4. any time and any place.

D. Bruno Bettelheim tells us that Joey, as a baby, "cried most of the time." In the Chapter 2 reading selection, "Learning Culture," you read that Cheyenne infants who cried were removed from camp and their baskets hung in the bushes till they stopped crying. Joey suffers from infantile autism; the Cheyenne produce remarkably well-adjusted children. How do you explain this apparent contradiction?

E. In the Chapter 5 reading selection, "Pygmalion in the Classroom," you read about the concept of the "self-fulfilling prophecy." Is Joey a good or a poor example of self-fulfilling prophecy? Explain.

Study Activity

SUMMARIZING THE CASE STUDY

The reading selection is an essay based on the case study of an autistic child. The study activity for this chapter is summarizing with a focus on the key points in the case study.

Summarizing, like outlining and notetaking, is condensing material to the essentials. In "Joey: 'A Mechanical Boy,'" the author summarizes in paragraphs 7 through 10 information from "intensive interviews" with Joey's parents. Without listening to tapes of those interviews or reviewing lengthy reports, the reader gets a clear impression of Joey's infancy and early childhood.

Unlike outlining, a summary is generally written in paragraph form. It includes a statement of the thesis or unifying idea of a selection and definitions of important technical terms. It does not include the reader's response. (Summarizing lengthy reading assignments is covered in Chapter 12.)

THE CASE STUDY

The case study is an exhaustive investigation of an individual, family or group. It may include (depending on the discipline in which it is being employed) the following: observable behavior or symptoms; family background and medical history; analysis of the causes of a condition; treatment; prediction of future success or failure.

Case studies are used to illustrate and explain abstractions such as autonomy as well as pathological conditions such as autism. You read them in texts and journals; hear them in lectures, and are trained to prepare them in advanced clinical courses or internships.

The case study summary adds substance to short response papers, term papers, and essay examinations.

CASE STUDY VOCABULARY

Just as story vocabulary (Chapter 9) and terms in the scientific method (Chapter 6) help us to summarize works of fiction and research experiments, case study vocabulary gives us a framework for organizing key points.

Some important terms are

Behavior observable actions and reactions

Symptoms evidence of disease or physical disturbance

History chronological account of medical and/or family background

Diagnosis identification of a disease based on its signs and symptoms; analysis of the causes of a condition

Intervention treatment

Prognosis prospects of recovery

THE SUMMARIZING PROCESS

As you read, underscore and annotate the selection. Important ideas and key statements will be restated in the summary. Identify the thesis, or central idea, and clearly indicate it in your notes. Remember that major points develop some aspect of the thesis.

> The thesis of "Joey: 'A Mechanical Boy,'" appears in paragraph 3: "In any age, when the individual has escaped into a delusional world, he has usually fashioned it from bits and pieces of the world at hand. Joey, in his time and world, chose the machine and froze himself in its image. His story has a general relevance to the understanding of emotional development in a machine age." In a summary of the selection, this thesis could be restated as the following single sentence: *Delusions usually reflect the time and place in which a person lives; therefore, Joey's condition helps us to understand emotional development in our own time and culture.*

Look for dominant patterns of organization; these will guide your writing as they do your reading.

> "Joey: 'A Mechanical Boy,'" is a case study which describes and explains a child's struggle from autism to autonomy; time order and cause-effect are

important patterns of organization. The author takes the reader back and forth in time, beginning in the past with Joey's arrival at the Orthogenic Institute and concluding at a point at which recovery seems a real possibility. Bettelheim is intent on explaining the factors (cause) that contributed to Joey's illness and delayed his recovery. Your summary, like Bruno Bettelheim's article, will recount what happened to Joey, when it happened in his development, and, most important, why one becomes a "mechanical boy."

Map the selection; that is, group together related paragraphs and note their unifying topic in the margin of the text. Then develop the unifying topics into sentences which encompass the information in the related paragraphs. Write your sentences on scrap paper under the heading "synthesis of information." See the example below:

A Student's Map of "Joey: 'A Mechanical Boy'"

Paragraphs	Unifying Topic	Synthesis of Information
1-6	Joey's condition when he arrived at the institute	Joey was autistic. His very convincing delusion was that he was a machine.
7-10	Joey's history	His mother was unaware of his existence. His father left. Joey changed from a bright baby into a sick child.
11-14	Observations of Joey's behavior: speech, rules	Joey reverses machines and humans. His speech and his rules make it very difficult to contact him.
15	Diagnosis/ explains behavior	He "explodes," has tantrums, because he is frustrated being a machine, but then he rebuilds the machine because it is too painful to be human.
16-20	Intervention/ (treatment)	The staff helped him with his toilet problem. Because they accepted him, he became more confident.
21-25	Diagnosis: Why Joey is a "mechanical boy"	His parents treated him as though he were a machine. They "had no emotional investment." They took no pride in his achievements. This could happen only in a "society of mechanized plenty."
26-31	Progress/prognosis	Joey expressed his fears in his drawings; he was reborn in his play.

GUIDED CASE STUDY SUMMARY

A. Refer to your notes and the map on page 221 to complete the following summary.

______________	______________	______________	______________
Title	Author	Publication	Date

is the case study of an autistic child. Autism is

Bettelheim's thesis is

The case study of Joey illustrates the thesis. When Joey arrived at the Orthogenic Institute in Chicago, the staff observed that

Joey's history revealed

Treating Joey was delayed because it was difficult to establish contact with him for several reasons:

The explanation for Joey's silent withdrawal followed by violent rage is

Overcoming Joey's mistrust was a difficult task for the staff. This was accomplished by

Bettelheim's diagnosis of Joey's illness is that

Joey's progress became apparent in his play and in his drawings. For example,

The prognosis for Joey is

B. Reread and summarize the reading selection in Chapter 4, "Learning Culture," by Serena Nanda. Use the checklist as a guide for evaluating your work:

	Yes	No
Is the bibliography complete?	______	______
Is the thesis quoted or restated?	______	______
Are all the major points included?	______	______
Are minor details omitted?	______	______

	Yes	No
Is your opinion omitted?	_____	_____
If the author has reached any conclusions, are they stated?	_____	_____
Is the length appropriate (15-25 percent of the original)?	_____	_____
Is the form correct (a well-organized paragraph)?	_____	_____
Are the mechanics (punctuation, spelling, grammar, handwriting) at an acceptable level for college work?	_____	_____

Connections

The following excerpt is from a biographical novel, *This Stranger, My Son,* by Louise Wilson, who is the mother of a schizophrenic child. Bettelheim sees Joey's environment as a decisive factor in his illness. What is Dr. Davis' theory regarding a similar pathological condition?

> The doctor spoke emphatically. "Schizophrenia is a physical illness. Your son, Tony, is as physically ill as he would be if he had diabetes. And his illness is no more your fault or anybody else's than it would be if he had diabetes. "Schizophrenia," he said, "is a biochemical abnormality. Certain chemicals within these patients, very complex secretions of the adrenal gland, somehow or other fall out of balance. We do not know how or why. But we do know that there are marked changes in behavior of certain people in which this imbalance exists. This 'changed behavior' is schizophrenia: a distortion of thought, of mood and perception. Of course, I am giving you the very simplest kind of summary." . . .
>
> I was astounded. "This is very different from what I have been accustomed to hearing. We have always been led to believe that Tony's sickness is the result of poor environment."
>
> "I know. And I am sorry. I have seen too many parents like you and I know how you suffer from guilt. There's always something wrong with the family, they tell you. It is too rich or it is too poor, too harsh or too lenient. Permissive, restrictive, overpossessive, rejecting, castrating. I know."
>
> "Doctor Davis, I wonder if you can imagine what it is to live all these years remembering everything you ever said, every time you were angry or unsympathetic or impatient. Blaming yourself and wishing you could have another chance. Wishing you could begin again in babyhood and do everything differently. 'Not

enough love, not the right kind of love.' But I know I always loved Tony and how I love him now."

Topic for Composition

Judge Joey's statement "Feelings are more important than anything under the sun," in light of the notion that our society appears to become more mechanized and less humane with every passing day.

10

The Green Decade

Summarizing the Essay

We have not inherited the earth from our fathers; we are borrowing it from our children.

—Native American Saying

Before Reading

University students around the world have come to regard the fate of the earth as the crucial problem of their generation. Earth Day, 1970, marked the formal beginning of the environmental movement in the United States. Since then, Human Ecology has become an increasingly attractive field of study. The following selection, required reading in many Human Ecology courses, is by Denis Hayes, lawyer, engineering professor, and Chairperson of Earth Day, 1990. A committed environmentalist, he makes points that you may wish to challenge in this carefully crafted argumentative essay. (Argument here is a technical writing term meaning persuasive.)

Before you read, consider your own position on this matter. Is the issue of primary or secondary importance? Explain. List the following in the order in which you think they are responsible for protecting the environment: governments, universities, industries, the individuals, advocacy groups, unions. What is the meaning of "green decade?"

READING SELECTION

Earth Day 1990: Threshold of the Green Decade

By Denis Hayes*

1 For many of my generation, involvement with serious issues—adult issues—began with some form of unconventional politics. Passive disobedience and freedom rides in support of civil rights. The endless town meetings of Vietnam Summer. Wearing gas masks down Fifth Avenue on Earth Day. Picketing a state legislature in support of the Equal Rights Amendment. Breaching the exclusion zone around the Seabrook or Diablo Canyon nuclear plants. Blocking a train carrying fissionable material to the Rocky Flats bomb factory in Colorado.

2 We were impatient and idealistic. The first generation with strontium-90 in our bones (from atmospheric nuclear testing), we

*Denis Hayes, chairman of Earth Day 1990, practices law in San Francisco and teaches engineering at Stanford University. This essay was adapted from the Natural Resources Defense Council's Marshall Lecture, delivered by Hayes at the American Museum of Natural History, New York.

trusted no one over thirty. Outraged over the state of the world we were inheriting, we vowed that we would pass on to our children a world that was peaceful, just, and ecologically sustainable.

3 That was twenty years ago . . . The angry young women and men of Earth Day, who poured sewage on corporate carpets and pounded polluting automobiles apart with sledgehammers, are now middle aged. The first generation with strontium-90 in its bones now has parented a post-Chernobyl* generation with iodine-131 in its thyroid.

4 Twenty years after Earth Day, those of us who set out to change the world are poised on the threshold of utter failure. Measured on virtually any scale, the world is in worse shape today than it was twenty years ago. How could we have fought so hard, and won so many battles, only to find ourselves now on the verge of losing the war? The answers are complex. But if we can understand the mistakes that led to our current dilemma, we may yet be able to redeem our youthful promises to the next generation.

What Went Wrong During the Last Twenty Years?

5 Occasionally we were blind sided. Problems snuck up on us before anyone recognized the threat they posed. We possess only a **rudimentary** understanding of the complex interactions of life in the biosphere and of the myriad subtle effects of human action upon long-established processes. If at the time of the first Earth Day a poll had been taken of industrial chemists, asking each to name ten triumphs of modern chemistry, most would probably have listed chlorofluorocarbons (CFCs). These compounds had an array of beneficial uses, and they appeared to have no undesirable side effects. They are not **toxic, carcinogenic**, or **mutagenic**. They do not corrode materials; they are not flammable; they don't explode.

6 Not until 1974—four years after Earth Day—did Prof. Sherwood Rowland and his colleagues at the University of California at Irvine discover that CFCs posed a theoretical danger to the stratospheric ozone layer that protects the earth from ultraviolet radiation. And it was not until 1985 that a British team discovered the huge seasonal thinning of the ozone layer over the Antarctic.

7 A CFC molecule requires about fifteen years to migrate up to the stratosphere. Once there, its chlorine will **catalyze** the destruction

* Site of nuclear plant accident.

of ozone, on average, for about a century, during which time it will destroy 100,000 ozone molecules. CFCs were in use for fifty years before they were found to have any negative side effects. Now we realize that the side effects could include the destruction of vital links in the food chain, increases in skin cancer, and harm to human immunological systems.

8 Ozone threats are not a unique example of our ignorance. Until recently, we used asbestos routinely, never dreaming that it could wreak havoc on human health. Today a thriving industry exists for the sole purpose of removing asbestos from locations where it poses a health hazard, and asbestos litigation is carving out new domains of law.

9 Another example of scientific uncertainty, one that has catapulted to widespread public attention only in the last year, is the debate over the health effects of non-ionizing electromagnetic radiation. Some evidence indicates that electromagnetic fields (EMFs) can promote childhood leukemia, fetal deformities, learning disabilities, depression, miscarriages, and cancer. Until recently, there was a consensus among mainstream scientists that EMFs had no biological effects. Today, virtually all scientists concede that such radiation does interact with tissue at the cellular level, but they disagree as to whether the effects are harmful. The debate is hindered because the Environmental Protection Agency's major study of the field was eliminated under President Reagan. If, like asbestos, EMFs are found to foster health risks, the consequences will be far reaching. Potentially dangerous EMFs are created by computers, photocopiers, cellular phones, and even household appliances. Last November, *Consumer Reports* recommended that pregnant women and infants avoid electric blankets.

10 Asbestos, EMFs, and CFCs have given us a degree of **humility**. When yesterday's "triumph of modern chemistry" turns out instead to be today's deadly threat to the global environment, we can legitimately ask, What else don't we know?

It Is Always Easier to Tackle Urgent Problems Than Distant Threats—Even When the Distant Threats Are More Important

11 The U.S. is what boxers call a counterpuncher. What we do best is respond. Bomb Pearl Harbor and America will pull out all the

stops. Launch Sputnik and America will have NASA functioning overnight. What we do not do well is anticipate and avoid problems. Unfortunately, many environmental phenomena involve **thresholds** that, when passed, cause irreversible damage. If we wait until the damage occurs and then respond, it will be too late.

12 We face numerous such thresholds in the years ahead. Some, such as rain forest destruction, are already causing **irrevocable** harm. Every area cleared is lost forever. Others, such as global warming, could eventually result in rising oceans covering huge tracts of land, including the rice-producing river deltas of East Asia. These are not problems we can experience and then respond to; they are problems we must avoid.

13 The root of this failing lies in discount rates. We tend, for fundamental economic reasons, to assign a higher value to a dollar of income we receive today than to a dollar promised for delivery a year from now. We "discount" the future dollar to a lower present value. In the same way, we discount future costs. To anyone other than an economist, of course, this is appalling.

14 This shortsightedness is what leads lumber companies to harvest 1,000-year-old redwoods, and also leads them never to plant a redwood sapling. The contemporary essayist Adam Smith has written that "killing whales is very profitable until the day when there are no more whales, because we have only been **amortizing** the ships and the radar and the depth charges and the harpoons. We haven't amortized the whales, and anyway, how do you replace whales?" You don't.

15 Government has the power to remove redwoods and whales from the financial marketplace before they disappear. But politicians also have discount rates—governed roughly by the next election, and loosely by the politician's expected political lifetime. Problems that will be felt only after a politician has retired from office are perceived to be "on someone else's beat."

The "Solutions" We Pursue for Today's Problems Can Create Tomorrow's Catastrophes

16 Despite all the environmental literature, both scholarly and poetic, describing how everything is connected to everything else, we have repeatedly ignored this elementary truth. Our departments and agencies were organized to solve problems on a piecemeal

basis. As a result, we frequently cleared the air by polluting the water, and cleaned the water by fouling the ground.

17 We face a serious possibility of making the same error again. For example, some are advocating biodegradable plastics as the answer to the plastic litter problem. Discarded plastic six-pack holders can strangle birds and other species; plastic "baggies" can destroy marine environments; plastic diapers are clogging our landfills. But the problems posed by biodegradable plastics are themselves serious. For example, when biodegradable plastic is mixed with other plastic, it renders the latter virtually impossible to recycle.

18 Similarly, many are advocating the construction of hundreds of large incinerators as the answer to the declining availability of landfills for garbage. However, such incinerators produce major air pollution problems, and their hazardous ash constitutes a difficult disposal problem.

19 Nuclear power is another example of a solution being worse than the problem. The nuclear industry is mounting a massive international campaign heralding a new generation of "inherently safe" reactors as the answer to the problem of global warming. But the innate problems of nuclear fission pose a threat that is at least as **intractable** as global warming.

20 As a thinking exercise, assume that after one more doubling the world's population will level off at 10 billion. Further posit a goal of meeting a per capita energy demand that is one-third of the current level in the United States—more than enough for a productive economy and comfortable lives. Meeting this level of demand with coal would have dire consequences for global warming. Atmospheric carbon dioxide would double in about twenty-five years. To meet this level of demand with nuclear energy would require the world to use 44 million pounds of plutonium per year. Every year. This is enough plutonium to manufacture 4 million Hiroshima-sized bombs. Every year. It is impossible to imagine this flood of **fissile** material continuing for many years without leading to widespread weapons proliferation among nations, terrorist groups, and even criminal gangs.

21 Coal versus plutonium is a false choice. We must not solve global warming by creating a nuclear garrison state. We must not approach problems with such tunnel vision that our solutions ultimately make things worse.

Time and Again, the Environmental Movement Has Relied too Heavily Upon the Government

22 Government is the nation's largest polluter, and it frequently exempts itself from rules it applies to industry. The toxic brews around nuclear weapons facilities may be the most contaminated sites in the world, and the estimated price tag to clean them up is more than $150 billion.

23 Most of the energy strategies that the government pursued were nonstarters, and the situation has deteriorated. U.S. production of oil has been declining since 1971; in July 1988, for the first time, we imported more than half of all the oil we consumed. Our vulnerability is far greater today than it was in 1973, at the time of the Arab **embargo**.

24 If we follow the current course, we can safely predict that the international price of oil will begin to rise in 1992-93 . . .

The obvious solution is to increase the price of oil ourselves—with a carbon dioxide tax and a gasoline tax—so that the revenues will stay at home to be redistributed and invested. Americans pay between one-half and one-third as much for gasoline as do our industrial allies—all of whom enjoy robust economies and comfortable life styles. (The 1990 fuel efficiency standard for France is 39 miles per gallon, versus 27.5 for the United States.) A dollar-per-gallon gasoline tax would be an important step toward sound energy policy and fiscal integrity. Instead, our leadership resolutely chants "no new taxes," thus guaranteeing that when crude oil prices soar, all the proceeds will flow to the Middle East.

25 Not to put too fine a point on it, our national energy program has been a bust, but this is not to suggest that the environmental movement should ignore the government. On the contrary, governments (local, state, federal, and international) must be a major focus of our efforts. Governments must set the rules and establish the framework if we are ever to build a sustainable society.

We Have Not Asked Enough of Our Supporters

26 All the most successful movements, and all the world's major religions, have succeeded in part because they ask people to improve their behavior. The civil rights movement and the women's movement, for example, ask their supporters for heroic changes in their

personal lives. Environmentalists, on the other hand, have often tried to convince the public that we could all eat our cake and have it, too. People were encouraged to believe that if only we could effect the necessary changes in government and industry, people would not have to change their habits at all.

27 The answer to air pollution was claimed to be catalytic converters on tailpipes and scrubbers on smokestacks. We have pursued this strategy, at enormous cost, for twenty years. Yet the sky today in Los Angeles resembles split pea soup. We have been spectacularly unsuccessful at cleaning up automobile exhaust. Meanwhile, our cities have grown larger. People have moved farther away from their jobs and they drive more miles; their cars idle more at stop lights, drive-through windows, and traffic jams.

28 It was necessary, but not sufficient, to scrub pollutants out of exhaust. We must also begin using cleaner fuels and more efficient engines. We should encourage widespread use of, and improvements in, public transportation and promote bicycle riding wherever possible (and bicycle lanes). We should create incentives for people to live closer to their workplaces to reduce urban commuting and the resultant congestion.

29 In Europe, the "green consumer" has become a force to be reckoned with. Environmental labels are commonplace; consumer magazines are devoted to the environmental impacts of products. In the United States, such consciousness is only beginning. Several of us are exploring criteria for an American environmental label to be awarded to the best products from the best companies.

30 Perhaps no American behavior is more ripe for change than recycling. Sending our natural resources on a one-way trip from the mine to the dump makes no sense no matter how you look at it. We throw away valuable resources, eliminate jobs, waste embedded energy, and destroy the environment—all because people don't put glass in one trash container and aluminum in another.

31 Comprehensive recycling and composting will require significant government involvement—to end its bias in favor of raw materials and its bias in favor of landfills and incinerators, provide curbside pickups, set standards, and provide near-term markets for recycled goods. But the necessary first step is to do our part. We must comprehensively recycle all used items, and we must purchase recycled goods whenever possible.

The Environmental Movement Must Broaden

32 The most dangerous environments are in communities that are the least powerful. Poor people and minorities are downwind from the most toxic incinerators. They are down gradient from most hazardous waste dumps. They are in the fields when pesticides are sprayed from planes. They work in factory jobs having the highest exposure to dangerous substances. Yet poor people are not well represented in the ranks of the environmental movement. In communities racked by the devastation of drugs, plagued with violent crime, suffering rising school dropout rates of more than 50 percent, and experiencing rising problems of homelessness and malnutrition, environmental issues are not considered a priority. But they should be. The problems are indivisible.

33 In an important speech in the 1960s at the Riverside Church in New York, the Reverend Martin Luther King, Jr., came out against the war in Vietnam. The wave of criticism he suffered was intense. To those who challenged him for getting involved in an issue other than civil rights, he replied that African-Americans were being drafted in disproportionate numbers, and returned home in body bags in disproportionate numbers. There is no more fundamental civil right, he said, than the right to live to be an adult.

34 Similarly, the right to lead healthy, productive lives means that environmental values should be of great importance to those communities most deeply scarred by environmental degradation.

35 Right now there are probably no more than 10 million dues-paying environmentalists in the country. They are powerful beyond their numbers because they tend to be highly educated, well paid, and politically active. That is enough to pass some good, narrowly tailored legislation. However, it was not enough to successfully withstand the full frontal assault of the Reagan administration.

36 Let me cite a particularly painful example. In 1980, the United States led the world in every renewable energy technology. Today, we lead in none. Most of our photovoltaic industry has been sold to foreign companies or abandoned. Renewable energy sales have declined by more than 95 percent. This was not an accident. The destruction of the U.S. renewable energy industry and the abandonment of solar research by many of our most prestigious scientists were the result of explicit governmental policies that served powerful economic interests—the conventional energy industry—

which were colorfully characterized during this period by budget director David Stockman as "pigs in the trough."

37 The environmental movement will face the same hard battles again and again in the years ahead. Global warming, for example, requires that we move swiftly off fossil fuels and on to renewable fuels. It demands . . . a swift transition from oil and gas to solar hydrogen, a universal use of passive solar architecture, and perhaps a trillion-dollar investment in energy efficiency. Such a transition will necessarily entail winners and losers. Conventional energy producers will be among the losers. These energy producers are some of the richest and most powerful institutions in the country, and they will fight like hell to avoid being phased out of existence.

38 But there are no powerful economic institutions on the solar side. A solar transition will only be achieved if it enjoys enthusiastic backing from a broad cross section of society.

Some Hard Issues to Face

39 It will not be possible to build a sustainable society without confronting some controversial, emotional issues. Many environmental organizations have avoided issues that should be of central concern; two are of paramount concern.

40 The proposed U.S. military budget for next year is $305 billion—all ostensibly to defend our national security. Far more vital threats to our security—global warming, ozone destruction, the ecological undermining of agricultural productivity, mounting dependence upon foreign oil, the crack epidemic, the creation of a permanent urban underclass, all cry out for more money. These threats cannot be averted as long as 75 percent of all federal research and development is devoted to military research.

41 This is not merely an American problem. The world cannot build a sustainable future so long as it spends $1 trillion annually—virtually all the discretionary capital—on military ends. To take just one poignant example, if Ethiopia had diverted one-third of its military budget to agriculture and tree planting, the recent tragic Ethiopian famine could have been *averted.*

42 Even as martin Luther King was told to stay out of the war issue, we have well-intentioned friends and allies cautioning environmentalists to stay out of the defense debate. We must quietly but firmly reject that advice. We can never save the planet if mankind spends $1 trillion a year on instruments designed to destroy it.

43 Similarly, we are frequently urged to sidestep the population issue. Environmental **advocacy** of family planning will alienate major religions, certain racial and ethnic leaders, and some heads of state from the environmental cause. Some feel we should avoid the issue and instead focus all our attention upon matters over which we can build a consensus. Again, we must ignore the advice. The human population, which has doubled since my birth, may quadruple before my death.

44 Current population levels are undermining the biological basis for our future. Water tables are plummeting far faster than they are recharged. Topsoil is eroding five times faster than it is replaced; in some parts of Ohio, farms lost two bushels of topsoil for every bushel of corn harvested. Deserts are on the march in Africa, Asia, Australia, and America. There is not a single important problem facing the planet that could not be more easily solved with a population of under five billion.

45 Global population growth is an urgent priority, and it must be addressed with substantial family-planning assistance and provisions for social mechanisms (for example, old age insurance) to undercut the motivations for large families while advancing social justice.

We Have the Power to Choose Our Future

46 A common feature of all the problems we have been discussing is that none are the result of forces beyond human control. None are caused by sunspots or the gravity pull of the moon or volcanic activity. All are the result of conscious human choices. All can be cured by making other choices.

47 First, we need to make our own lives **congruent** with our values. For most of us, there is room for improvement in virtually all spheres. We should conserve energy with easy things, such as replacing incandescent light bulbs with folded fluorescents, which are five times as efficient, insulating our water heaters, and doing laundry in cold water. Then we should do the more expensive and difficult things, such as superinsulating our dwellings and buying a more efficient furnace and more efficient appliances.

48 We should pledge not to purchase another new car until we can buy one that meets our needs while getting at least fifty miles per gallon. We should install flow restricters in our faucets and showers and dams in our toilets. We should plant **indigenous** vegetation,

search our environmentally sensible soaps and cosmetics, and look for recycled paper and other products.

49 We should eat lower on the food chain and develop a preference for fresh organic products grown nearby. We should carry our own, reusable string bags to the supermarket and search out ways to eliminate other, unnecessary packaging. We should recycle our meals, glass, paper, and plastics and compost all organic waste.

50 In the **aggregate**, such life-style changes make a huge difference. If everyone used the most efficient refrigerators available, we could save an amount of energy equivalent to that produced by twelve large nuclear power plants. Using the most efficient cars with the same internal dimensions as our current vehicles would cut gasoline consumption in half. Every year, we send more iron and steel to our dumps than we use in the entire automobile industry. The aluminum we throw away every three months could replace the nation's entire fleet of airplanes.

51 What should an individual do to make a difference? Leading a life that is congruent with your values is a necessary and important first step, but it does not discharge your responsibilities. Next you need to explore what you can do as an employee, an investor, a parent, and a member of your church and civic clubs. You should be alert to ways you can lessen the environmental impact of your job, from avoiding styrofoam coffee cups to suggesting modifications in industrial processes. . . . You should set a good example for your children.

52 Integrating your values into your job and your other activities is another important step, but it still does not discharge your responsibilities. Next, join local and national organizations that share your goals and your philosophy, and **proselytize** on their behalf.

53 Working on behalf of environmental groups that represent your views is vitally important, but this still does not fully discharge your responsibilities. Become actively involved in politics. Support candidates who share your vision; vigorously oppose those who do not. Invest the time, energy, and financial support needed to win elections. Play the sort of role that causes political friends and foes alike to view you as a person to be reckoned with. Communicate your environmental goals and values to your candidate and make clear that there are narrow limits on how much compromise is acceptable.

54 Time is running out. We have, at most, ten years to embark on some undertakings if we are to avoid crossing some dire environmental thresholds. Individually, each of us can do only a little.

Together, we can save the world.

Vocabulary

The following words are boldfaced in the reading selection. Write a synonym or brief definition for each. Add other unfamiliar terms and their meanings to the list.

WORD OR PHRASE	SYNONYM OR BRIEF DEFINITION
rudimentary (5)	
carcinogenic (5)	
mutagenic (5)	
immunological (7)	
catalyze (7)	
wreak havoc (8)	
consensus (9)	
hindered (9)	
threshold (11)	
irrevocable (12)	
amortize (14)	
intractable (18)	

WORD OR PHRASE	**SYNONYM OR BRIEF DEFINITION**
fissile (19)	
embargo (22)	
averted (32)	
advocacy (43)	
indigenous (47)	
aggregate (50)	
proselytize (52)	

YOUR ADDITIONS

A. Complete these sentences with adjectives from the vocabulary list.

1. Extinction is ________________.

2. Sorting material for recycling is a ________________ skill.

3. Cats with 28 "toes" may have been exposed to ________________ material.

4. It's important to check food labels for ________________ ingredients.

5. ________________ matter is split with a tremendous release of energy.

6. The ________________ system protects us from disease.

B. Match these verbs to their synonyms.

1. catalyze
2. amortize
3. proseltyze
4. ionize

A. convert; recruit
B. eliminate a debt
C. create a reaction
D. charge by adding or subtracting an electron

C. Match these nouns to their antonyms.

1. aggregate
2. threshold
3. consensus
4. avert

A. disagreement
B. collide
C. exit
D. individual

D. Rewrite these sentences by paraphrasing the underscored words.

1. Asbestos can <u>wreak havoc</u> on human health.
2. Debate was <u>hindered</u> when the study was eliminated.
3. Nuclear fission and global warming pose <u>intractable</u> problems.
4. <u>Advocacy</u> of family planning will alienate major religions.
5. We must make our lives <u>congruent</u> with our values.
6. We should plant <u>indigenous</u> vegetation.

Comprehension

SPECIFIC INFORMATION

A. According to Denis Hayes, environmental problems have resulted from

1. natural forces beyond our control.
2. conscious human choices.
3. poorly administered social services.
4. discount rates for informed consumers.

B. Which is not an effect of CFCs?

1. childhood leukemia
2. destruction of links in the food chain
3. harm to the immunological system
4. skin cancer

C. Asbestos, CFCs, EMFs are examples of

1. better living through chemistry.
2. mistakes that should make us humble.
3. algebraic equations.
4. scientific advancements.

D. Americans pay ________________ for oil than other industrialized countries.

1. more
2. the same
3. less
4. a fairer price

E. The author proposes a carbon dioxide and a gas tax in order to

1. motivate improved fuel efficiency.
2. create revenues to invest in the United States.
3. limit the outward flow of money.
4. all of the above.

F. The author favors

1. recycling.
2. building larger incinerators.
3. developing nuclear energy.
4. mining more coal.

G. Two sensitive issues that the government must confront are

1. family planning and old age assistance.
2. destruction of the ozone and electromechanical radiation.
3. global population growth and defense spending.
4. Pearl Harbor and Sputnik.

H. In this essay, the onus for environmental problems is on

1. industry and government.
2. technical solutions that make things worse.
3. individuals.
4. all of the above.

I. The author indicates that Americans use ________________ more energy than is necessary for a comfortable, productive life.

1. 5%
2. up to 3 times
3. no
4. 20%

ANALYSIS

J. The essay is particularly rich in

1. figurative language.
2. statistical data.
3. science fiction.
4. none of the above.

K. The thesis or overall main idea is

1. We must scrutinize past mistakes in order to fulfill our promise to future generations.
2. The environmental movement must broaden its membership.
3. We must learn more about the effects of human action on long established processes.
4. We must make life style changes that reflect our values.

L. The most common thought pattern is

1. causal effect.
2. key points illustrated with lists of examples.
3. comparison-contrast.
4. historical (time order).

There *may* be more than one answer to the following questions. Explain your choices in the space provided.

M. The purpose of this essay is

1. to entertain.
2. to motivate action.
3. to obfuscate or cover up.
4. to attack.

N. To support his point that nuclear fission is a threat, the author

1. tells a story.
2. gives research data.
3. creates grotesque images.
4. presents a hypothetical situation.

O. The function of introductory paragraphs 1. 2, and 3 is to

1. attract the reader's interest.
2. present the author's credentials as a social activist.
3. establish a time frame.
4. connect the past to the present.

P. The concluding paragraphs contain

1. generalizations.
2. disturbing images.
3. a list of specific suggestions.
4. steps in procedures.

Critical Thinking

INFERENCE QUESTIONS FOR INDEPENDENT AND GROUP WORK

A. The word green as used here suggests or connotes

1. envy.
2. innocence.
3. life.
4. fog.

B. Why might old age insurance undercut the motivation for large families in some parts of the world?

C. Why was Martin Luther King criticized for taking a stand against the Vietnam War?

What connection is the author making with this reference?

Is it valid?

D. When you "eat lower on the food chain," what's on the menu?

E. Design an environmental label that could be awarded to the "best products from the best companies." Your label may include art work, text, or both.

Study Activity

SUMMARIZING THE ESSAY

A. Map the essay by grouping related paragraphs, noting their topics and writing out the important ideas. Use the elements of the argumentative essay as a framework for your summary. These include introduction, thesis, argument (points that support and develop the thesis), and conclusion.

Paragraphs	Unifying Topic	Synthesis of Information
1–3	1970-1990	
4	mistakes and their consequences	
5–10		
11–14		
15–20		
21–24		
25–30		
31–37		

Paragraphs	Unifying Topic	Synthesis of Information
38–44		
45–53		

B. Summarize the reading selection using the completed map and your underlinings and marginal notes.

Connections

The following "letters to the editor" were in response to Denis Hayes' essay. Is either congruent with your own opinion of his work?

EARTH DAY PROS AND CONS

"Earth Day 1990: Threshold of the Green Decade" is a reminder of how selfish environmentalists are: They are more concerned with whales and redwoods than they are with human beings. And they're much too willing to spend other peoples' money.

Thank you for printing "Earth Day 1990 by Denis Hayes. It was both comprehensive and comprehensible. Everyone working at the local, state, national or global level should use this essay as the foundational starting point for developing specific policy programs.

Topic for Composition

Environmentalists have been called elitists, more sensitive to the needs of animals and vegetation than to the needs of human beings. Agree or disagree with this statement in an argumentative essay.

Try to model your writing after Denis Hayes'.

- In your introduction, establish yourself as a person who is aware of environmental and social problems.
- State your thesis; agree or disagree with the given statement.

- Support your thesis with two or three major points. Develop each point with examples or explanations.
- Conclude with a list of suggestions or predictions.
- Tie everything together by restating your thesis as the conclusion of your essay.

Look carefully at A, B, and C. To you, are they characters with human identities and capacities or are they caricatures, exaggerations of human types?

11

Easy as A, B, and C

Reading Mathematics

"... no problem"

Before Reading

Stephen Leacock, a mathematics professor at McGill University in Montreal, was one of North America's best loved humorists. How do you rate yourself as a math student? Good? Average? Do you think that you have a "math block?" Leacock describes math problems, as ". . . short stories of adventure and industry with the end omitted, and having . . ." "a strong family resemblance" as well as "a certain element of romance." Have you ever found adventure, industry, a relative, or romance in a math problem? As you read this satirical piece, you may find some surprising answers to this question.

READING SELECTION

A, B, and C
The Human Element in Mathematics

By Stephen Leacock

1 The student of arithmetic who has mastered the first four rules of his art, and successfully striven with money sums and fractions, finds himself confronted by an unbroken expanse of questions known as problems. These are short stories of adventure and industry with the end omitted, and, though betraying a strong family resemblance, are not without a certain element of romance.

2 The characters in the plot of a problem are three people called A, B, and C. The form of the question is generally of this sort:

3 'A, B, and C do a certain piece of work. A can do as much work in one hour as B in two, or C in four. Find how long they work at it.'

4 Or thus:

'A, B, and C are employed to dig a ditch. A can dig as much in one hour as B can dig in two, and B can dig twice as fast as C. Find how long, etc. etc.'

5 Or after this [model]:

'A lays a wager that he can walk faster than B or C. A can walk half as fast again as B, and C is only an **indifferent** walker. Find how far, and so forth.'

6 The occupations of A, B, and C are many and varied. In the older arithmetics they contented themselves with doing 'a certain piece of work.' This statement of the case, however, was found too sly and mysterious, or possibly lacking in romantic charm. It became the

fashion to define the job more clearly and to set them at walking matches, ditch-digging, **regattas** and piling cord-wood. At times they became commercial and entered into partnership, having with their old mystery a 'certain' capital. Above all they revel in motion. When they tire of walking matches, A rides on horseback, or borrows a bicycle and competes with his weaker-minded associates on foot. Now they race on locomotives; now they row; or again they become historical and engage stagecoaches; or at times they are aquatic and swim. If their occupation is actual work they prefer to pump water into **cisterns**, two of which leak through holes in the bottom and one of which is water-tight. A, of course, has the good one; he also takes the bicycle, and the best locomotive, and the right of swimming with the current. Whatever they do they put money on it, being all three sports. A always wins.

7 In the early chapters of arithmetic, their identity is concealed under the names John, William and Henry, and they wrangle over the division of marbles. In algebra they are often called X, Y, Z. But these are only their Christian names, and they are really the same people.

8 Now to one who has followed the history of these men through countless pages of problems, watched them in their leisure hours dallying with cord-wood, and seen their panting sides heave in the full frenzy of filling a cistern with a leak in it, they become something more than mere symbols. They appear as creatures of flesh and blood, living men with their own passions, ambitions, and **aspirations** like the rest of us. Let us view them in turn. A is a full-blooded blustering fellow, of energetic temperament, hot-headed and strongwilled. It is he who proposes everything, challenges B to work, makes the bets, and bends the others to his will. He is a man of great physical strength and phenomenal endurance. He has been known to walk forty-eight hours at a stretch, and to pump ninety-six. His life is **arduous** and full of peril. A mistake in the working of a sum may keep him digging a fortnight without sleep. A repeating decimal in the answer might kill him.

9 B is a quiet, easy-going fellow, afraid of A and bullied by him, but very gentle and brotherly to little C, the weakling. He is quite in A's power, having lost all his money in bets.

10 Poor C is an undersized, frail man, with a **plaintive** face. Constant walking, digging, and pumping has broken his health and ruined his nervous system. His joyless life has driven him to drink and

smoke more than is good for him, and his hand often shakes as he digs ditches. He has not the strength to work as the others can; in fact, as Hamlin Smith has said, 'A can do more work in one hour than C in four.'

11 The first time that ever I saw these men was one evening after a regatta. They had all been rowing in it, and it had transpired that A could row as much in one hour as B in two, C in four, B and C had come in dead fagged and C was coughing badly. 'Never mind, old fellow,' I heard B say, 'I'll fix you up on the sofa and get you some hot tea.' Just then A came blustering in and shouted, 'I say, you fellows, Hamlin Smith has shown me three cisterns in his garden and he says we can pump them until to-morrow night. I bet I can beat you both. Come on. You can pump in your rowing things, you know. Your cistern leaks a little, I think, C.' I heard B growl that it was a dirty shame and that C was used up now, but they went, and presently I could tell from the sound of the water that A was pumping four times as fast as C.

12 For years after that I used to see them constantly about town and always busy. I never heard of any of them eating or sleeping. Then, owing to a long absence from home, I lost sight of them. On my return I was surprised to no longer find A, B, and C at their accustomed tasks; on inquiry I heard that work in this line was now done by M, N, and O, and that some people were employing for algebraical jobs four foreigners called Alpha, Beta, Gamma, and Delta.

13 Now it chanced one day that I stumbled upon old D, in the little garden in front of his cottage, hoeing in the sun. D is an aged labouring man who used occasionally to be called in to help A, B, and C. 'Did I know 'em, sir?' he answered, 'why, I knowed 'em ever since they was little fellows in **brackets**. Master A, he were a fine lad, sir, though I always said, give me Master B for kind-heartedness-like. Many's the job as we've been on together, sir, though I never did no racing nor aught of that, but just the plain labour, as you might say. I'm getting a bit too old and stiff for it nowadays, sir—just scratch about in the garden here and grow a bit of a logarithm, or raise a common denominator or two. But Mr. Euclid he use me still for them propositions, he do.'

14 From the **garrulous** old man I learned the **melancholy** end of my former acquaintances. Soon after I left town, he told me, C had been taken ill. It seems that A and B had been rowing on the river for a wager, and C had been running on the bank and then sat in a

draught. Of course the bank had refused the **draught** and C was taken ill. A and B came home and found C lying helpless in bed. A shook him roughly and said 'Get up, C, we're going to pile wood.' C looked so worn and pitiful that B said, 'Look here, A, I won't stand this, he isn't fit to pile wood to-night.' C smiled feebly and said, 'Perhaps I might pile a little if I sat up in bed.' Then B, thoroughly alarmed, said, 'See here, A, I'm going to fetch a doctor; he's dying.' A flared up and answered, 'You've no money to fetch a doctor.' 'I'll reduce him to his lowest terms,' B said firmly, 'that'll fetch him.'

15 C's life might even then have been saved but they made a mistake about the medicine. It stood at the head of the bed on a bracket, and the nurse accidentally removed it from the bracket without changing the sign. After the fatal blunder C seems to have sunk rapidly. On the evening of the next day, as the shadows deepened in the little room, it was clear to all that the end was near. I think that even A was affected at the last as he stood with bowed head, aimlessly offering to bet with the doctor on C's laboured breathing. 'A,' whispered C, 'I think I'm going fast.' 'How fast do you think you'll go, old man?' murmured A. 'I don't know,' said C, 'but I'm going at any rate.'—the end came soon after that. C rallied for a moment and asked for a certain piece of work that he had left downstairs. A put it in his arms and he expired. As his soul sped heavenward, A watched its flight with melancholy admiration. B burst into a passionate flood of tears and sobbed, 'Put away his little cistern and the rowing clothes he used to wear, I feel as if I could hardly ever dig again.'

16 The funeral was plain and unostentatious. It differed in nothing from the ordinary, except that out of deference to sporting men and mathematicians, A engaged two hearses. Both vehicles started at the same time, B driving the one which bore the sable parallelopiped containing the last remains of his ill-fated friend. A on the box of the empty hearse generously consented to a **handicap** of a hundred yards, but arrived first at the cemetery by driving four times as fast as B. (Find the distance to the cemetery.) As the sarcophagus was lowered, the grave was surrounded by the broken figures of the first book of Euclid.—It was noticed that after the death of C, A became a changed man. He lost interest in racing with B, and dug but languidly. He finally gave up his work and settled down to live on the interest of his bets.—B never recovered from the shock of C's death; his grief preyed upon his intellect and it became deranged. He grew

moody and spoke only in monosyllables. His disease became rapidly aggravated, and he presently spoke only in words whose spelling was regular and which presented no difficulty to the beginner. Realizing his precarious condition he voluntarily submitted to be incarcerated in an asylum, where he **abjured** mathematics and devoted himself to writing the History of the Swiss Family Robinson in words of one syllable.

Vocabulary

The following words are boldfaced in the reading selection. Write a synonym or brief definition for each. Add other unfamiliar terms and their meanings to the list.

WORD OR PHRASE	SYNONYM OR BRIEF DEFINITION
indifferent (5)	
regatta (6)	
cistern (6)	
aspirations (8)	
arduous (8)	
plaintive (10)	
brackets (13)	
garrulous (14)	
melancholy (14)	
draught (14)	
abjured (16)	

YOUR ADDITIONS

A. Match these adjectives to their synonyms.

1. indifferent
2. arduous
3. plaintive
4. garrulous
5. aspiring

a. talkative
b. melancholy
c. difficult; strenuous
d. mediocre; unconcerned
e. sable
f. hopeful

B. An important aspect of Leacock's humor is the use of words and phrases that have special meaning when used in a mathematical context. Give the general and the math-related meanings for these terms as they are used in paragraphs 14 and 15:

1. draught
2. bracket
3. reduce to lowest terms
4. rate

C. Leacock concludes his story with several math puns, jokes that are based on words and expressions that have double meanings. Quote or retell some of these puns here.

Comprehension

SPECIFIC INFORMATION

A. A, B, and C do not engage in which of these activities?

1. business
2. computer programming
3. racing
4. construction

B. B is in A's power because of

1. debts.
2. draughts.
3. drinking.
4. drugs.

C. Who is responsible for turning $^{2}/_{3} + ^{1}/_{4}$ into $^{8}/_{12} + ^{3}/_{12}$?

1. A
2. B
3. C
4. D

ANALYSIS

D. Leacock has written *A, B, and C: The Human Element in Mathematics* for an audience

1. of math tutors.
2. that is general but educated.
3. that crosses educational levels.
4. of English and Speech majors.

E. The purpose is to

1. refine math curriculum.
2. increase math requirements.
3. entertain.
4. teach skills.

F. The story is told from the perspective of

1. A, B, C
2. X
3. D
4. I

G. Leacock's prose is particularly rich in

1. illustrative examples.
2. restatements.
3. statistics.
4. opinions.

H. Why can't we figure out the distance to the cemetery where C is buried?

1. not enough time
2. not enough information
3. no calculator
4. C's unfair advantage

I. ________________ are Euclidian figures.

1. [tic-tac-toe grid]
2. ♀ ♂
3. [stick figures]
4. □ △ [cube] ○

J. Answer A, B, C, or X (for neither) to each of the following questions and explain your choice:

1. Who would you hire?
2. Who would you fire?
3. Who is like you?
4. Who would you like on your team?
5. Whose cistern would you never borrow?
6. Who is autonomous?

Study Activity

READING MATHEMATICS

This study activity includes a series of eight math exercises designed by mathematics professor Marjorie Tenner to improve her students' problem solving abilities. The exercises are followed by an explanation of the steps used in problem solving. As you work through the exercises, which increase in difficulty, you may consult the corresponding answer keys to monitor your progress. If a term is unfamiliar, check your dictionary or an algebra text for the mathematical meaning.

BASIC MATH TERMS

Review this list of basic math terms and their antonyms, then complete the exercise by circling the appropriate term(s) in the given sentence. The first item has been completed for you.

multiply	divide
add	subtract
minus	plus
greater	less
increase	decrease
positive	negative
odd	even
numerator	denominator
equal	unequal
sum	difference
product	quotient

1. The coach had to multiply/divide the pizza among the players.
2. Two, eight, sixty-six, and one hundred are all odd/even numbers.
3. If the temperature is below zero degrees, it is reported as a positive/negative number.
4. The sum/difference between twelve and seven is five.
5. The product/quotient of twenty-four and six is four; the product/quotient is 144.
6. If you have two quarters and three dimes and I have sixteen nickels, the amount of money we each have is equal/unequal.
7. One quarter is greater/less than one-third.

8. In the fractional representation of two-thirds, two is the numerator/denominator of the fraction and three is the numerator/denominator.

9. If you spend $10.00 you increase/decrease the amount of money you have.

10. Seven minus/plus eight is positive/negative one.

Key

1. divide; 2. even; 3. negative; 4. difference; 5. quotient; 6. equal; 7. less; 7. less; 8. numerator, denominator; 9. decrease; 10. minus, negative.

LANGUAGE OF MATHEMATICS

In the language of mathematics, symbols replace words and phrases. Write the letter of the mathematical expression in Column B next to the phrase it represents in Column A.

	Column A	Column B
		a. 8×9
g	1. two plus seven	b. $6 - 8$
____	2. eight multiplied by nine	c. $^1/_{10} \times 2$
____	3. one hundred divided by twenty-five	d. $^1/_2 - ^2/_3$
____	4. twenty-five divided by one hundred	e. $25 \div 100$
		f. $100 \div 25$
____	5. one-seventh	g. $2 + 7$
____	6. two-thirds plus one-half	h. $^1/_7$
____	7. eleven times two equals twenty-two	i. $^2/_3 - ^1/_2$
		j. 11×2
____	8. one-tenth times two	k. $8 - 6$
____	9. the difference between eight and six	l. $^2/_3 + ^1/_2$
____	10. two-thirds minus one half	m. $11 \times 2 = 22.$

Key

1. g; 2. a; 3. f; 4. e; 5. h; 6. l; 7. m; 8. c; 9. k; 10. i.

ALGEBRAIC SYMBOLS

Let *a* represent the first number and *b* the second number and write the following in algebraic symbols.

1. a + b the sum of two numbers
2. ______________ the difference of two numbers
3. ______________ the product of two numbers
4. ______________ the square of the first number *
5. ______________ the square of the second number
6. ______________ the difference of the squares of the numbers
7. ______________ the square of the difference of the numbers
8. ______________ the sum of the squares of the numbers
9. ______________ the square of the sum of the numbers
10. ______________ the square of the product of the numbers

Key

a. $a+b$; b. $a-b$; c.ab; d. a^2; e. b^2; f. a^2-b^2; g. $(a-b)^2$; h. a^2+b^2; i. $(a+b)^2$; j. $(ab)^2$.

MATHEMATICAL STATEMENTS

Rewrite the following expressions as mathematical statements. (When the letter to be used to represent an unknown number is not specified, use any letter you like.)

1. the sum of x and y x + y
2. the difference between a and b ______________
3. the difference between b and a ______________
4. 3 more than n ______________

* The square of a number is the number times itself.

5. 3 times n ________________

6. 4 times the product of x and y ________________

7. 19 less than the product of 3 and y ________________

8. r decreased by the quotient of 2 and 3 ________________

9. two thirds of r ________________

10. 4 times the sum of x and y ________________

11. twenty-five percent of x ________________

12. x decreased by twenty-five percent ________________

13. a number plus seven added to the difference of the number and 3 ________________

14. the sum of a number and twice the square of the number ________________

15. a number plus 10 percent of the number ________________

16. Three more than twice a number is the number plus six. ________________

17. The sum of a number and twelve is ten. ________________

18. Seven less than twice a number is eleven. ________________

19. The difference between five times a number and twice the number is nine. ________________

20. Twenty is two minus the product of six and a number. ________________

Key

1. $x + y$; 2. $a - b$; 3. $b - a$; 4. $n + 3$; 5. $3n$; 6. $4(xy)$; 7. $3y - 19$; 8. $r - 2/3$; 9. $(2/3)r$; 10. $4(x + y)$; 11. $.25x$; 12. $x - .25x$; 13. $(n + 7) + (n - 3)$; 14. $n + 2n^2$; 15. $m + .10m$; 16. $3 + 2x = x + 6$; 17. $n + 12 = 10$; 18. $2x - 7 = 11$; 19. $5y - 2y = 9$; 20. $20 = 2 - 6k$.

WORD PROBLEMS

Following each word problem is a paragraph that restates the problem focusing on the operation the student must perform. Complete the restatement by filling in the blanks with word(s) that make sense to you.

A. A store is having an end-of-year sale. All items are marked down 25%. What is the sale price of a pair of jeans that regularly sells for $20.00?

The problem is asking you to find the ___price___ of the jeans after they have been ________________ by an amount that is ________________ of the regular selling price. One way to solve the problem is by finding out how much you will ________________ by buying the jeans on sale. The next step is to ________________ the amount you save from ________________. The result is the ________________ of the jeans.

B. Maria has grades of 73, 95, and 82 on the first three tests in a course. What grade must Maria get on the fourth test so that her average for the four tests will be 85?

The problem is asking what Maria must get on the ________________ test in order to have an average grade of ________________ on all ________________. One way to solve the problem is to determine that all ________________ test grades must add up to ________________ which is ________________ times 85. Then, you ________________ the sum of the three grades already received from ________________. The result is the ________________ Maria must get on the ________________ test.

C. John's car is worth $7,200.00 today. This is 90% of its value a year ago. How much was John's car worth last year.

The problem asks how much John's car was worth ________________. One way to find out is to find the number that when ________________ by .90 is ________________. To do that you must ________________ 7200. by ________________. This will give you last year's value for John's car.

D. The perimeter of a triangle is 40 inches. Two sides of the triangle are equal and the third side is 5 inches less than each of the equal sides. Find the length of each side of the triangle.

The problem is asking for the ________________ of each ________________ of the triangle. The lengths of all three sides add up to ________________ inches. Two of the sides measure ________________ each and the third side is 5 inches ________________ than each of the others. If x represents the length of one of the equal sides, then ________________ represents the length of the unequal side and ________________ adds up to 40. An equation which will allow us to solve for x is ________________.

Key

A. price, reduced, 25%, save, subtract, 20, cost; B. fourth, 85, 4 tests, 4, 340, 4, subtract, 340, grade, fourth; C. one year ago, multiplied, 7,200, divide, .90; D. length, side, 40, the same, less, $x - 5$, $3x - 5 = 40$, $3x = 40 + 5$.

DIAGRAMMING AND DESIGNING A TABLE

Two important problem-solving skills are diagramming (making a graphic representation of a mathematical representation) and designing a table (an orderly display of data). Study the following diagrams for the given problems and consider how they help to solve the problems. Then, draw a diagram or make a table to assist you to solve each of the remaining problems.

A. Juan owes Sam \$27.00. Sam owes Fred \$6.00 and he owes Linda \$15.30. If, with Sam's permission, Juan pays off Sam's debts to Fred and Linda, how much does he still owe to Sam?

Solution:

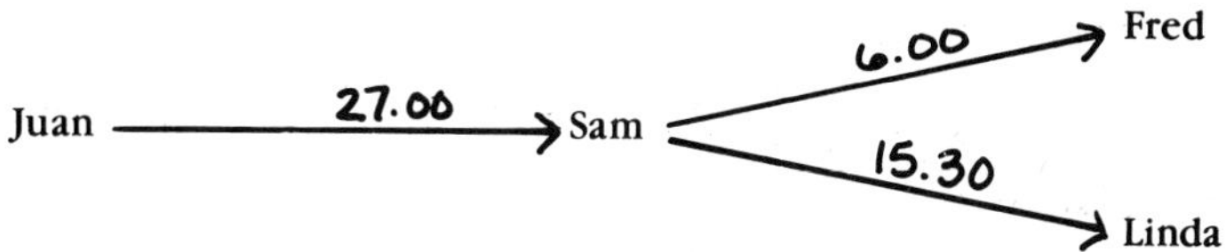

Sam owes a total of $21.30 to Fred and Linda. Subtracting this amount from $27.00 leaves $5.70 which Juan must give to Sam.

B. Mike and Sue started 28 miles apart and walked toward each other, meeting in 4 hours. If Sue walked 1 mile an hour faster than Mike, find the rate at which each of them walked.

Solution:

	Rate	Time	Distance
Mike	x	4	4x
Sue	x + 1	4	4(x + 1)

The total distance they traveled is 28 miles.

$4x + 4(x + 1) = 28$ and $x = 3$. Mike's rate is 3 miles per hour and Sue's is 4 miles per hour.

C. The length of a rectangle is 20 inches more than its width. Find the length and width if the perimeter of the rectangle is 160 inches.

D. A square has an area of 144 square feet. How long is each side?

E. Jack is shorter than Phil but taller than Dick. Dick is shorter than Jack but taller than Greg. Which man is the tallest and which is the shortest?

F. Jim was 5 years old when his father was 32 years old. How old will Jim be when his father is exactly four times Jim's age?

G. The Ace, King, Queen and Jack of Hearts are placed on a table. In how many different ways can they be placed in a row?

H. A train travels 30 miles in the time a car travels 20 miles. How far will the train have gone when the car has traveled 90 miles?

Key

C. 30 inches and 50 inches; D. 12 feet; E. Phil is the tallest and Greg is the shortest; F. 9 years old; G. 24; H. 135 miles.

IDENTIFYING ESSENTIAL INFORMATION

Every word problem contains essential information that the solver must understand. Practice identifying essential information by determining whether the following problems are complete. If the problem lacks some information needed to solve it, note what is missing.

1. A school trip costs $3,562. How much did it cost per student?
   The number of students.
2. The sum of two numbers is 23. One number is larger than the other. Find the two numbers.
3. Mary was in Macy's and bought some items at an end of season sale. If the original cost of the items was $75.00, how much did they cost after having been marked down?
4. The parking lot where I park my car charges $3.00 for the first hour and $1.50 for each additional hour. If I pull into the lot at 9:00 A.M. and pull out at 3:00 P.M. how much will the charge for parking be?
5. If the expenses for a concert are $600.00 and tickets sell for $5.00 each, how much will the profit be?

Key

1. the number of students; 2. the difference between the numbers; 3. percentage of markdown; 4. complete; 5. number of tickets sold.

ESTIMATING

An estimate is a preliminary calculation. Estimating is a familiar part of our daily lives. For example, when we go to the supermarket we estimate how much money we will need for our purchases. Estimating, based on given information, is a crucial step in the problem-solving process. On a short answer math test, an estimate enables us to select an answer without doing much calculation. This is the case in the first example which is worked out for you.

1. The selling price of a particular shirt is $23.89. If sales tax is 4%, which of the following choices represents the total cost of the shirt?

   1) $0.96 2) $23.93 3) $24.85 4) $96.00

   Estimate: $25.00 Correct answer: 3

2. The student government of my school showed a movie to raise money. The total expenses for this event were $800.00. If 491 tickets were sold at $1.99 each, how much profit was made?

   Estimate: Correct answer:

3. You are planning a bike trip from New York City to Orlando, Florida, after school is over for the year. You will have exactly four weeks to complete the trip. It is 1,327 miles from New York to Orlando and you can average 112 miles per day. How many full days will you be able to spend in Orlando?

   Estimate: Correct answer:

4. If you have $50.00 to spend, indicate which of the following you would be able to purchase.
   a. Both a radio ($29.95) and a hair dryer ($19.88)
   b. Both a lamp ($34.95) and a footstool ($10.99)
   c. Both a camera ($37.50) and a flash attachment ($15.99)
   d. Both a tire ($38.98) and a TV antenna ($9.99)
   e. Both a calculator ($19.95) and a sweater ($27.95)

5. Each carton holds 94 textbooks. If the bookstore receives 189 cartons, how many books are in the delivery?

   1) 1,766 2) 17,766 3) 177,660 4) 19,966

   Estimate: Correct answer:

Key

1. Estimate: $25 Answer: $24.85; 2. Estimate: $200 Answer: $177.09; 3. Estimate: 6 Answer: 4; 4. a., b., d., and e.; 5. Estimate: 19,000 Answer: 17,766 (2).

STEPS IN PROBLEM SOLVING

Problem solving usually requires a series of steps. Following is one list of the steps you may go through when solving a word problem. Each and every step is not appropriate for every problem, but keep the steps in mind as you approach the problems in this and the final math exercise.

1. Read the problem.
   - Read the problem slowly and carefully.
   - Note the key words and expressions.
   - Ask yourself, "What do I know?"
   - Ask yourself, "What is being asked for?"
   - Paraphrase, that is, restate the problem in your own words.
2. Approach the problem.
   - Draw a diagram or make a chart.
   - Write down the facts that are necessary to answer the question(s).
   - Experiment.
3. Select a strategy.
   - Decide what you will do and the order in which you will do it.
   - Estimate what you think the answer should be and try out your estimate in the problem to be sure it makes sense.
4. Carry through your strategy.
   - Work the problem out entirely.
   - Compare your result with your estimate.

5. Review what you have done.

   • Check your work and try your answer out in the original problem.

Each of the problems in this set is followed by a series of questions that reflect the steps in the problem solving process. As you complete each question, think about the techniques that you are using. After you answer each question indicate the step you used by putting the appropriate number and letter next to your response.

A. In a bin there are 150 pounds of a combination of peanuts and cashews which is 20% cashews. How many pounds of cashews must be added to produce a combination which is 40% cashews?

1. To determine what the problem is asking, answer the following true or false. If a choice is false, correct it.

   a. ______ The original mixture is 40% peanuts.

   b. ______ You cannot add peanuts.

   c. ______ You are not to remove cashews.

   d. ______ The final mixture will have more peanuts than the original mixture did.

2. What are you asked to find?

   a. x

   b. the amount of peanuts to be added

   c. the pounds of mixture

   d. the number of pounds of cashews to add.

3. What is the original amount of cashews? There may be more than one correct response.

   a. 40% of 150

   b. 30 lbs.

c. .20° × 150

d. .40 (150 + x).

4. After the proper amount of cashews have been added, the amount of mixture can be represented by:

a. x + 30

b. 150 + x

c. 20 + x

d. .20x + 150

5. The final amount of cashews is:

a. 40% of 150

b. 20 lbs.

c. .20 × 150

d. .40 (150 + x)

6. Which mathematical expression of the problem is true?

a. .40x = 150 + 30

b. 50 = 50

c. .40 (150 + x) = 30 + x

d. .20x = .40 (150 + y)

7. Estimate the correct response.

8. Solve the problem:

B. The sales price for a car tire is $35.75, which is 45% off the regular price. Find the regular price.

1. Answer the following true or false. If a choice is false, correct it.

   a. The regular selling price is less than $35.75.

   b. The sales price is less than the regular selling price.

   c. $35.75 is 45% of the regular selling price.

   d. The sales price is less than one-half of the original price.

2. What are you asked to find?

   a. x

   b. the amount of the discount

   c. the original selling price of the tire

   d. y

3. If p is the regular price of the tire, then (there may be more than one correct response)

   a. the sales price is .45p,

   b. the sales price is p − .45p,

   c. the amount of savings is $35.75, or

   d. the sales price is .55p.

4. Which mathematical expression of the problem is true?

   a. $.45p = 35.75$

   b. $.55p = 35.75$

   c. $p = 35.75 + .45$

   d. $p + .45p = 35.75$

5. Estimate the regular price.

6. Solve the problem:

C. A living room is 16 feet by 20 feet. A rug, also rectangular, measures 12 feet by 15 feet. How many square feet of floor remain uncovered when the rug is put down?

1. Draw a rectangle to represent the living room.

   a. Label the length and width.

   b. Draw in the rug.

   c. Label the length and width of the rug.

2. What does the problem ask you to find?

   a. Shade in the area you must find on your diagram.

3. Which of the following relationships are you dealing with in this problem?

   a. Floor area plus rug area,

   b. Floor area minus rug area,

   c. Floor area times rug area, or

   d. None of these.

4. Estimate your answer.

5. Solve the problem.

Key

A: 1. a. f, b. t, c. t, d. f; 2. d; 3. b, c; 4. b; 5. d; 6. c; 7. 40 pounds; 8. 50 pounds
B: 1. a. f b. t c. f d.; 2. c; 3. b, d; 4. b; 5. $70; 6. $65; C: 1.

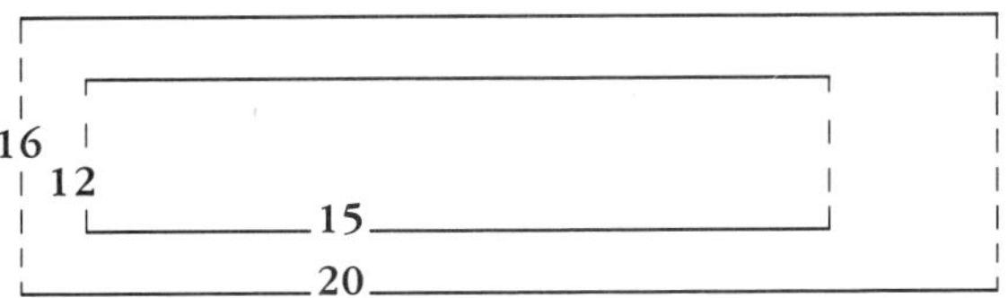

2. the area not covered by the rug; 3. b; 4. 150 square feet; 5. 140 square feet.

MORE WORD PROBLEMS

Here is a selection of different types of word problems. Remember the steps and apply them to find the solutions.

1. The sales tax on a car that costs $9,600.00 is $624.00. Find the rate of sales tax as a percent.

2. In a certain company, 3 out of 5 employees are men. How many women work for the company if there are 600 men working there?

3. Mark is three years younger than twice Luis' age. The difference between their ages is 14. How old is each?

4. An attorney spent 80 hours on two cases. Four times as many hours were spent on one case as on the other. Find the number of hours spent on each case.

5. The World Trade Center is 150 feet taller than the Empire State Building and 108 feet shorter than the Sears Tower. If the total height of the three buildings is 3,984 feet, find the height of each building.

6. A financial manager has determined that the cost per unit to manufacture a radio is $23.00. If the fixed costs for rent, utilities and other items are $3,000. per month, find the total number of radios produced during a month when the total expenditures were $7,600.

7. One printer takes 16 minutes longer to produce a report than does a second printer. Working together the printers can produce the report in 6 minutes. How long would it take each machine working separately to produce the report?

Key

1. 6.5%; 2. 400 women; 3. Luis is 17 years old and Mark is 31 years old; 4. 16 and 64 hours; 5. Sears—1,450 feet, World Trade Center—1,342 feet and Empire State—1,192 feet; 6. 200 radios; 7. 8 minutes and 24 minutes.

Connections

Read *Boarding House Geometry* by Stephen Leacock and estimate how much time it would take you to move out of such an establishment.

Boarding-House

By Stephen Leacock

Definitions and Axioms

1 All boarding-houses are the same boarding-house.

2 Boarders in the same boarding-house and on the same floor are equal to one another.

3 A single room is that which has no parts and no magnitude.

4 The landlady of a boarding-house is a parallelogram—that is, an oblong angular figure, which cannot be described, but which is equal to anything.

5 A wrangle is the disinclination for each other of two boarders that meet together but are not in the same line.

6 All the other rooms being taken, a single room is said to be a double room.

Postulates and Propositions

7 A pie may be produced any number of times.

8 The landlady can be reduced to her lowest terms by a series of propositions.

9 A bee line may be made from any boarding-house to any other boarding-house.

10 The clothes of a boarding-house bed, though produced ever so far both ways, will not meet.

11 Any two meals at a boarding-house are together less than two square meals.

12 If from the opposite ends of a boarding-house a line be drawn passing through all rooms in turn, then the stovepipe which warms the boarders will lie within that line.

13 On the same bill and on the same side of it there should not be two charges for the same thing.

14 If there be two boarders on the same floor, and the amount of side of the one be equal to the amount of side of the other, each to each, and the wrangle between one boarder and the landlady be equal to the wrangle between the landlady and the other, then shall the weekly bills of the two boarders be equal also, each to each.

15 For if not, let one bill be the greater.

16 Then the other bill is less than it might have been—which is absurd.

Topic for Composition

Select another field that uses symbols such as computers, chemistry, music, physics, science, biology, engineering. Note two or three symbols from the particular field. Anthropomorphize these symbols by giving them human physical and personality traits. Design a cartoon and/or devise a plot for your characters that reveals the human element in your selected field or discipline.

Drafting the Declaration of Independence.

12

Common Sense: Declaring Independence

The Formal Outline

"... in America, the law is King."

—Tom Paine, "Common Sense"

Before Reading

This chapter examines autonomy from the perspective of American history. It focuses on the 13 colonies' struggle to achieve autonomy within the British Empire. Particular attention is given to the causes and consequences of that struggle. Like the final decades of the eighteenth century, the last decade of the twentieth century is a time of revolutionary activity in different parts of the world. Can you discuss some of these current struggles for autonomy or independence, their causes, and possible consequences?

For college students not educated in the United States, the following terms and images may be unfamiliar. What do they mean to you?

"taxation without representation"

"Boston Tea Party"

"minute men" and "lobsterbacks"

"I know not what course others may take, but as for me, give me liberty or give me death."

"life, liberty and the pursuit of happiness"

These terms will help you to understand concepts presented in the reading selection.

Enlightenment The term applied to the mainstream of intellectual thought in the eighteenth century (1700–1800). New advances and discoveries in science suggested the presence of order and harmony in nature. "Enlightened" thinkers believed that ordinary persons were capable of establishing and maintaining order and harmony in human society. The spirit of Enlightenment found political expression in the ideas of the English philosopher John Locke. Locke conceived of government as a contract between those who govern and the people, who are governed. If the government fails to meet the terms of the contract, the people have the right, in fact the obligation, to dissolve the contract.

Mercantile Theory The belief that colonies, foreign territorial possessions, exist to benefit the parent country, and to add to its wealth, prosperity, and self-sufficiency. Colonists are regarded, therefore, as tenants who are expected to pay the parent country for the expense of governing and protecting them.

READING SELECTION

"A Struggle for Autonomy Leads to 'The Declaration of Independence'"

By John B. Harris and Richard E. Sullivan

One Tradition: Two Societies

1 Although there were by 1776 wide differences between American and British society, these differences did not spell revolution. Most Americans were still Englishmen and still closely attached to a European tradition. Their economic ideas, their political system, their religion and their social concepts were fundamentally European, adapted to fit a new environment but not magically transformed into something new. Their revolt was inspired by the conviction that Britain was violating the very tradition that the colonists had inherited from her. The revolution was not a case of the Americans **repudiating** Europe; it was more nearly a case of the Americans seeking to put into practice some of Europe's most prized and most advanced concepts in order to fulfill the promise of the society they had planted and nourished in America.

The Quarrel with Great Britain

2 Nowhere was there less understanding of the **ferment** in colonial society than in eighteenth century Great Britain. British interest in her overseas colonies was primarily economic. In true merchantilistic fashion the ruling aristocracy was convinced that British prosperity and power depended upon the **exploitation** of colonial resources. Little thought was given to the human factors involved in colonial relationships. Great Britain's policy toward her colonies was set forth in a series of Navigation Acts which required that certain items produced be sold only in Great Britain, that colonists purchase manufactured goods only from Great Britain and that all shipping be carried in British or colonial ships. Britain's goal was to create a closed self-sufficient economic system. She did not **conspire** to **pillage** the colonies for her benefit; she merely insisted that her interests have priority over colonial interests.

Actions and Reactions

3 For many years Britain was extremely **lax** in administering her colonies; the governors Britain sent to enforce her regulations got little backing from the parent country. The conclusion of the Seven Years' War between France and England (1756–1763) spurred her into a program of reform intended to correct years of neglect. Britain's major concerns after 1763 lay with paying her war debt, colonial defense and economic regulation of the colonists who had long been guilty of ignoring the Navigation Acts.

4 The strife between Great Britain and the colonists gradually intensified in the decade between 1763 and 1773. Under Prime Ministers Grenville (1764–1765) and Townshend (1767) Parliament imposed a series of measures aimed at raising money and tightening colonial administration. Specifically, she closed the western territory to further settlement, laid taxes on numerous imports into the colonies and on business documents ("Stamp Act," 1765) and took steps to give British businesses preferential treatment over colonial businesses. Of all these measures the most detestable to the colonists were the Stamp Act and the "Townshend Duties" (1767) which taxed among other imports, tea.

5 The colonists fought back with boycotts, fiery speeches, acts of violence and protest meetings, and in 1766, in the face of colonial resistance, the crown **repealed** the Stamp Act. At the same time, however, she persisted in her general policy of tightening control by passing the "Declaratory Act" which asserted that Parliament had authority over the colonies, "in all cases whatsoever." By 1768 Britain had sent troops to America. The colonists began to question British authority on much wider grounds than taxation. Many became convinced that they were being deprived of all traditional English liberties while their wealth was being stolen through taxation.

6 A crisis occurred in 1773 when, angered by the tax on tea, a group of Boston citizens disguised themselves as Indians and destroyed a cargo of tea which belonged to the British East India Company. As punishment, Britain enacted the "Intolerable Act," legislation which closed the port of Boston, placed Massachusetts under the control of a military commander, quartered troops in Boston homes and threatened those suspected of a major crime with transportation to Britain for trial in the English courts. As if this were not enough, the British passed the "Quebec Act" (1774) which joined

all territory north of the Ohio River to the Canadian province of Quebec under a non-representative royal administration.

The Colonies Draw Together

7 The handful of American radicals began to gain recruits. The First Continental Congress composed of delegates from the colonies met in Philadelphia in 1774 to discuss the troubled situation. The growing spirit of rebellion was revealed in their adoption of a bold statement which proclaimed the "Intolerable Acts" illegal and stated that Parliament had violated man's natural rights.

8 The increasing reference to "natural rights" in the arguments of the colonists was **momentous**. It signified that many believed in a natural law superior to English law and in a right, perhaps even an obligation, to revolt if the English violated the natural law. Thus, Britain and the colonies slowly drifted toward war. Blood was first shed in **skirmishes** at Lexington and Concord on April 18, 1775.

9 Three weeks after the battles of Lexington and Concord, when the Second Continental Congress met in Philadelphia, the delegates agreed in their determination to support the war but disagreed about its objectives. At one extreme John and Samuel Adams leaned toward independence (though they did not yet **avow** it), and at the other extreme John Dickinson of Pennsylvania hoped for an early reconciliation with Great Britain. Most of the delegates held views that ranged between those of Dickinson and the Adamses. They disregarded Parliament's "Conciliatory Propositions" as insincere but voted reluctantly for one last appeal to the King in the "Olive Branch Petition." Then, on July 6, 1775, they adopted a "Declaration of the Causes and Necessity of Taking Up Arms," announcing that the British government had left the American people with only two alternatives, "unconditional submission to the **tyranny** of irritated ministers or resistance by force," and the people had decided to resist.

10 So for the first year of the war, the Americans were fighting for a redress of grievances within the British Empire, not for independence. During that year, however, many of them began to change their minds, for various reasons. For one thing, they were making sacrifices so great as in the Battle of Bunker Hill, the bloodiest engagement of the entire war and one of the most sanguinary anywhere in the eighteenth century, that their original war aims seemed unequal

to the cost. For another thing, they lost much of their lingering affection for the mother country when she prepared to use Indians, slaves and foreign **mercenaries** (the hated Hessians) against them. And, most important, they felt that they were being forced into independence when the British government replied to the Olive Branch Petition with the Prohibitory Act, which closed the colonies to all overseas trade and made no concession except an offer of pardon to **repentant** rebels. The Americans desperately needed military supplies to continue the war and now they could get them from abroad in adequate amounts only if they broke completely with Great Britain and proceeded to behave in all respects as if they comprised a **sovereign** nation.

Independence Is Common Sense

11 These feelings were not caused, but were clarified and crystallized by the publication in January, 1776 of the pamphlet "Common Sense." Its author was Thomas Paine, who with letters of introduction from Benjamin Franklin had emigrated from England less than two years earlier. Though long a failure in various trades, Paine proved a brilliant success as a revolutionary propagandist. In his pamphlet he argued with flashing phrases that it was plain common sense for Americans to separate from an England rotten with the corrupt monarchy of George III, brutal as an unnatural parent toward her colonies, responsible for dragging them in to fight her wars in the past, and no more fit as an island kingdom to rule the American continent than a **satellite** was fit to run the sun.

Declaration of Independence

12 Despite the persuasion of "Common Sense" the American people were far from unanimous, and they entered upon a bitter debate over the merits of dependence and independence. While the debate raged, the Continental Congress advanced step by step toward a final break. Congress opened the ports of America to all the world except Great Britain, entered into communication with foreign powers and recommended to the various colonies that they establish governments without authority from the Empire, as in fact they were already doing. Congress also appointed a committee to draft a formal declaration which it adopted on July 4, 1776.

13 The document was primarily the work of the young radical from Virginia, Thomas Jefferson. His fellow committee members, Benjamin Franklin and John Adams, and Congress made more

drastic changes, striking out passages that condemned the British people and the slave trade. As Adams afterwards observed, Jefferson said nothing new in composing the document. Its very virtue, in fact, lay in his noble phrasing of beliefs already widespread in America. He planned the document in two main parts. In the first part, the preamble, he restated the familiar contract theory of Enlightenment philosopher John Locke, who had held that governments were formed to protect the rights of life, liberty and property, but Jefferson gave the theory a more humane twist by referring instead to the rights of "life, liberty and the pursuit of happiness." In the second part he listed the alleged crimes of the British King who, with the backing of Parliament, had violated his contract with the colonists and thus had forfeited all claims to their loyalty.

14 Once adopted, the Declaration of Independence exerted an incalculable influence on later history. With its democratic principle that "all men are created equal," it stimulated humanitarian movements of various kinds in the United States, and abroad it helped to inspire the French Revolution with its "Declaration of the Rights of Man." More immediately, it led to increased foreign aid for the struggling rebels and prepared the way for France's allout intervention on their side. It **steeled** American patriots to carry on without regard to offers of a peace short of the stated goal. And at the same time it divided Americans more cruelly and more extensively than they ever had been divided before.

Vocabulary

The following words are boldfaced in the reading selection. Write a synonym or brief definition for each. Add other unfamiliar terms and their meanings to the list.

WORD OR PHRASE	SYNONYM OR BRIEF DEFINITION
repudiating (1)	
ferment (2)	
conspire (2)	
pillage (2)	

WORD OR PHRASE	SYNONYM OR BRIEF DEFINITION
exploitation (2)	
lax (3)	
repealed (5)	
skirmishes (8)	
momentous (8)	
avow (9)	
tyranny (9)	
repentant (10)	
sovereign (10)	
mercenaries (10)	
satellite (11)	
steeled (14)	

YOUR ADDITIONS

Review of Word Forms and Functions

Form	Function	Example
Noun	Names a person, place, thing, or idea	*Tom Paine* *Philadelphia* *Stamp Act* *Allegiance*
Verb	States action in time	A government which *violates* Paine *emigrated* from England.
Adjective	Describes	The most *sanguinary* battle A *momentous* event
Adverb	Tells how an action is performed; modifies the meaning of an adjective	The colonists moved *rebelliously.* Supervision was *extremely* lax.

A. Find the missing word in the vocabulary list and use its appropriate form (noun, verb, adjective or adverb) to complete these sentences.

1. The British ________________ the colonists' wealth by imposing harsh taxes.
2. Americans didn't ________________ enlightened European ideas.
3. ________________ administrators neglected to enforce the Navigation Acts.
4. The colonists came to regard George III as a ________________.
5. The British responded to the colonists' boycott by ________________ the Stamp Act.
6. The Declaration of Independence was an ________________ of America's sovereignty.
7. By 1774, the radical movement was gaining ________________.
8. Skirmishes at Lexington and Concord ________________ the soldiers for the ensuing battle.
9. When we do anything solely for money, we do it ________________.
10. There wasn't a ________________ to loot the colonial treasury.

Comprehension

Scan, that is, look closely over the reading selection focusing on details in order to answer these true/false questions. Give the number of the paragraph(s) that contain(s) the answer. Correct the false statements in the space provided.

Examples The influence of the Enlightenment idea that a contract must exist between those who govern and those who are governed is evident in the "Intolerable Acts."

The influence of the Enlightenment idea that a contract must exist between those who govern and those who are governed is evident in the Declaration of Independence.

The Seven Years' War had a direct effect on Britain's colonial policies.

3 T

1. British reforms beginning in 1763 improved the quality of colonial life. ______ ______

2. The Crown regarded the Boston Tea Party as a joke; its response to it was restrained. ______ ______

3. The Intolerable Acts of the Quebec Act were direct attacks on the right to representative government. ______ ______

4. For Tom Paine, it was common sense to cling to Britain for protection and economic stability. ______ ______

5. During the first year of fighting, the colonists' objective shifted from autonomy as British subjects to independence. ______ ______

6. The slave trade is condemned in the Declaration of Independence. ______ ______

7. In the Second Continental Congress, there was no consensus regarding the radical sentiment for revolution. ______ ______

8. The French "Declaration of the Rights of Man" was an inspiration to American revolutionaries. ______ ______

9. The First Continental Congress reflected the ideals of the Enlightenment philosophers. ______ ______

10. The Olive Branch Petition offered by Parliament motivated the decision to go to war. ______ ______

Study Activity

THE FORMAL OUTLINE

An outline is a framework of related ideas. In an outline, the visual pattern in which information appears on a page is significant. It indicates how the ideas in a reading assignment or lecture relate to each other and to the work as a whole.

Major concepts, the general, umbrella ideas that often encompass several supporting statements and terms, are recorded at the left margin. Major and minor supporting details are indented. The more specific and finite a detail, the more it is indented.

NOTATION

A formal outline follows a universally recognized system, which is called *notation*. The notations are the symbols which precede the various items of information: Roman numerals are placed in front of major concepts. Capital letters are placed in front of major details. Arabic numerals precede minor details, and the most finite, subordinate to minor details are preceded by lowercase letters. Notation indicates the degree of subordination of an item, as does its position on the page.

To achieve consistency, notations are followed with periods, the first letter of each item is a capital and all levels have at least two units. (Roman I is followed by Roman II, capital A by capital B, number 1 by number 2, and lowercase a by lowercase b.)

A. Read the following paragraph. Then, study the outline for its important points.

Tom Paine fought for justice with a pen not a musket. Soon after his arrival from England in 1774, he became editor of "Pennsylvania

Magazine" and instituted an editorial policy for social reform. He opposed aristocratic customs which supported privileges of class and rank such as inherited titles and exclusionary rights to employment. He denounced dueling as a decadent aristocratic indulgence. Moreover, Paine championed causes that other reformers ignored or feared: abolition of slavery; women's rights including suffrage (the vote) and more liberalized divorce laws. (Both were considered outrageously radical ideas at the time.) He wrote in favor of old-age pensions and humane treatment of animals. Finally, with the publication of the forty-two page pamphlet, "Common Sense" Tom Paine took on King George III, the English parliament and the whole institution of monarchy.

(Title) Tom Paine—reformer journalist

I. (Major concept) Paine edited "Pennsylvania Magazine" 1774–75
   A. (Major detail supports I.) Opposed aristocratic customs
      1. (Minor detail supports I.A.) Inherited titles
      2. (Minor detail supports I.A.) Exclusionary employment
      3. (Minor detail supports I.A.) Dueling
   B. (Major detail supports I.) Championed unpopular causes
      1. (Minor detail supports I.B.) Abolition of slavery
      2. (Minor detail supports I.B.) Women's rights
         a. (Minor detail supports I.B.2.) Suffrage
         b. (Minor detail supports I.B.2.) Liberalized divorce laws
      3. (Minor detail supports I.B.) Old-age pensions
      4. (Minor detail supports I.B.) Humane treatment of animals

II. (Major concept) Pamphlet "Common Sense" challenged English monarchy

B. Sort the following related items into general and subordinate points and record them in the appropriate places in the outline pattern:

Tea	Taxes on business documents
Sugar	Lead
Paint	Contracts
Licenses	Reports
Leases	

I. British outrages

A. Threats to colonial economy

1. Taxes on imports

a.

b.

c.

d.

2.

a.

b.

c.

d.

C. Complete the outline pattern by recording the following items in the appropriate places:

Intolerable Acts
Closed the port of Boston
Transportation for trial
Declaratory Act
Quartered troops in Boston
Threats to civil liberties
Quebec Act
Joined territory to Canada
Disbanded Boston legislature
Royal nonrepresentative government

B.

1.

2.

a.

b.

3.

a.

b.

c.

d.

OUTLINING DETAILED FACTUAL MATERIAL

In the formal outline, notes should be recorded either entirely in sentences or entirely in short phrases. The complex, detailed factual information in a history text or lecture, however, requires a more flexible approach, one that allows for combining sentences and phrases. With a text, the student previews the entire work and then works section by section through it, formulating major concepts from section headings, summarizing central ideas, and listing details in as few words as possible.

The following model outline is based on the first three sections of the reading selection (paragraphs 1 through 6). In section I, the author expresses the source of colonial discontent with the British authorities. In section II, the author explains British economic policy in the years prior to the revolution. Reread these sections, including your underscorings and annotations. Then examine the following outline of the material.

Two Societies: One Tradition

I. Reasons for revolt
    A. American colonists and English tied to same European traditions (1776)
        1. Economic ideas
        2. Political system
        3. Social concepts
        4. Religious concepts
    B. Colonists rebelled to protect traditional English rights
II. Quarrel with Great Britain
    A. Insensitive to colonial ferment
    B. Interests purely economic
        1. Colonists could sell only in Great Britain
        2. Colonists could buy only from Great Britain
        3. Shipping only in British or colonial ships

D. In your notebook, outline section III, "Actions and Reactions." Check your notes with the following ones:

III. Actions and Reactions (1763–1773)
   A. Conclusion Seven Years' War (1763) spurred reforms
   B. Prime Ministers Grenville (1764–1765), Townshend (1767), imposed measures to raise money, tighten colonial administration
      1. West closed to settlement
      2. Taxes on business documents (Stamp Act, 1765)
      3. Taxes on imports (Townshend duties, 1767)
      4. British business favored
   C. Colonists' civil disorder affects British policy
      1. Stamp Act repealed (1776)
      2. Declaratory Act gave British "complete authority" (1768)
      3. Troops sent (1768)
   D. Boston Tea Party forces crisis
      1. Intolerable Acts
         a. Closed port of Boston
         b. Military commander in control
         c. Troops in colonists' homes
         d. Transportation for trial to Britain
      2. Quebec Act
         a. Northern territory joined to Quebec
         b. Royal nonrepresentative government

Observe that actions (A, B, C, D) and reactions (1, 2, 3, and so forth) are noted. Under reactions 1, "Intolerable Acts," and 2, "Quebec Act," there is further listing of the specifics of these acts, which are designated with lowercase letters.

E. Preview the following incomplete outline, and reread the fourth and fifth sections of the reading selection (paragraphs 7 through 14). Then complete the outline with the missing factual details.

IV. Colonies draw together
   A. First Continental Congress meets in spirit of rebellion

   B. First bloodshed at Lexington and Concord, April 18, 1775

C. Second Continental Congress not united on war objective

D. War aims change to independence

E. Tom Paine's "Common Sense" brings the message to the people

V. Declaration of Independence

A.

1. Opened ports to all but British
2. Entered into communications with foreign powers
3. Recommended colonies establish govts. with no authority of empire
4. Appointed committee to draft declaration
5. Adopted declaration on July 4, 1776

B. Content

C. Composition

F. Work from your outline to construct a time line of the events that led to the Declaration of Independence on July 4, 1776.

Critical Thinking

QUESTIONS FOR INDEPENDENT AND GROUP WORK

A. Words are used and abused in politics.

1. Give the literal meanings of each of these terms.

radical

reform

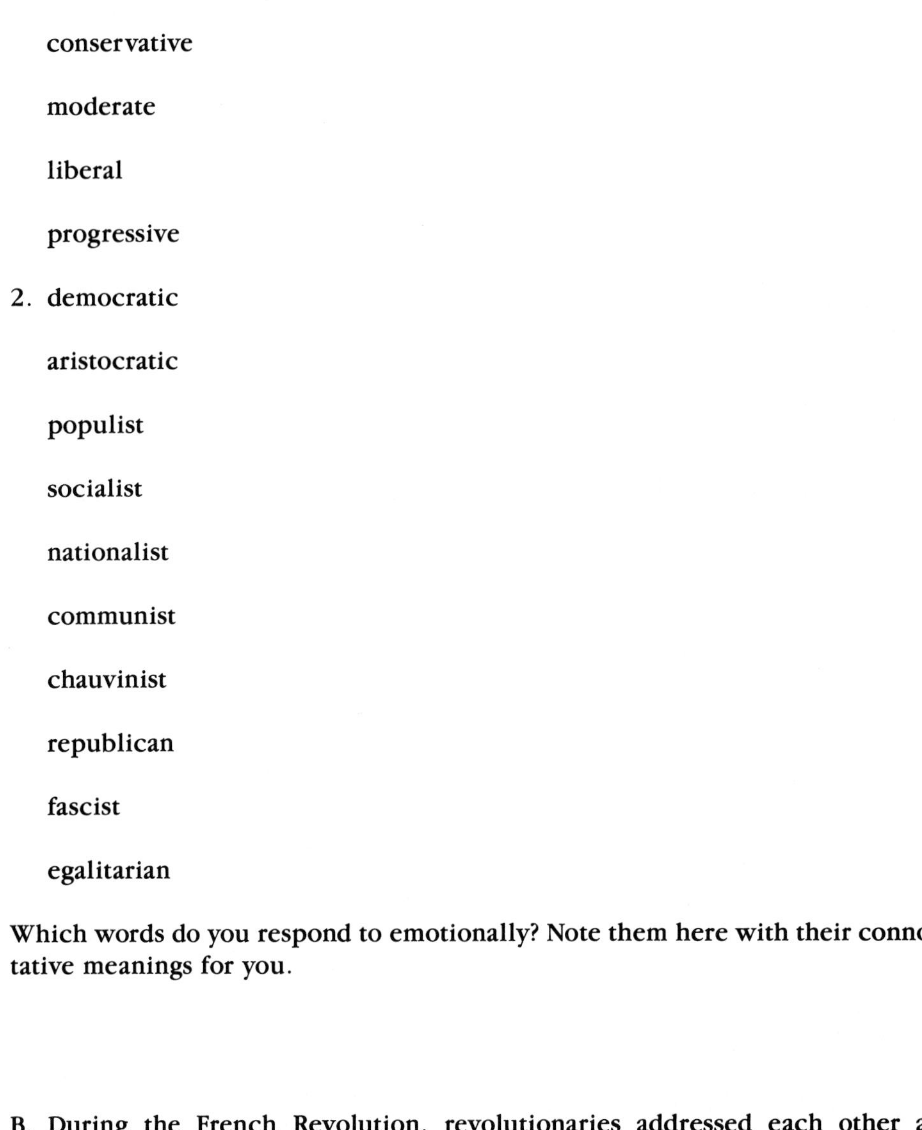

reactionary

conservative

moderate

liberal

progressive

2. democratic

aristocratic

populist

socialist

nationalist

communist

chauvinist

republican

fascist

egalitarian

Which words do you respond to emotionally? Note them here with their connotative meanings for you.

B. During the French Revolution, revolutionaries addressed each other as "Citizen" and "Citizeness." What similar titles are used in English and other languages to indicate equality among people and a disdain for rank and inherited privilege?

C. When the First French National Assembly met in Versaille, the members were seated according to their loyalty to Louis XIV. Those who favored keeping the King's head on his neck and his body on the throne sat at the far right; those who wished to end the monarchy quickly and establish an entirely new kind of society sat at the far left. The words left and right have retained a political meaning. Where would you place the terms in Exercise A 1 on the political spectrum from left to right?

D. As citizens, Americans have the right and responsibility to renew or break their contract with the administration every four years. However, Supreme Court justices, appointed by the President with the advice and consent of the legislature, may serve for life. Through such appointments, the influence of a particular administration is felt for many decades.

1. Who today are the nine justices of the Supreme Court?

2. Where would you place each of the judges on the political spectrum from left to right?

3. Are justices expected to be autonomous in reaching their decisions? Explain.

4. What are some momentous cases before the court at this time? What are your hopes and expectations for their decisions?

Connections

Artists—musicians, poets, painters, sculptors, writers—have found inspiration and given inspiration to those who seek freedom from oppression. In 1774, writer Tom Paine brought the message of revolution to the colonists when he said it was common sense for the American continent to free itself from an island kingdom.

There is irony in history. In 1897, the Caribbean island colony, Puerto Rico won autonomy from Spain. A year later, during the Spanish American War it was invaded and colonized once again, this time by the United States.

Immediately, a movement for independence from the "American continent" was born.

The poet José de Diego brought the message of resistance to the people. A century later, Puerto Rico is still struggling with its political identity. José de Diego's poetry speaks to oppressed women and men everywhere, who though surrounded and outnumbered hold fast to their ideals.

Here is one of his poems from the collection *Cantos de Rebeldia, Songs of Rebellion* which was published in 1916. If you know of complementary works written, musical, or visual on this theme, share them with your class.

"En La Brecha"

By José de Diego (1916)

A un perseguido
¡Ah desgraciado si el dolor te abate,
si el cansancio tus miebros entumece!
Haz como el árbol seco: reverdece:
y como el germen enterrado: late.
Resurge, alienta, grita, anda, combate,
vibra, ondula, retruena, resplandece . . .
Haz como el rio con la lluvia: ¡crece!
y como el mar contra la roca: ¡bate!
De la tormena al iracundo empuje,
no has de balar, como el cordero triste,
sino rugir, como la fiera ruge.
¡Levantate! ¡revuelvete! ¡resiste!
Haz como el toro acorralado: ¡muge!
O como el toro que no muge: ¡¡embiste!!

In The Breach (Surrounded)

To one who is persecuted
Oh misfortune if the pain crushes you,
if exhustion paralyzes your limbs!
Be like the dry tree: turn green again:
and like the buried seed: pulse.
Resurge, take heart, shout, stride, fight,
vibrate, undulate, thunder, shimmer . . .
Like the river with rain: swell!
and like the sea against the rock: pound!

As the angry storm sweeps ahead,
no bleating like a sad sheep,
but roar, like a wild animal roars.
Stand! writhe! resist!
Be like the cornered bull: bellow!
Or like the bull that doesn't bellow: charge!!

Topics for Composition

A. Struggles for political autonomy and independence have been universal. If you were not born on the United States mainland, did such a struggle occur in your homeland? Who were the leaders? What were the circumstances? What were the consequences?

B. Movements for self-determination are an important aspect of contemporary life. Consider groups here in the United States or in other countries who are currently involved in such struggles? Discuss the circumstances and the possible consequences.

Appendix I
Vocabulary

Word Inventory

This alphabetical inventory of words from reading selections and exercises includes words not defined in the text.

WORD	*PART OF SPEECH*	*BRIEF DEFINITION*
abhor	verb	to loath, to shrink from
abjure	verb	reject
abreast	adverb	alongside of
accrue	verb	to gain
acquisition	noun	something gained
actualize	verb	to make actual, to realize
adamantine	adjective	hard like a diamond
advocacy	noun	support
aesthetic	adjective	artistic, dealing with the beautiful
aggregate	noun	sum total
aggression	adjective	anger
alienation	noun	separation from the mainstream
alleged	adjective	supposed, so-called
altruistic	adjective	generous, giving, idealistic
ambivalent	adjective	confused, shifting
amortize	verb	pay a debt gradually
anarchy	noun	no government, absence of political order
animate	adjective	living
anonymous	adjective	unknown
antedated	verb	came before
anthropology	noun	comparative study of human beings

WORD	PART OF SPEECH	BRIEF DEFINITION
apparatus	noun	device or tool for a specific purpose
appreciation	noun	recognition, gratitude, increase in value
appurtenances	noun	objects (job or skill related)
archaeologist	noun	one who studies the remains of human activity
arduous	adjective	difficult, laborious
ascertain	verb	figure out
aspirations	noun	ambition
auspices	noun	protection, support
avert	verb	turn from
autonomous	adjective	in control of self
avarice	noun	greed
beggar	verb	make destitute
benevolent	adjective	kind, charitable
bond	noun	link, connection
bountiful	adjective	abundant
boycott	noun	policy restricting trade
brutish	adjective	having the qualities of a brute
carcinogenic	adjective	cancer producing
carnal	adjective	physical, sensual
catalyze	verb	change, produce, alter
celibate	noun	an unmarried person not sexually active
chasm	noun	a wide difference of views
cistern	noun	tank for storing water
cognitive	adjective	aware
collateral	adjective	parallel, corresponding
colic	noun	abdominal pain, usually in babies
competent	adjective	capable
compliance	noun	a disposition to yield to the wishes or demands of others
component	noun	evidence of the use of a site
compulsive	adjective	coercive, obligatory; must be obeyed
conspiracy	noun	plot; agree-upon plan to commit an illegal act
culture shock	noun	barrier to effective fieldwork
customarily	adverb	usually
data	noun	information compiled for analysis
datum point	noun	indication that excavation occurred
deformation	noun	alteration
denunciation	noun	open condemnation
designate	verb	to indicate or specify

WORD	PART OF SPEECH	BRIEF DEFINITION
devoid	adjective	empty
differentiation	noun	distinction
discontinuity (cultural)	noun	contradiction between what is expected of children and what is expected of adults
disengage	verb	to free oneself
disrupt	verb	to create confusion
distinguished	verb	see as separate or different
domain	noun	territory, field of influence
domestic	adjective	of the household, pertaining to the home
draught (draft)	noun	air current, payment
embargo	noun	trade restriction
encumber	verb	to burden
ensue	verb	to follow as a result
ensure	verb	to guarantee
essence	noun	basic nature of something
ethnographer	noun	one who studies particular groups
excavation	noun	hole or cavity
exploit	verb	use to one's own advantage
famine	noun	starvation
feasible	adjective	capable of being accomplished
feign	verb	to pretend
fey	adjective	other worldly
fidelity	noun	loyalty
fissile	adjective	can be split
foster	verb	to encourage, cultivate
frantically	adverb	in a frenzy, panic
garrulous	adjective	talkative
genesis	noun	beginning, origin
gerontocracy	noun	society of elders
hallmark	noun	distinctive feature
hampered	adjective	impeded, restrained
havoc	noun	destruction, confusion
hierarchy	noun	a body of entities arranged in a graded series
hostile	adjective	feeling or showing anger
idealize	noun	to regard or to represent as an ideal
immune	adjective	having a resistance to disease
imperceptible	adjective	faint
inadequacies	noun	weakness
incongruous	adjective	out of place
indifference	noun	lack of interest

WORD	PART OF SPEECH	BRIEF DEFINITION
idle	adjective	inactive
inhibitions	noun	restraints
insulate	verb	to isolate
intractable	adjective	unruly, obstinate
intrinsically	adverb	essentially
inured	adjective	used to, accustomed to
invariably	adverb	constantly
inviolate	adjective	pure, undisturbed
irrevocable	adjective	unalterable, can't be revoked
laison	noun	close relationship, connection
livery	noun	distinctive dress
lore	noun	accumulated fact, tradition, and belief
macabre	adjective	gruesome, ghastly
malevolent	adjective	malicious, wishing harm to others
manipulate	verb	control
maze	noun	confusing passage
mediate	verb	to settle differences by intercession
melancholy	adjective	pensive, dejected
melodrama	noun	a drama with exaggerated characters and plot
mercenary	noun	soldier serving in a foreign army for pay
momentous	adjective	very important
monogamous	adjective	married to one person
monopolist	noun	one who has exclusive control of a service or commodity
mutagenic	adjective	capable of inducing mutation
mutation	noun	change in genetic makeup
mute	adjective	silent
nuance	noun	slight variation in meaning, color or quality
neologism	noun	a newly coined word
oblige	verb	to please
obscure	adjective	unknown
obsession	noun	preoccupation
occidental	adjective	Europe and the Western hemisphere
ominous	adjective	threatening
ostentatiously	adverb	with outright display
paraphernalia	noun	articles used in an activity; gear
parasitic	adjective	pertaining to taking advantage of or exploiting
partake	verb	to take or have a share in

WORD	*PART OF SPEECH*	*BRIEF DEFINITION*
paternalism	noun	relating in a fatherly manner by creating dependence and not requiring responsibility
pathological	adjective	pertaining to disease
peers	noun	equals
peripheral	adjective	pertaining to the boundary, relatively unimportant
perspective	noun	point of view, relationship of aspects of a subject to each other and to the whole
phenomenon	noun	an observable fact or event, usually extraordinary
physiological	adjective	pertaining to the physical, biological
pilot experiment	noun	tentative model for future modifications
plaintive	adjective	melancholy, woeful
preclude	verb	to make impossible
prestige	noun	reputation
primatologist	noun	one who studies primates
prior	adjective	earlier
procreate	verb	to generate offspring; reproduce
proselytize	verb	to recruit, to make converts
pronounced	adjective	strongly marked
prophecy	noun	prediction
prudence	noun	good sense
quid pro quo	noun	equal exchange
rail	verb	speak bitterly
random	adjective	haphazard
rebuff	verb	to repulse or refuse abruptly
recapitulate	verb	to repeat in summary form
reconcile	verb	to bring warring factions together
redolent	noun	fragrant, pleasantly odorous
reform	verb	to improve by stopping abuses
reform	noun	a correction, improvement
reinforcement	noun	additional strength
repellent	adjective	repulsive
repudiate	verb	to deny, reject
rigged	adjective	arranged, fixed dishonestly
rite	noun	a solemn ceremonial act
sanctify	verb	to make sacred
sanguinary	adjective	bloody

WORD	**PART OF SPEECH**	**BRIEF DEFINITION**
schism	noun	split
shoddy	adjective	poorly made
siblings	noun	brothers and sisters
solitude	noun	state of being alone
spontaneously	adverb	without a plan; on impulse; naturally
spurt	noun	burst of matter, energy or activity
squelch	verb	to crush or suppress
standardize	verb	to make uniform
status	noun	relative position; high position; general situation
stipulate	verb	specify
strain	noun	ancestry
submissive	adjective	obedient
subservience	noun	the quality of being submissive
subtle	adjective	elusive, difficult to detect
sultry	adjective	oppressively hot and moist
threshold	noun	gate, door
thwarted	adjective	frustrated
transgression	noun	broken law
uncanny	adjective	weird
uniform	adjective	consistent
universal	adjective	transcending limited time and place
unobtrusively	adjective	unseen
vanquish	verb	to defeat, overcome
zeal	noun	intense enthusiasm
zenith	noun	summit, highest point

Prefixes, Suffixes, Stems

The stem of a word is its basic form, the fundamental element which is common to all other forms of the word. A *prefix* is a syllable affixed to the beginning of the stem; a *suffix* is one or more syllables affixed to the end of the stem. Prefixes generally change meaning; suffixes generally change the word's function or part of speech.

Example

base word or stem	*justify*
suffix	*justifiable*
prefix	*unjustifiable*

In this example, the suffix changes the verb *justify* into the adjective *justifiable,* and the prefix *un-* changes the meaning to the opposite. The easiest way to form new words is to add prefixes and to add or change suffixes.

The following charts of common prefixes, suffixes, and stems provide space for you to give additional examples.

Prefix	*Meaning*	*Example*	*Your Example*
a	not	atypical	
ad	to, toward	addict	
ante	before	antedate	
anti	against	antidote	
bi	two, twice	bicycle	
com/co	with, together	communal	
con	with, together	conformist	
de	down, from	descend	
dis	apart, away	disinfect	
ex	out	exorcist	
hyper	extremely	hyperactive	
il, im, in, ir, un	not	impossible	
inter	between, among	interact	
macro	large	macroeconomics	
mal	bad	maladapt	
micro	small	microbe	
mini	small	minimal	
mis	badly, wrong	misunderstand	
mono	alone, one	monotone	
multi	many	multitude	
pan	all	pantheon	
post	after	posterity	
pre	before	prejudice	
prim	first	primary	
pro	before, in favor	promote	
re	again, back	reinforce	
semi	part, half	semicircle	
sub	under, below	subdue	
sup	under, below	support	
trans	across, over	transcend	
uni	one, single	union	
un	not, reverse	unjustifiable	

Noun Suffix	*Example*	*Your Example*
er	ethnographer	
ist	anthropologist	
ary	mercenary	
ment	reinforcement	
tion/sion	aggression, alienation	
ism	paternalism	
ship	apprenticeship	
ty	variability	
acy	conspiracy	
ence/ance	appurtenance, ambivalence	
ness	goodness	

Adjective Suffix	*Example*	*Your Example*
ic	prophetic	
ible/able	feasible/defensible	
al	hierarchical	
ant/ent	dominant/competent	
mous/ous	autonomous, ambiguous	
y	uncanny	
ive	compulsive	
ful	vengeful	
ary	imaginary	
ish	brutish	
ly	brotherly	

Verb Suffix	*Example*	*Your Example*
ize/ise	socialize/compromise	
ate	automate	
ify	justify	
en	strengthen	
y	defy	
er	foster	

Adverb Suffix	*Example*	*Your Example*
ly	socially	

WORD STEMS

Some word stems, such as *duct* or *script*, are complete words. Generally, however, stems combine with prefixes and/or suffixes to form words.

Stem	*Meaning*	*Example (Stem in Combination with an Affix)*	*Your Example*
auto	self	autism	
bibl	book	bibliography	
cept, capt	take, seize	capture, intercept	
cess	go, move, yield	procession	
chron	time	chronological	
dict, dec	say, tell, speak	declaration, dictate	
duc, duct	take, lead	introduce, conduct	
fac	do, make	manufacture	
fort	strong	fortress	
geo	earth	geology	
graph, gram	write	telegram	
gress	go	regress, digress	
hetero	other	heterogeneous	
homo	same	homogeneous	
log, logy	speech, study	dialogue, biology	
man	hand	manual	
mater	mother	maternal	
miss	send, let go	transmit, dismiss	
nym	name	pseudonym	
pathy	feeling	sympathy	
patr, patra	father	paternal, patriot	
pend, pens	hang, weigh	pensive	
phil	like, love	philosophy	
phon	sound	phonograph	
port	carry	portable	
pseudo	false	pseudonym	
psyche	soul	psychology	
sequ	follow	sequence	
script, scrib	write	transcript	
sist	stand	persist	
soph	wise	sophisticated	
spec	look	spectacles	
tang, tact	touch	tangled, tactile	
tele	far, distant	telegram	
tract	draw	attract	
vers, vert	turn	divert, versatile	
vid, vis	see	evident, visual	
vok	call	evoke, vocal	
volve	roll, turn	evolve, ambivalent	

Suggestions for Extending Vocabulary

GENERAL WORDS

Keep a general word list in a separate section of your notebook. Use context and word elements to arrive at tentative definitions. Consult your dictionary and after you have verified and refined your tentative definition of a word, record it.

Note the various suffixes that work with the word stem, and record the word in its various grammatical forms—noun, verb, adjective, adverb.

Write a synonym for the word.

Write an antonym for the word.

Write the word in a sentence.

SPECIALIZED OR TECHNICAL WORDS

Keep a word list for each course in your notebook.

Group words and their definitions according to topic.

To drill terms and definitions, use the index card system described in Appendix II.

Critical Reading and Writing Terms

Writing that intends primarily to inform is called expository prose. Textbooks, articles in general periodicals and professional journals, students' essays and research papers, are all types of expository prose. The characteristics of good expository writing include the following:

Precision	Topics are narrowed and words are selected to communicate *exactly* what the *writer* intends to *communicate*.
Conciseness	The work is to the point. The writer eliminates the unnecessary: wordiness (verbosity), redundancies (repetitions), clichés, and puffery (expressions that have become meaningless with overuse and misuse such as *fantastic, tremendous, incredible,* and *beautiful*). To achieve conciseness, you may follow this "concise advice:" *Tell them (your readers) what you are going to say. Say it. Tell them what you said.*

Completeness	All points are elaborated with *sufficient explanation and illustration.*
Coherence	Literally, the parts *cohere*. That is they "stick together." There are no pointless digressions or contradictions. Details focus on the thesis, contribute to the argument, and lead to the logical conclusion.
Direct language	*Literary prose* relies heavily on *figurative* language to evoke experience. Ambiguity is often valued for the types and levels of interpretation which it affords. *Expository prose,* on the other hand, *tends to use denotative language: Meaning is single, easily paraphrased, and grasped in one or two readings*. The writer *avoids slang and colloquialisms.*
Organization	Patterns of discourse are familiar—list, time order, cause-effect, comparison-contrast. *Development of ideas is predictable*—central idea, explanation, illustration and restatement; thesis, argument, conclusions; term, definition, example.

APPENDIX II

Techniques for Taking Short Answer Tests

A short answer, or objective, test requires you to select correct answers from among two or more possible choices. Matching, true-false, and multiple choice are all types of short answer questions. Short answer tests require as much review and thinking as essay questions, but do not require sustained writing. Short answer tests are also called objective tests because they do not involve the instructor's subjective interpretation and evaluation of your work. Answers are either completely right or completely wrong. If the answer is correct, it is worth a specified number of points. If it is incorrect, no credit is given. (Occasionally instructors deduct points for incorrect answers.)

The short answer test does not measure your ability to communicate what you have learned; it can, however, give your instructor a comprehensive indication of your mastery of course material. It measures your ability to recall specifics—dates, technical terms and definitions, steps in a procedure, phases in a process, events and their causes and consequences, points of contrast and similarity, and universals. Such tests can also measure your ability to explain and to combine concepts and to apply them to specific situations.

Preparing for Short Answer Tests

OVERVIEW AND INTEGRATE COURSE CONTENT

Most instructors spell out their testing policy and procedures early in the semester. When in doubt, ask for clarification regarding the date, scope, type, and method of grading any test.

To prepare for either a short answer or an essay test, begin by getting an overview of the material for which you are responsible—specific lectures, text chapters, outside reading, lab and fieldwork experiences. An overview entails your gathering together and assembling information in proper order (the order in which the instructor has presented the material). It is now necessary for you to work with this material and the corresponding text assignments, integrating text markings and lecture and written notes into the briefer lists, visuals, and study frames which you will commit to memory.

The Index Card System

The index card system is a good technique for memorizing dates, definitions, major points, and their supportive details. Try this technique with 4 × 6-inch index cards. Prepare the cards by recording a point that you anticipate your instructor will want to know on one side of the card. On the other side, record the specifics related to the concept. Test your recall by focusing on the front of the card and then writing the information on the back. Turn the card to check your answer. Set the cards that you have mastered aside; continue to review the others.

Study the sample index cards.

Front	Back
1 Maslow's deficiency needs — 4	1 1. psysiological 2. safety 3. love and belonging 4. esteem
2 socialization def.	2 learning process: social roles; moral values; obey authority

3
rites of passage why? reasons:

3
public implications everyone shifts position at birth, marriage, death

Charts and Study Frames

Study frames include questions that direct attention to important points and that anticipate questions which will appear on an examination. Here is an example of a study frame for reviewing the content of Chapter 6, Lucy.

Perspectives on Human Development

	Geology	Biology	Paleontology	Archaeology	Physical Anthropology	Cultural Anthropology
What is the subject of inquiry?						
Where does research occur? (field, laboratory)						
How far back in time does the subject take us?						
What are the major contributions to our knowledge of human development? (key concepts, theories)						
What is the relevance to modern life?						

General Suggestions for Taking Short Answer Tests

1. Be on time. Your ability to answer questions under a degree of time pressure is evaluated in a short answer test. You want to take full advantage of the time that you have. Furthermore, if you are late, you may miss verbal directions and corrections that you must record on the test.
2. Assume that you will remain in the room for the entire test period. Leave only if you must.
3. Have the correct supplies—sharpened pencils, eraser, scrap paper, and (if you have one) a watch.
4. Sit as close to the front of the room as possible so that you will have a good view of the board.
5. Ignore everyone except the instructor or proctor and everything except the test.
6. Listen carefully to all directions. Make corrections on the test as they are announced and written on the board.
7. Write your name on the answer sheet or fill out the identification grid according to directions.
8. Preview the test. Turn each page over. Students often lose points because they omit questions on the backs of pages. Decide how you are going to budget your time.
9. Read directions very carefully. Make clear, bold marks on the answer sheet. If you must write letters, be sure that they are clearly recognizable as As, Bs, and so forth.
10. Work through the whole exam, answering questions that you know first.
11. Read each question very carefully and predict the answer before you turn to the choices.
12. Consider all possible choices before making your decisions.
13. Make marks in the margin next to questions you want to rethink.
14. When you have worked through the test, return to the unanswered questions. Use any insights that you have gained from the test to answer these questions.
15. Check over the test. Use any additional information that you have gained from the test to assess your work, but do not rush to change answers.
16. Get as much as you can from test review sessions. Clearly note correct answers that you missed. Be sure that you understand your mistakes (why the correct answer is correct, why your choice is incorrect).
17. If you disagree with answers to particular questions and are generally disturbed by your performance on the test, request an appointment with your

instructor to discuss the test and your progress in the course. Your instructor may have helpful suggestions about class preparation, participation, and studying techniques.

Specific Suggestions for Different Types of Short Answer Tests

TRUE-FALSE

1. Read directions carefully. Usually you are simply required to indicate whether a statement is true or false. Occasionally, however, it is also necessary to specify the words in a statement that make it false and/or to revise a false statement to make it true.

2. Assume that a statement is true until you determine that it is false. Statistically, most statements are true. This may be because it is easier for the testmaker to quote or to paraphrase a point than it is to create one.

3. If you think that a statement is true, be sure that all parts of it are true. Except for the last two words the following statement is true. Still, the correct answer is false.

Socialization is learned and inherent.

MATCHING

The matching test requires you to match various kinds of items such as dates and events, terms and definitions, individuals and their works or significant contributions, schools and their representative theories. An orderly process of elimination which works for most students involves the following steps: Concentrate on the first item on the left. Bring to mind what you know about the item. Make a mental note of the possible answer, then skim the column on the right to find the answer. Consider each possible choice. Draw lines between the matches. Lightly cross out your chosen answer and return to the column on the left, item number 2. Repeat the procedure until all items on the left are paired with items on the right.

MULTIPLE CHOICE

The multiple-choice question consists of the stem, which is either a question or an incomplete statement, and the "multiple choices," which include the correct answer and all incorrect answers (called distractors). Study the following examples:

Which of the following does Mead *not* include among the contributions the elderly could make?

1. their warm bodies
2. their dead bodies
3. their experience
4. their Social Security benefits

Mead's "new style of aging" is for the elderly to

1. become less autonomous, more dependent.
2. use their autonomy to benefit society.
3. dye their hair in the most modern color.
4. develop their creative and artistic potential.

Turn stems and choices into true-false questions and accept or reject them on that basis.

Try every possible answer before you make a decision in a multiple-choice question. "None of the above" or "all of the above" may be a final choice. If none of the above is a possible response, try the true-false technique. Use the process of elimination, rejecting all choices as false before you select none of the above.

In the case of all of the above, if one answer is requested and among the choices two are correct, then all of the above is your answer.

Look for answers using familiar language, particularly statements that are italicized or boldfaced in your texts. Outrageous or irrelevant statements, unfamiliar technical language, or jargon usually indicate distractors.'

General Suggestions About Language

Regardless of the type of short answer problem, take careful note of statements that contain specific determiners such as every, all, only, never, none, always, best, worst, invariable. They tend to be false because they exclude all possibilities.

Be aware of qualifying words such as many, most, some, few, generally, frequently, ordinarily, often, sometimes, seldom. Statements with qualifying words are more likely to be true than statements with specific determiners.

For example, the following statement is true: Margaret Mead observed that people in different generations are *often* unable to communicate. Whereas this statement is false: Margaret Mead observed that people in different generations are *always* unable to communicate.

Your awareness of word elements (prefixes, suffixes, and stems), word forms, and grammar will assist you. A suffix such as "ist" indicates a particular role or occupation; it may also refer to an individual who fulfills the role or occupation. "Ism" may indicate a doctrine, theory, or system. The same word forms generally match nouns to nouns, verbs to verbs, and so forth. Grammatical consistency should be apparent between matches: subject-verb agreement as well as agreement in gender, and number.

Complete the following matching exercise and indicate your reason for making the match: r = recall, wp = word-part clue, wf = word form clue, g = grammar clue.

______ 1. propagandist
______ 2. minute man
______ 3. boycott
______ 4. steeled
______ 5. a diary or letter
______ 6. mercenaries
______ 7. mercantilism

a. is a primary source ______
b. Tom Paine ______
c. a citizen soldier ______
d. are hired to fight by a foreign country ______
e. refuse to patronize ______
f. hardened ______
g. economic principle of colonial exploitation ______

Key

1.b; 2.c; 3.e; 4.f; 5.a; 6.d; 7.g.

ANTICIPATING THE ANSWER

With both matching and multiple choice problems, allow yourself the opportunity to think, to tap the information stored in your memory. Then turn to the choices.

Practice anticipating answers before you survey your choices. Following is one column of a matching exercise. It contains the names of several social scientists whose work is known to you. In the next exercise, you will be asked to match the individual to a theory which he or she has contributed to our knowledge of human behavior. Focus on the item, make an association, and record it in the space provided:

Example:

1. Ruth Benedict

studied Cheyenne — continuity from childhood to adulthood.

2. Margaret Mead

3. Kalvero Oberg

4. Abraham Maslow

5. Rosenthal and Jacobson

Now practice the matching technique by drawing lines between the social scientist and his or her theory of human behavior. The first match is made for you.

Example:

1. Ruth Benedict	a. generation gap
2. Margaret Mead	b. culture shock
3. Kalvero Oberg	c. self-fulfilling prophecy
4. Abraham Maslow	d. hierarchy of needs
5. Rosenthal and Jacobson	e. cultural discontinuity

Key

1.e; 2.a; 3.b; 4.d; 5.c.

Reading Tests

You can find practice tests and keys in commercial test preparation books. Reading tests are generally timed. The best way to pick up speed is to read fairly challenging material on a regular daily basis. As your vocabulary and your information base grows, so will the amount of material you can cover in a given period of time.

See how long it takes you to complete a test or a given amount of reading without time constraints. Then use an alarm clock. Set it for the time generally allotted for such a test (usually thirty minutes) and see how close you come to completing all items within that time. Continue working with the alarm, setting it at shorter and shorter intervals until you are within the thirty-minute time frame. Rather than work for speed, try to develop a rhythm as you read, progressing from one question to the next, making text-based answers and inferential guesses at a fairly even rate.

Try to categorize the question before you turn to the choices. Three types of questions are usually found: central of summarizing ideas, details, and inferences. Less common but certainly possible are questions on writer's technique and figurative language.

Signal words are crucial. In reviewing many forms of short answer reading tests, one gets the impression that the entire English language hangs on the word *but* and signal expressions with a similar meaning such as *yet, however, in contrast,* and *on the other hand.* The point that these words signal is usually a key point and an answer to a question on a reading test.

Some students feel that reading the questions before reading the passage helps them to be more efficient with their time. You might want to experiment with this technique.

Always read directions thoroughly before beginning the test. Answer all questions unless directions indicate that incorrect answers are penalized.

Acknowledgments

Chapter 1: P. xxiv, photo by Fabiola Lopez. Reprinted by permission of Cathy Yelverton M.S., Fitness Consultant, Movement Matters, Inc., Brooklyn, N.Y. Pp. 2–4 from *Psychology for the Classroom,* by Janice T. Gibson, © 1976, pp. 189–192. Reprinted by permission of Prentice-Hall, Inc., Englewood Cliffs, NJ.

Chapter 2: P. 16, United Nations/photo by M. Grant. Pp. 18–22, from "A New Style of Aging" by Margaret Mead. Reprinted with permission. Copyright 1971, Christianity & Crisis, 537 West 121st Street, New York, NY 10027. P. 30, from *Selected Poems of Langston Hughes.* Copyright © 1959 by Langston Hughes. Reprinted by permission of Alfred A. Knopf, Inc. Pp. 31–32, adapted from "The Sampler" by I.V. Morris in *Best Short Stories of 1934*. Reprinted by permission of Harold Ober Associates.

Chapter 3: P. 34, © Gregory Heisler. P. 44, from *The Portable Dorothy Parker,* revised and "Indian Summer" enlarged edition edited by Brendan Gill. Copyright 1926, 1954 by Dorothy Parker. Reprinted by permission of Viking Penguin, Inc. P. 55, translation by Joan Gregory. Reprinted by permission. P. 55, excerpt from *In Praise of Krishna* by Edward C. Dimock and Denise Levertov, copyright © 1967 by The Asia Society, Inc. Used by permission of Doubleday, a division of Bantam Doubleday Dell Publishing Group, Inc. P. 56, reprinted from *The Prophet* by Kahlil Gibran, by permission of Alfred A. Knopf Inc. Copyright 1923 by Kahlil Gibran and renewed 1951 by Administrators of C.T.A. of Kahlil Gibran Estate, and Mary G. Gibran.

Chapter 4: P. 58 (left), reprinted by permission. P. 58 (right), negative no. 334083 (Photo by Murl Deusing). Pp. 60–63, from *Cultural Anthropology* by Serena Nanda © 1980 by Litton Educational Publishing, Inc. Reprinted by permission of Wadsworth, Inc. P. 82, "If" from Rudyard Kipling's *Definitive Edition.* Copyright 1910 by Doubleday & Company, Inc. Used by permission of The National Trust, The Macmillan Company of London & Basingstoke and Doubleday & Company, Inc.

Chapter 5: P. 84 (top), United Nations/Photo by S. Stokes. P. 84 (bottom), United Nations/photo by A. Jongen. Pp. 86–90, adapted from *Pygmalion in the Classroom,* by Robert Rosenthal and Lenore Jacobson. Copyright © 1968 by Holt, Rinehart and Winston, Inc. Reprinted by permission of Holt, Rinehart, and Winston, Inc. Pp. 99–101, from *Growing Up,* copyright © 1982 by Russell Baker. Reprinted by permission of Congdon & Weed, Chicago.

Chapter 6: P. 102, reprinted by permission of Simon and Schuster. Pp. 104–111, from *Lucy: The Beginnings of Humankind,* by Donald Johanson and Maitland Edey, copyright © 1981 by Donald C. Johanson and Maitland A. Edey. Reprinted by permission of Simon & Schuster, Inc. Pp. 119–120, from *Fossil Man* by Michael H. Day. © 1970 by Grosset & Dunlap, Inc., © 1969 by The Hemlyn Group. Reprinted by permission of Grosset & Dunlap, Inc. Pp. 118–119, excerpt adapted from *Invitation to Archaeology* by James Deetz. Copyright © 1967 by James Deetz. Reprinted by permission of Doubleday & Company, Inc. Pp. 123–126, from *Cultural Anthropology: Understanding Ourselves and Others,* 2nd Edition, by Richly H. Crapo, 1990. Copyright © 1990, The Dushkin Publishing Group Inc., Guilford, CT. All rights reserved. P. 124 (top), BISON Grotte d'Altamira (Espagne) Paleolithic superieur, Releve H. Breuil. Reprinted by permission of the Musee De L'Homme. P. 124 (bottom right), LES EYZIES, Grotte de Font de Gaume, Boef en noir plat, releve de l'abbe Breuil, (extrait de "La caverne de Font de Gaume" Caipton, Breuil, Peyrony, Institut de paleontologie humaine) Reprinted by permission of the Musee De L'Homme. P. 124 (bottom left), Venus de Lespuque, vue de profil. Reprinted by permission of the Musee De L'Homme.

Chapter 7: P. 128, photo courtesy of Rhoden Studios, Brooklyn Heights, N.Y. P. 139, from the *Readers' Guide to Periodical Literature,* copyright © 1980, 1981, by the H.W. Wilson Company. Material reproduced by permission of the publisher. P. 143, from *The Index to Periodical Articles* *by and About Negroes: 1984.* Copyright 1987 G.K. Hall & Co. Boston, MA. P. 142, copyright by The New York Times Company. Reprinted by permission. Pp. 149–151, from *Slavery Remembered: A Record of Twentieth Century Slave Narratives,* by Paul Escott. Copyright © 1979, The University of North Carolina Press. Reprinted by permission of the publisher. Pp. 152–153, letter from Anthony Chase provided by the Otho Holland Williams Papers, MS. 908, Manuscripts Division, Maryland Historical Society. Pp. 154–156, from *Twelve Years a Slave* by Solomon Northrup, copyright © 1968. Reprinted by permission of Louisiana State University Press. Pp. 157–160, from *Early American Negro Writers* by Benjamin Brawley. Copyright © 1935 by The University of North Carolina Press. Reprinted with permission. Pp. 163–167, from *My Bondage and My Freedom,* by Frederick Douglass, 1969, Dover Publications, N.Y., N.Y., 10014.

Chapter 8: P. 168, photo courtesy of Beverly Mathias. Pp. 170–177, reprinted by permission of Farrar, Strauss, & Giroux, Inc. "A Summer's Reading," by Bernard Malamud; originally appeared in *The New Yorker.* Pp. 189–197, from *Fires,* copyright © 1983 by Raymond Carver Estate. Reprinted by permission of Copra Press, Santa Barbara.

Chapter 9: P. 202, courtesy of Marcos A. Pacheco. Pp. 205–212, reprinted with permission. Copyright © 1959 by SCIENTIFIC AMERICAN, Inc. All rights reserved. P. 213, reprinted courtesy of Bruno Bettelheim. P. 224, "This Stranger My Son" by Louise Wilson, © 1969.

Chapter 10: P. 226, reprinted courtesy of Marcos A. Pacheco. Pp. 228–239, reprinted with permission of *Natural History,* © 1990.

Chapter 11: P. 248, reprinted courtesy of Marcos A. Pacheco. Pp. 250–254, copyright © Stephen Leacock. P. 257, from "Reading and Solving Problems in Mathematics" by Dr. Marjorie Tenner, Chairperson, Mathematics Department, New York City Technical College, City University of New York. Reprinted with permission. Pp. 272–273, copyright © Stephen Leacock.

Chapter 12: P. 274, copyright © J.L.G. Ferris, Archives of 76, Bay Village, Ohio. Pp. 277–281, from *A Short History of Western Civilization,* 2nd Edition, by John B. Harris and Richard E. Sullivan. Copyright © 1960, 1966 by John B. Harris and Richard E. Sullivan. Reprinted by permission of McGraw Hill, Inc. Pp. 279–281, from *American History: A Survey,* 4th Edition by Richard N. Current, T. Harry Williams, and Frank Friedel. Copyright © 1975 by Richard N. Current, T. Harry Williams, and Frank Friedel. Reprinted by permission of McGraw-Hill, Inc. Pp. 293–294, translation by Benjamin Pacheco, "En La Brecha" by Jose de Diego, 1916.